# Free Video    Free Video

## *Essential Test Tips* Video from Trivium Test Prep

Dear Customer,

Thank you for purchasing from Trivium Test Prep! We're honored to help you prepare for your exam.

To show our appreciation, we're offering a **FREE *HESI Essential Test Tips* Video by Trivium Test Prep.*** Our video includes 35 test preparation strategies that will make you successful on the HESI exam. All we ask is that you email us your feedback and describe your experience with our product. Amazing, awful, or just so-so: we want to hear what you have to say!

To receive your **FREE *HESI Essential Test Tips* Video**, please email us at 5star@triviumtestprep.com. Include "Free 5 Star" in the subject line and the following information in your email:

1. The title of the product you purchased.
2. Your rating from 1 – 5 (with 5 being the best).
3. Your feedback about the product, including how our materials helped you meet your goals and ways in which we can improve our products.
4. Your full name and shipping address so we can send your **FREE *HESI Essential Test Tips* Video**.

If you have any questions or concerns please feel free to contact us directly at 5star@triviumtestprep.com.

Thank you!

– Trivium Test Prep Team

*To get access to the free video please email us at 5star@triviumtestprep.com, and please follow the instructions above.

# HESI® A² STUDY GUIDE 2025-2026:
3 Practice Tests and HESI Admission Assessment Exam Review for Nursing [7th Edition]

Jeremy Downs

Copyright © 2025 by Ascencia Test Prep

ISBN-13: 9781637982983

ALL RIGHTS RESERVED. By purchase of this book, you have been licensed one copy for personal use only. No part of this work may be reproduced, redistributed, or used in any form or by any means without prior written permission of the publisher and copyright owner. Ascencia Test Prep; Trivium Test Prep; Cirrus Test Prep; and Accepted, Inc. are all imprints of Trivium Test Prep, LLC.

Elsevier was not involved in the creation or production of this product, is not in any way affiliated with Ascencia Test Prep, and does not sponsor or endorse this product. All test names (and their acronyms) are trademarks of their respective owners. This study guide is for general information only and does not claim endorsement by any third party.

Image(s) used under license from Shutterstock.com

# Table of Contents

Online Resources ............................................. i
Introduction ................................................. iii

## 1 Mathematics ............................................. 1
- Types of Numbers ......................................... 1
- Scientific Notation ...................................... 2
- Positive and Negative Numbers ............................ 2
- Order of Operations ...................................... 4
- Decimals and Fractions ................................... 5
- Rounding and Estimation .................................. 7
- Ratios ................................................... 8
- Proportions .............................................. 8
- Percentages .............................................. 9
- Comparison of Rational Numbers ........................... 10
- Algebraic Expressions .................................... 10
- Operations with Expressions .............................. 10
- Linear Equations ......................................... 11
- Building Equations ....................................... 13
- Inequalities ............................................. 13
- Units of Measurement ..................................... 13
- Geometric Figures ........................................ 15
- Statistics ............................................... 18
- Data Presentation ........................................ 20

## 2 Reading ................................................. 33
- The Main Idea ............................................ 33
- Summarizing Passages ..................................... 35
- Supporting Details ....................................... 35
- Text Structure ........................................... 37
- Drawing Conclusions ...................................... 37
- The Author's Purpose ..................................... 38
- Words in Context ......................................... 39

## 3 Vocabulary .............................................. 43
- Word Structure ........................................... 43
- Homophones and Homographs ................................ 49

## 4 Grammar ................................................. 53
- Parts of Speech .......................................... 53
- Constructing Sentences ................................... 61
- Capitalization ........................................... 65
- Common Language Errors ................................... 66

## 5 Biology ................................................. 77
- Biological Macromolecules ................................ 77
- The Cell ................................................. 80
- Genetics ................................................. 84

## 6 Chemistry ............................................... 89
- Properties of Atoms ...................................... 89
- Intramolecular Bonds ..................................... 95
- Intermolecular Bonds ..................................... 97
- Properties of Substances ................................. 98
- States of Matter ......................................... 101
- Chemical Reactions ....................................... 102
- Catalysts ................................................ 105
- Acids and Bases .......................................... 106

## 7 Anatomy and Physiology ............... 111
- ANATOMICAL TERMINOLOGY ........................... 111
- THE RESPIRATORY SYSTEM ............................ 113
- THE CARDIOVASCULAR SYSTEM ..................... 115
- THE NERVOUS SYSTEM .................................. 118
- THE GASTROINTESTINAL SYSTEM ................... 121
- THE SKELETAL SYSTEM .................................. 123
- THE MUSCULAR SYSTEM ................................ 126
- THE IMMUNE SYSTEM .................................... 128
- THE REPRODUCTIVE SYSTEM ......................... 130
- THE ENDOCRINE SYSTEM ............................... 132
- THE INTEGUMENTARY SYSTEM ....................... 135
- THE GENITOURINARY SYSTEM ........................ 136

## 8 Physics ........................................ 139
- MOTION ........................................................ 139
- FORCES ........................................................ 140
- WORK ........................................................... 141
- ENERGY ........................................................ 141
- WAVES .......................................................... 143
- ELECTRICITY AND MAGNETISM ..................... 145

## 9 Practice Test .............................. 149
- MATHEMATICS ............................................... 149
- READING ...................................................... 155
- VOCABULARY ................................................ 166
- GRAMMAR .................................................... 173
- BIOLOGY ...................................................... 180
- CHEMISTRY ................................................... 183
- ANATOMY AND PHYSIOLOGY ......................... 186
- PHYSICS ....................................................... 189
- ANSWER KEY ................................................ 193

# Want More?

## TRY OUR ONLINE HESI A² PREP COURSE

Dear Reader,

Here at Trivium Test Prep, we understand how important scoring well on the HESI A² exam is for your future. We believe you can never be "too prepared" for such a life-changing test. We are excited to offer you a comprehensive online course devoted to the HESI A²! Our *HESI A2 Prep Course* includes:

- a <u>complete review</u> of all content on the HESI A² exam, with **trackable course progress** so you know exactly what you still need to review;
- <u>subject quizzes</u> at the end of each section, so you can **assess your retention** before moving on to new units;
- <u>two full practice exams</u> with **fully explained answer rationales** and **trackable scoring**, so you can measure your progress and understand what you need to improve on;
- and <u>full accessibility</u> via your computer, tablet, and mobile phone 24/7, enabling you to **learn at home or on-the-go!**

Best of all, our unique material and practice questions are available exclusively through *HESI A² Prep Course*, ensuring you get double the study time when coupled with this book!

Trivium Test Prep's *HESI A² Prep Course* is available to current customers like you at the following promotional prices:

- Month to month: $14.99
- 3-months: $39.99
- 6-months: $49.99

Many less convenient programs retail for hundreds of dollars online. To enroll today and start learning immediately, please visit:

https://course.triviumtestprep.com/hesi-a2/

Thank you for choosing Trivium Test Prep for all your HESI A² study needs!

Best of luck with your studies,

– The Trivium Test Prep Team

# Online Resources

Ascencia Test Prep includes online resources with the purchase of this study guide to help you fully prepare for your HESI A² exam.

### PRACTICE TESTS

In addition to the practice test included in this book, we also offer an online exam. Since many exams today are computer based, practicing your test-taking skills on the computer is a great way to prepare.

### REVIEW QUESTIONS

Need more practice? Our review questions use a variety of formats to help you memorize key terms and concepts.

### FLASH CARDS

Ascencia Test Prep's flash cards allow you to review important terms easily on your computer or smartphone.

### CHEAT SHEETS

Review the core skills you need to master the exam with easy-to-read Cheat Sheets.

### FROM STRESS TO SUCCESS

Watch "From Stress to Success," a brief but insightful YouTube video that offers the tips, tricks, and secrets experts use to score higher on the exam.

### REVIEWS

Leave a review, send us helpful feedback, or sign up for Ascencia Test Prep promotions—including free books!

Access these materials at: **https://www.ascenciatestprep.com/hesi-a2-online-resources**

# INTRODUCTION

The HESI Admission Assessment (HESI $A^2$) exam is a part of the admissions process for nursing and allied health programs around the country. Schools use the test to assess applicants' capabilities in high-school level reading, writing, math, and science. This guide will allow you to review your knowledge in these subject areas, apply your knowledge, and answer test questions.

## What's on the HESI $A^2$?

The HESI $A^2$ is a computer-based exam with eight sections. Different schools require different sections as part of their applications. Check with the institution or program you are interested in to find out what sections you need to take on test day.

You can work through the sections on the HESI $A^2$ in any order.

Most candidates take about four hours to complete the HESI $A^2$. Some programs allow candidates more time, depending on the required tests, or do not impose a time limit at all. The time limits listed below are suggested by the administrators of the HESI $A^2$ exam.

### HESI $A^2$ Content

| Subject | Topics | Number of Questions | Suggested Time Limit |
| --- | --- | --- | --- |
| Mathematics | arithmetic, fractions and decimals, proportions, units and measurements, calculating dosages | 55 | 50 minutes |
| Reading | main idea, supporting idea, inferences, details, interpreting information | 55 | 60 minutes |
| Vocabulary | knowledge of English vocabulary, particularly related to health and medicine | 55 | 50 minutes |
| Biology | biological molecules, cells, cellular respiration, genetics, photosynthesis | 30 | 25 minutes |
| Chemistry | atomic structure, chemical bonding, chemical equations, chemical reactions, nuclear chemistry, the periodic table | 30 | 35 minutes |

## HESI A² Content (continued)

| Subject | Topics | Number of Questions | Suggested Time Limit |
| --- | --- | --- | --- |
| Anatomy and Physiology | body systems (muscular, skeletal, nervous, renal/urinary, reproductive, endocrine, circulatory, and respiratory) | 30 | 25 minutes |
| Physics | mechanics, energy, forces, waves, and light (This section is typically excluded by many programs; the mathematics and other sciences are more important.) | 30 | 25 minutes |

### OTHER UNSCORED SECTIONS

*Learner profile* exams are **UNSCORED** tests to help students better understand their strengths and weaknesses, learning styles and habits, and other personality traits. Some schools may require them.

All sections on the HESI A² will include some pilot, unscored questions. The test writers use these questions to test new material. These questions do not count toward your final score. However, these questions are not indicated on the exam, so you must answer every question.

## How is the HESI A² Scored?

There is no way to pass or fail the HESI A². A candidate's score simply shows their level of comprehension and skill. Schools and programs have their own entrance requirements, so candidates must check with the institutions that they want to attend for details on required scores.

## How to Use This Guide

The chapters in this book are divided into a review of the topics covered on the exam. This is not intended to teach you everything you'll see on the test: there is no way to cram all of that material into one book! Instead, we are going to help you recall information that you've already learned, and even more importantly, we'll show you how to apply that knowledge. Each chapter includes an extensive review with practice questions at the end to test your knowledge. With time, practice, and determination, you'll be well prepared for test day.

## Ascencia Test Prep

With health care fields such as nursing, pharmacy, emergency care, and physical therapy becoming the fastest-growing industries in the United States, individuals looking to enter the health care industry or rise in their field need high-quality, reliable resources. Ascencia Test Prep's study guides and test preparation materials are developed by credentialed industry professionals with years of experience in their respective fields. Ascencia recognizes that health care professionals nurture bodies and spirits, and save lives. Ascencia Test Prep's mission is to help health care workers grow.

# ONE: MATHEMATICS

## Types of Numbers

Numbers are placed in categories based on their properties.

- A **natural number** is greater than zero and has no decimal or fraction attached. These are also sometimes called counting numbers. {1, 2, 3, 4, ...}
- **Whole numbers** are natural numbers and the number zero. {0, 1, 2, 3, 4, ...}
- **Integers** include positive and negative natural numbers and zero. {. . ., −4, −3, −2, −1, 0, 1, 2, 3, 4, ...}
- A **rational number** can be represented as a fraction. Any decimal part must terminate or resolve into a repeating pattern. Examples include −12, $-\frac{4}{5}$, 0.36, 7.$\overline{7}$, 26$\frac{1}{2}$, etc.
- An **irrational number** cannot be represented as a fraction. An irrational decimal number never ends and never resolves into a repeating pattern. Examples include $-\sqrt{7}$, $\pi$, and 0.34567989135 ...
- A **real number** is a number that can be represented by a point on a number line. Real numbers include all the rational and irrational numbers.

**HELPFUL HINT**
If a real number is a natural number (e.g. 50), then it is also an integer, a whole number, and a rational number.

Every natural number (except 1) is either a prime number or a composite number. A **prime number** is a natural number greater than 1 which can only be divided evenly by 1 and itself. For example, 7 is a prime number because it can only be divided by the numbers 1 and 7.

On the other hand, a **composite number** is a natural number greater than 1 which can be evenly divided by at least one other number besides 1 and itself. For example, 6 is a composite number because it can be divided by 1, 2, 3, and 6.

Composite numbers can be broken down into prime numbers using factor trees. For example, the number 54 is 2 × 27, and 27 is 3 × 9, and 9 is 3 × 3, as shown in Figure 1.1.

Once the number has been broken down into its simplest form, the composite number can be expressed as a product of prime factors. Repeated factors can be written using exponents. An **exponent** shows how many times a number should be multiplied by itself. As shown in the factor tree, the number 54 can be written as 2 × 3 × 3 × 3 or 2 × 3$^3$.

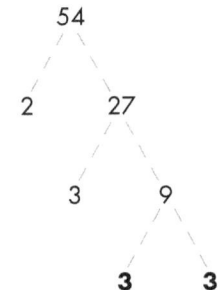

**Figure 1.1. Factor Tree**

PRACTICE QUESTIONS

*Classify the following numbers as natural, whole, integer, rational, or irrational. (The numbers may have more than one classification.)*

1. 72

2. $-\frac{2}{3}$

3. $\sqrt{5}$

# Scientific Notation

**Scientific notation** is a method of representing very large and small numbers in the form $a \times 10^n$ where $a$ is a value between 1 and 10, and $n$ is an integer. For example, the number 927,000,000 is written in scientific notation as $9.27 \times 10^8$. Multiplying 9.27 by 10 eight times gives 927,000,000. When performing operations with scientific notation, the final answer should be in the form $a \times 10^n$.

Table 1.1. Place Value

| 1,000,000 | 100,000 | 10,000 | 1,000 | 100 | 10 | 1 | . | $\frac{1}{10}$ | $\frac{1}{100}$ |
|---|---|---|---|---|---|---|---|---|---|
| $10^6$ | $10^5$ | $10^4$ | $10^3$ | $10^2$ | $10^1$ | $10^0$ | | $10^{-1}$ | $10^{-2}$ |
| Millions | Hundred Thousands | Ten Thousands | Thousands | Hundreds | Tens | Ones | Decimal | Tenths | Hundreths |

When adding and subtracting numbers in scientific notation, the power of 10 must be the same for all numbers. This results in like terms in which the $a$ terms are added or subtracted and the $10^n$ remains unchanged. When multiplying numbers in scientific notation, multiply the $a$ factors and add the exponents. For division, divide the $a$ factors and subtract the exponents.

PRACTICE QUESTIONS

4. Simplify: $(3.8 \times 10^3) + (4.7 \times 10^2)$

5. Simplify: $(8.1 \times 10^{-5})(1.4 \times 10^7)$

# Positive and Negative Numbers

**Positive numbers** are greater than zero, and **negative numbers** are less than zero. Both positive and negative numbers can be shown on a **number line**.

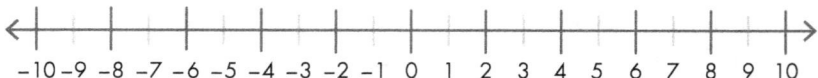

**Figure 1.2. Number Line**

Positive and negative numbers can be added, subtracted, multiplied, and divided. The sign of the resulting number is governed by a specific set of rules shown in the table below.

Table 1.2. Operations with Positive and Negative Numbers

| **Adding Real Numbers** | |
| --- | --- |
| Positve + Positive = Positive | 7 + 8 = 15 |
| Negative + Negative = Negative | −7 + (−8) = −15 |
| Negative + Positive = Keep the sign of the number with the larger absolute value | −7 + 8 = 1<br>7 + (−8) = −1 |
| **Subtracting Real Numbers** | |
| Change the subtraction to addition, change the sign of the second number, and use addition rules. | |
| Negative − Positive = Negative | −7 − 8 = −7 + (−8) = −15 |
| Positive − Negative = Positive | 7 − (−8) = 7 + 8 = 15 |
| Negative − Negative = Keep the sign of the number with the larger absolute value. | −7 − (−8) = −7 + 8 = 1<br>−8 − (−7) = −8 + 7 = −1 |
| Positive − Positive =<br>Positive if the first number is larger<br>Negative if the second number is larger | 8 − 4 = 4<br>4 − 8 = −4 |
| **Multiplying Real Numbers** | |
| Positive × Positive = Positive | 8 × 4 = 32 |
| Negative × Negative = Positive | −8 × (−4) = 32 |
| Negative × Positive = Negative | 8 × (−4) = −32<br>−8 × 4 = −32 |
| **Dividing Real Numbers** | |
| Positive ÷ Positive = Positive | 8 ÷ 4 = 2 |
| Negative ÷ Negative = Positive | −8 ÷ (−4) = 2 |
| Positive ÷ Negative OR<br>Negative ÷ Positive = Negative | 8 ÷ (−4) = −2<br>−8 ÷ 4 = −2 |

## PRACTICE QUESTIONS

*Add or subtract the following real numbers:*

**6.** −18 + 12

**7.** −3.64 + (−2.18)

**8.** 9.37 − 4.25

**9.** 86 − (−20)

**MATHEMATICS**

*Multiply or divide the following real numbers:*

10. $\frac{10}{3}(-\frac{9}{5})$

11. $\frac{-64}{-10}$

12. $(2.2)(3.3)$

13. $-52 \div 13$

## Order of Operations

When solving a multi-step equation, the **order of operations** must be used to get the correct answer. Generally speaking, the problem should be worked in the following order: 1) parentheses and brackets; 2) exponents and square roots; 3) multiplication and division; 4) addition and subtraction. The acronym PEMDAS can be used to remember the order of operations.

**P**lease **E**xcuse (**M**y **D**ear) (**A**unt **S**ally)

1. **P** — Parentheses: Calculate expressions inside parentheses, brackets, braces, etc.
2. **E** — Exponents: Calculate exponents and square roots.
3. **M** — Multiply and **D** — Divide: Calculate any remaining multiplication and division in order from left to right.
4. **A** — Add and **S** — Subtract: Calculate any remaining addition and subtraction in order from left to right.

The steps "Multiply-Divide" and "Addition-Subtraction" go in order from left to right. In other words, divide before multiplying if the division problem is on the left.

For example, the expression $(3^2 - 2)^2 + (4)5^3$ is simplified using the following steps:

1. Parentheses: Because the parentheses in this problem contain two operations (exponents and subtraction), use the order of operations within the parentheses. Exponents come before subtraction. $(3^2 - 2)^2 + (4)5^3 = (9 - 2)^2 + (4)5^3 = (7)^2 + (4)5^3$
2. Exponents: $(7)^2 + (4)5^3 = 49 + (4)125$
3. Multiplication and division: $49 + (4)125 = 49 + 500$
4. Addition and subtraction: $49 + 500 = 549$

### PRACTICE QUESTIONS

14. Simplify: $2(21 - 14) + 6 \div (-2) \times 3 - 10$

15. Simplify: $-3^2 + 4(5) + (5 - 6)^2 - 8$

16. Simplify: $\frac{(7 - 9)^3 + 8(10 - 12)}{4^2 - 5^2}$

# Decimals and Fractions

## DECIMALS

A **decimal** is a number that contains a decimal point. The place value for a decimal includes **tenths** (one place after the decimal point), **hundredths** (two places after the decimal point), **thousandths** (three places after the decimal point), etc.

| 5 | 4 | • | 3 | 2 |
|---|---|---|---|---|
| $5 \times 10^1$ | $4 \times 10^0$ | Decimal Point | $3 \times 10^{-1}$ | $2 \times 10^{-2}$ |
| $5 \times 10$ | $4 \times 1$ | | $3 \times \frac{1}{10}$ | $2 \times \frac{1}{100}$ |
| 50 | 4 | | 0.3 | 0.02 |
| Tens | Ones | | Tenths | Hundredths |

$50 + 4 + 0.3 + 0.02 = 54.32$

**Figure 1.3. Decimals and Place Value**

Decimals can be added, subtracted, multiplied, and divided:

To add or subtract decimals, line up the decimal points and perform the operation, keeping the decimal point in the same place in the answer.

$$12.35$$
$$+ \ 3.63$$
$$= 15.98$$

To multiply decimals, first multiply the numbers without the decimal points. Then, add the number of decimal places to the right of the decimal point in the original numbers and place the decimal point in the answer so that there are that many places to the right of the decimal.

$$12.35 \times 3.63 =$$
$$1235 \times 363 = 448305 \rightarrow 44.8305$$

When dividing decimals move the decimal point to the right in order to make the divisor a whole number and move the decimal the same number of places in the dividend. Divide the numbers without regard to the decimal. Then, place the decimal point of the quotient directly above the decimal point of the dividend.

$$\frac{12.35}{3.63} = \frac{1235}{363} =$$

$$363 \overline{)1235.0}^{\ 3.4}$$

## PRACTICE QUESTIONS

**17.** Simplify: $24.38 + 16.51 - 29.87$

**HELPFUL HINT**
If you're unsure which way to move the decimal after multiplying, remember that changing the decimal should always make the final answer smaller.

18. Simplify: (10.4)(18.2)

19. Simplify: 80 ÷ 2.5

## FRACTIONS

A **fraction** is a number that can be written in the form $\frac{a}{b}$ where $b$ is not equal to zero. The $a$ part of the fraction is the numerator (top number) and $b$ part of the fraction is the denominator (bottom number).

If the denominator of a fraction is greater than the numerator, the value of the fraction is less than 1 and it is called a **proper fraction** (e.g., $\frac{3}{5}$ is a proper fraction).

In an **improper fraction**, the denominator is less than the numerator and the value of the fraction is greater than one (e.g., $\frac{8}{3}$ is an improper fraction). An improper fraction can be written as a whole number or a mixed number. A **mixed number** has a whole number part and a proper fraction part. Improper fractions can be converted to mixed numbers by dividing the numerator by the denominator, which gives the whole number part, and the remainder becomes the numerator of the proper fraction part (for example: improper fraction $\frac{25}{9}$ is equal to mixed number $2\frac{7}{9}$ because 9 divides into 25 two times, with a remainder of 7).

**HELPFUL HINT**
$a\frac{m}{n} = \frac{n \times a + m}{n}$

Conversely, mixed numbers can be converted to improper fractions. To do so, determine the numerator of the improper fraction by multiplying the denominator by the whole number, then adding the numerator. The final number is written as the (now larger) numerator over the original denominator.

Fractions with the same denominator can be added or subtracted by simply adding or subtracting the numerators; the denominator will remain unchanged. If the fractions to be added or subtracted do not have a common denominator, the least common multiple of the denominators must be found. The quickest way to find a common denominator of a set of values is simply to multiply all the values together. The result might not be the least common denominator, but it will get the job done.

In the operation $\frac{2}{3} - \frac{1}{2}$, the common denominator will be a multiple of both 3 and 2. Multiples are found by multiplying the denominator by whole numbers until a common multiple is found:

- multiples of 3 are **3** (3 × 1), **6** (3 × 2), **9** (3 × 3) …
- multiples of 2 are **2** (2 × 1), 4 (2 × 2), **6** (2 × 3) …

Since 6 is the smallest multiple of both 3 and 2, it is the least common multiple and can be used as the common denominator. Both the numerator and denominator of each fraction should be multiplied by the appropriate whole number:

$$\frac{2}{3}\left(\frac{2}{2}\right) - \frac{1}{2}\left(\frac{3}{3}\right) = \frac{4}{6} - \frac{3}{6} = \frac{1}{6}.$$

When multiplying fractions, simply multiply each numerator together and each denominator together, reducing the result if possible. To divide two fractions, invert the second fraction (swap the numerator and denominator) then multiply normally. If there are any mixed numbers when multiplying or dividing, they should first be changed to improper fractions. Note that multiplying proper fractions creates a value smaller than either original value.

$$\frac{5}{6} \times \frac{2}{3} = \frac{10}{18} = \frac{5}{9}$$

$$\frac{5}{6} \div \frac{2}{3} = \frac{5}{6} \times \frac{3}{2} = \frac{15}{12} = \frac{5}{4}$$

## PRACTICE QUESTIONS

**20.** Simplify: $2\frac{3}{5} + 3\frac{1}{4} - 1\frac{1}{2}$

**21.** Simplify: $\frac{7}{8}(3\frac{1}{3})$

**22.** Simplify: $4\frac{1}{2} \div \frac{2}{3}$

## CONVERTING BETWEEN FRACTIONS AND DECIMALS

A fraction is converted to a decimal by using long division until there is no remainder or a pattern of repeating numbers occurs.

$$\frac{1}{2} = 1 \div 2 = 0.5$$

To convert a decimal to a fraction, place the numbers to the right of the decimal over the appropriate base-10 power and simplify the fraction.

$$0.375 = \frac{375}{1000} = \frac{3}{8}$$

## PRACTICE QUESTIONS

**23.** Write the fraction $\frac{7}{8}$ as a decimal.

**24.** Write the fraction $\frac{5}{11}$ as a decimal.

**25.** Write the decimal 0.125 as a fraction.

# Rounding and Estimation

**Rounding** is a way of simplifying a complicated number. The result of rounding will be a less precise value that is easier to write or perform operations on. Rounding is performed to a specific place value, such as the thousands or tenths place.

The rules for rounding are as follows:

1. Underline the place value being rounded to.
2. Locate the digit one place value to the right of the underlined value. If this value is less than 5, keep the underlined value and replace all digits to the right of the underlined value with zero. If the value to the right of the underlined digit is more than 5, increase the underlined digit by one and replace all digits to the right of it with zero.

**Estimation** is when numbers are rounded and then an operation is performed. This process can be used when working with large numbers to find a close, but not exact, answer.

**HELPFUL HINT**

Estimation can often be used to eliminate answer choices on multiple choice tests without having to completely work the problem.

### PRACTICE QUESTIONS

**26.** Round the number 138,472 to the nearest thousand.

**27.** The populations of five local towns are 12,341, 8,975, 9,431, 10,521, and 11,427. Estimate the population to the nearest 1,000 people.

## Ratios

A **ratio** is a comparison of two numbers and can be represented as $\frac{a}{b}$ ($b \neq 0$), $a:b$, or $a$ to $b$. The two numbers represent a constant relationship, not a specific value: for every $a$ number of items in the first group, there will be $b$ number of items in the second. For example, if the ratio of blue to red candies in a bag is 3:5, the bag will contain 3 blue candies for every 5 red candies. So the bag might contain 3 blue candies and 5 red candies, or it might contain 30 blue candies and 50 red candies, or 36 blue candies and 60 red candies. All of these values are representative of the ratio 3:5 (which is the ratio in its lowest, or simplest, terms).

To find the "whole" when working with ratios, simply add the values in the ratio. For example, if the ratio of boys to girls in a class is 2:3, the "whole" is five: 2 out of every 5 students are boys, and 3 out of every 5 students are girls.

### PRACTICE QUESTIONS

**28.** There are 10 boys and 12 girls in a first grade class. What is the ratio of boys to the total number of students? What is the ratio of girls to boys?

**29.** A family spends $600 a month on rent, $400 on utilities, $750 on groceries, and $550 on miscellaneous expenses. What is the ratio of the family's rent to their total expenses?

## Proportions

A **proportion** is an equation which states that two ratios are equal. Proportions are given in the form $\frac{a}{b} = \frac{c}{d}$, where the $a$ and $d$ terms are the extremes and the $b$ and $c$ terms are the means. A proportion is solved using **cross-multiplication** to create an equation with no fractional components: $\frac{a}{b} = \frac{c}{d} \rightarrow ad = bc$

### PRACTICE QUESTIONS

**30.** Solve the proportion for $x$: $\frac{3 - 5x}{2} = \frac{-8}{3}$

**31.** A map is drawn such that 2.5 inches on the map equates to an actual distance of 40 miles. If the distance between two cities measured on the map is 17.25 inches, what is the actual distance between them in miles?

**32.** At a certain factory, every 4 out of 1,000 parts made will be defective. If in a month there are 125,000 parts made, how many of these parts will be defective?

# Percentages

A **percent** (or percentage) means per hundred and is expressed with a percent symbol (%). For example, 54% means 54 out of every 100. A percent can be converted to a decimal by removing the % symbol and moving the decimal point two places to the left, while a decimal can be converted to a percent by moving the decimal point two places to the right and attaching the % sign.

A percent can be converted to a fraction by writing the percent as a fraction with 100 as the denominator and reducing. A fraction can be converted to a percent by performing the indicated division, multiplying the result by 100 and attaching the % sign.

The percent equation has three variables: the part, the whole, and the percent (which is expressed in the equation as a decimal). The equation, as shown below, can be rearranged to solve for any of these variables.

$$\text{part} = \text{whole} \times \text{percent}$$
$$\text{percent} = \frac{\text{part}}{\text{whole}}$$
$$\text{whole} = \frac{\text{part}}{\text{percent}}$$

This set of equations can be used to solve percent word problems. All that is needed is to identify the part, whole, and/or percent, then to plug those values into the appropriate equation and solve.

## PRACTICE QUESTIONS

**33.** Write 18% as a fraction.

**34.** Write $\frac{3}{5}$ as a percent.

**35.** Write 1.125 as a percent.

**36.** Write 84% as a decimal.

**37.** In a school of 650 students, 54% of the students are boys. How many students are girls?

## PERCENT CHANGE

Percent change problems involve a change from an original amount. Often percent change problems appear as word problems that include discounts, growth, or markups. In order to solve percent change problems, it is necessary to identify the percent change (as a decimal), the amount of change, and the original amount. (Keep in mind that one of these will be the value being solved for.) These values can then be plugged into the equations below:

$$\text{amount of change} = \text{original amount} \times \text{percent change}$$
$$\text{percent change} = \frac{\text{amount of change}}{\text{original amount}}$$
$$\text{original amount} = \frac{\text{amount of change}}{\text{percent change}}$$

## PRACTICE QUESTIONS

**38.** A Smart HDTV that originally cost $1,500 is on sale for 45% off. What is the sale price for the item?

**39.** A house was purchased in 2000 for $100,000 and sold in 2015 for $120,000. What was the percent growth in the value of the house from 2000 to 2015?

# Comparison of Rational Numbers

Rational numbers can be ordered from least to greatest (or greatest to least) by placing them in the order in which they fall on a number line. When comparing a set of fractions, it is often easiest to convert each value to a common denominator. Then, it is only necessary to compare the numerators of each fraction.

When working with numbers in multiple forms (for example, a group of fractions and decimals), convert the values so that the set contains only fractions or only decimals. When ordering negative numbers, remember that the negative number with the largest absolute value is furthest from 0 and is therefore the smallest number. (For example, −75 is smaller than −25.)

**HELPFUL HINT**
Drawing a number line can help when comparing numbers: the final list should go in order from left to right (least to greatest) or right to left (greatest to least) on the line.

## PRACTICE QUESTIONS

**40.** Order the following numbers from greatest to least: $-\frac{2}{3}$, 1.2, 0, −2.1, $\frac{5}{4}$, −1, $\frac{1}{8}$.

**41.** Order the following numbers from least to greatest: $\frac{1}{3}$, $-\frac{5}{6}$, $1\frac{1}{8}$, $\frac{7}{12}$, $-\frac{3}{4}$, $-\frac{3}{2}$.

# Algebraic Expressions

The foundation of algebra is the **variable**, an unknown number represented by a symbol (usually a letter such as $x$ or $a$). Variables can be preceded by a **coefficient**, which is a constant (i.e., a real number) in front of the variable, such as $4x$ or $-2a$. An **algebraic expression** is any sum, difference, product, or quotient of variables and numbers (for example $3x^2$, $2x + 7y - 1$, and $\frac{5}{x}$ are algebraic expressions). **Terms** are any quantities that are added or subtracted (for example, the terms of the expression $x^2 - 3x + 5$ are $x^2$, $3x$, and 5). A **polynomial expression** is an algebraic expression where all the exponents on the variables are whole numbers. A polynomial with two terms is known as a **binomial**, and one with three terms is a **trinomial**.

## PRACTICE QUESTION

**42.** If $m = 4$, find the value of the following expression: $5(m - 2)^3 + 3m^2 - \frac{m}{4} - 1$

# Operations with Expressions

## ADDING AND SUBTRACTING

Expressions can be added or subtracted by simply adding and subtracting **like terms**, which are terms with the same variable part (the variables must be the same, with the same exponents on each variable). For example, in the expressions $2x + 3xy - 2z$ and

$6y + 2xy$, the like terms are $3xy$ and $2xy$. Adding the two expressions yields the new expression $2x + 5xy - 2z + 6y$. Note that the other terms did not change; they cannot combine because they have different variables.

## PRACTICE QUESTION

**43.** If $a = 12x + 7xy - 9y$ and $b = 8x - 9xz + 7z$, what is $a + b$?

## DISTRIBUTING AND FACTORING

Often, simplifying expressions requires distributing and factoring, which can be seen as two sides of the same coin. **Distribution** multiplies each term in the first factor by each term in the second factor to clear off parentheses, while **factoring** reverses this process, taking a polynomial in standard form and writing it as a product of two or more factors.

When distributing a monomial through a polynomial, the expression outside the parentheses is multiplied by each term inside the parentheses. Remember, coefficients are multiplied and exponents are added, following the rules of exponents.

The first step in factoring a polynomial is always to "undistribute," or factor out, the greatest common factor (GCF) among the terms. The GCF is multiplied by, in parentheses, the expression that remains of each term when the GCF is divided out of each term. Factoring can be checked by multiplying the GCF factor through the parentheses again.

**HELPFUL HINT**
Operations with polynomials can always be checked by plugging the same value into both expressions.

## PRACTICE QUESTIONS

**44.** Expand the following expression: $5x(x^2 - 2c + 10)$

**45.** Expand the following expression: $x(5 + z) - z(4x - z^2)$

# Linear Equations

An **equation** states that two expressions are equal to each other. Polynomial equations are categorized by the highest power of the variables they contain. For instance, the highest power of any exponent of a linear equation is 1, a quadratic equation has a variable raised to the second power, a cubic equation has a variable raised to the third power, and so on.

## SOLVING LINEAR EQUATIONS

Solving an equation means finding the value(s) of the variable that make the equation true. To solve a linear equation, it is necessary to manipulate the terms so that the variable being solved for appears alone on exactly one side of the equal sign while everything else in the equation is on the other side.

The way to solve linear equations is to "undo" all the operations that connect numbers to the variable of interest. Follow these steps:

1. Eliminate fractions by multiplying each side by the least common multiple of any denominators.
2. Distribute to eliminate parentheses, braces, and brackets.
3. Combine like terms.

**HELPFUL HINT**
On multiple-choice tests, you can avoid solving equations by just plugging the answer choices into the given equation to see which value makes the equation true.

4. Use addition or subtraction to collect all terms containing the variable of interest to one side, and all terms not containing the variable to the other side.

5. Use multiplication or division to remove coefficients from the variable being solved for.

Sometimes there are no numeric values in the equation, or there will be a mix of numerous variables and constants. The goal will be to solve the equation for one of the variables in terms of the other variables. In this case, the answer will be an expression involving numbers and letters instead of a numeric value.

## PRACTICE QUESTIONS

**46.** Solve for $x$: $\left(\dfrac{100(x+5)}{20}\right) = 1$.

**47.** Solve for $x$: $2(x+2)^2 - 2x^2 + 10 = 20$

## GRAPHS OF LINEAR EQUATIONS

The most common way to write a linear equation is **slope-intercept form**:

$$y = mx + b$$

In this equation, $m$ is the **slope**, and $b$ is the **y-intercept**. Slope is often described as "rise over run" because it is calculated as the difference in $y$-values (rise) over the difference in $x$-values (run). The slope of the line is also the **rate of change** of the dependent variable $y$ with respect to the independent variable $x$. The $y$-intercept is the point where the line crosses the $y$-axis, or where $x$ equals zero.

To graph a linear equation, identify the $y$-intercept and place that point on the $y$-axis. Then, starting at the $y$-intercept, use the slope to count up (or down if negative) the "rise" part of the slope and to the right the "run" part of the slope to find a second point. These points can then be connected to draw the line. To find the equation of a line, identify the $y$-intercept, if possible, on the graph and use two easily identifiable points to find the slope.

**HELPFUL HINT**
Use the phrase **begin, move** to remember that $b$ is the $y$-intercept (where to begin) and $m$ is the slope (how the line moves).

## PRACTICE QUESTIONS

**48.** What is the equation of the following line?

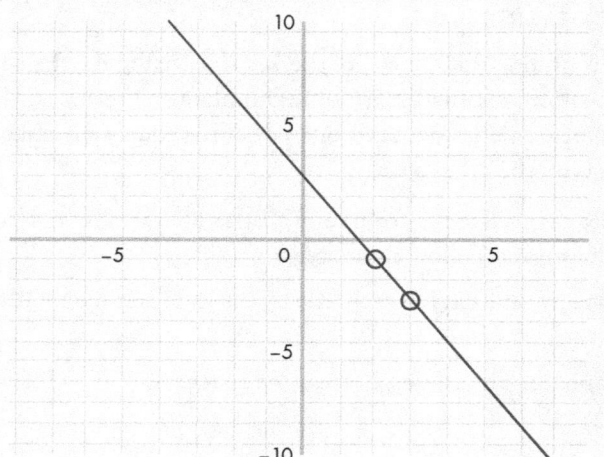

**49.** What is the slope of the line whose equation is $6x - 2y - 8 = 0$?

## Building Equations

In word problems, it is often necessary to translate a verbal description of a relationship into a mathematical equation. No matter the problem, this process can be done using the same steps:

1. Read the problem carefully and identify what value needs to be solved for.
2. Identify the known and unknown quantities in the problem, and assign the unknown quantities a variable.
3. Create equations using the variables and known quantities.
4. Solve the equations.
5. Check the solution: Does it answer the question asked in the problem? Does it make sense?

**HELPFUL HINT**
Use the acronym **STAR** to remember word problem strategies. **S**earch the problem, **T**ranslate into an expression or equation, **A**nswer, and **R**eview.

### PRACTICE QUESTIONS

**50.** A school is holding a raffle to raise money. There is a $3.00 entry fee, and each ticket costs $5.00. If a student paid $28.00, how many tickets did he buy?

**51.** Abby needs $395 to buy a new bicycle. She has borrowed $150 from her parents, and plans to earn the rest of the money working as a waitress. If she makes $10 per hour, how many hours will she need to work to pay for her new bicycle?

## Inequalities

**Inequalities** are similar to equations, but both sides of the problem are not equal ($\neq$). Inequalities may be represented as follows: greater than ($>$), greater than or equal to ($\geq$), less than ($<$), or less than or equal to ($\leq$). For example, the statement "12 is less than 4 times $x$" would be written as $12 < 4x$.

Inequalities can be solved by manipulating them much like equations. However, the solution to an inequality is a set of numbers, not a single value. For example, simplifying $4x + 2 \leq 14$ gives the inequality $x \leq 3$, meaning every number less than 3 would also be included in the set of correct answers.

### PRACTICE QUESTIONS

**52.** Solve the inequality: $4x + 10 > 58$

**53.** The students on the track team are buying new uniforms. T-shirts cost $12, pants cost $15, and a pair of shoes costs $45. If they have a budget of $2,500, write a mathematical sentence that represents how many of each item they can buy.

## Units of Measurement

The standard units for the metric and American systems are shown below along with the prefixes used to express metric units.

### Table 1.3. American and SI Units

| Dimension | American | SI |
|---|---|---|
| length | inch/foot/yard/mile | meter |
| mass | ounce/pound/ton | gram |
| volume | cup/pint/quart/gallon | liter |
| force | pound-force | newton |
| pressure | pound-force per square inch | pascal |
| work and energy | cal/British thermal unit | joule |
| temperature | Fahrenheit | kelvin |
| charge | faraday | coulomb |

### Table 1.4. Metric Prefixes

| Prefix | Symbol | Multiplication Factor |
|---|---|---|
| tera | T | 1,000,000,000,000 |
| giga | G | 1,000,000,000 |
| mega | M | 1,000,000 |
| kilo | k | 1,000 |
| hecto | h | 100 |
| deca | da | 10 |
| base unit | -- | -- |
| deci | d | 0.1 |
| centi | c | 0.01 |
| milli | m | 0.001 |
| micro | $\mu$ | 0.000001 |
| nano | n | 0.000000001 |
| pico | p | 0.000000000001 |

### Table 1.5. Conversion Factors

| | |
|---|---|
| 1 in. = 2.54 cm | 1 lb. = 0.454 kg |
| 1 yd. = 0.914 m | 1 cal = 4.19 J |
| 1 mi. = 1.61 km | 1°F = $\frac{9}{5}$°C + 32°C |
| 1 gal. = 3.785 L | 1 cm$^3$ = 1 mL |
| 1 oz. = 28.35 g | 1 hr = 3600 s |

**HELPFUL HINT**

A mnemonic device to help remember the metric system between kilo- and milli- is King Henry Drinks Under Dark Chocolate Moon (KHDUDCM).

Units can be converted within a single system or between systems. When converting from one unit to another unit, a **conversion factor** (a fraction used to convert a value with a unit into another unit) is used. For example, there are 2.54 centimeters in 1 inch, so the conversion factor from inches to centimeters is $\frac{2.54 \text{ centimeters}}{1 \text{ inch}}$.

To convert between units, multiply the original value by a conversion factor (or several if needed) so that the original units cancel, leaving the desired unit. Remember that the original value can be made into a fraction by placing it over 1.

$$\frac{3 \text{ inches}}{1} \times \frac{2.54 \text{ centimeters}}{1 \text{ inch}} = 7.62 \text{ centimeters}$$

Units can be canceled (meaning they disappear from the expression) when they appear on the top and the bottom of a fraction. If the same unit appears in the top (or bottom) of both fractions, you probably need to flip the conversion factor.

PRACTICE QUESTIONS

**54.** Convert 4.25 kilometers to meters.

**55.** Convert 12 feet to inches.

# Geometric Figures
## CLASSIFYING GEOMETRIC FIGURES

**Geometric figures** are shapes comprised of points, lines, or planes. A **point** is simply a location in space; it does not have any dimensional properties like length, area, or volume. A collection of points that extend infinitely in both directions is a **line**, and one that extends infinitely in only one direction is a **ray**. A section of a line with a beginning and end point is a **line segment**. Lines, rays, and line segments are examples of **one-dimensional** objects because they can only be measured in one dimension (length).

**Figure 1.4. One-Dimensional Object**

Lines, rays, and line segments can intersect to create **angles**, which are measured in degrees or radians. Angles between zero and 90 degrees are **acute**, and angles between 90 and 180 degrees are **obtuse**. An angle of exactly 90 degrees is a **right angle**, and two lines that form right angles are **perpendicular**. Lines that do not intersect are described as **parallel**.

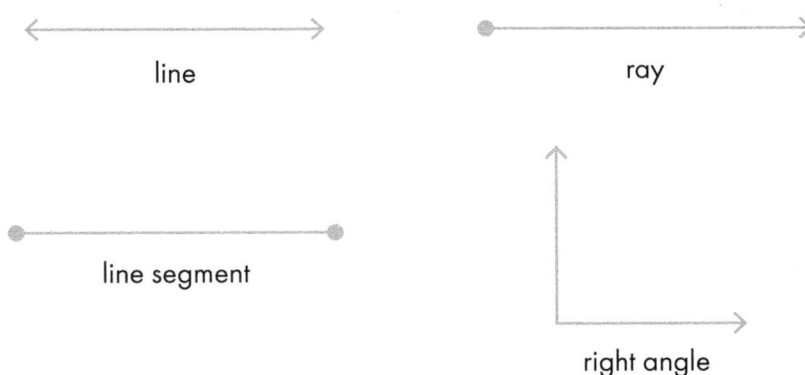

**Figure 1.5A. Lines and Angles**

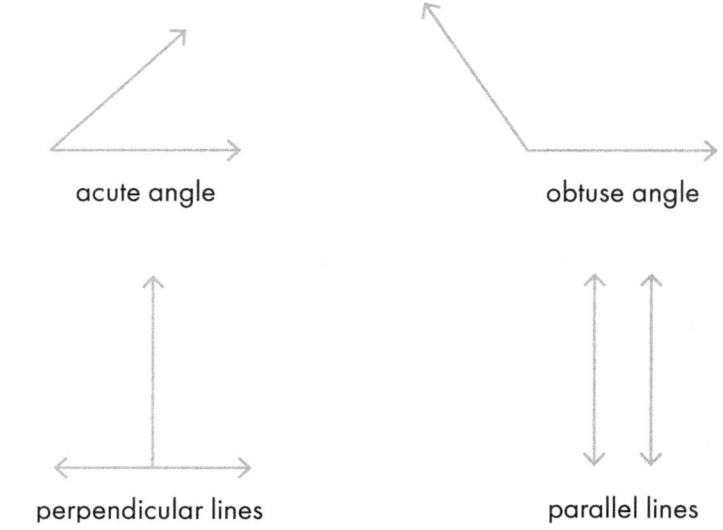

Figure 1.5B. Lines and Angles

**Figure 1.6. Two-Dimensional Object**

**Figure 1.7. Three-Dimensional Object**

**Two-dimensional** objects can be measured in two dimensions—length and width. A **plane** is a two-dimensional object that extends infinitely in both directions. **Polygons** are two-dimensional shapes, such as triangles and squares, which have three or more straight sides. Regular polygons are polygons whose sides are all the same length.

**Three-dimensional** objects, such as cubes, can be measured in three dimensions—length, width, and height.

## CALCULATING GEOMETRIC QUANTITIES

The **length**, or distance from one point to another on an object, can be determined using a tape measure or a ruler. The size of the surface of a two-dimensional object is its **area**. Generally, finding area involves multiplying one dimension of an object by another, such as length by width. For example, if a window is 3 feet long and 2 feet wide, its area would be 6 ft².

The distance around a two dimensional figure is its **perimeter**, which can be found by adding the lengths of all the sides. The distance around a circle is referred to as its **circumference**.

Table 1.6. Area and Perimeter of Basic Shapes

| Shape | Example | Area | Perimeter |
|---|---|---|---|
| Triangle | | $A = \frac{1}{2}bh$ | $P = s_1 + s_2 + s_3$ |
| Square | | $A = s^2$ | $P = 4s$ |

16   HESI A² Study Guide

| Shape | Example | Area | Perimeter |
|---|---|---|---|
| Rectangle | | $A = l \times w$ | $P = 2l + 2w$ |
| Trapezoid | | $A = \frac{1}{2}h(b_1 + b_2)$ | $P = b_1 + b_2 + l_1 + l_2$ |
| Circle | | $A = \pi r^2$ | $C = 2\pi r$ |
| Sector | | $A = \frac{x°}{360°}(\pi r^2)$ | arc length = $\frac{x°}{360°}(2\pi r)$ |

For the rectangle below, the area would be 8 m² because 2 m × 4 m = 8 m². The perimeter of the rectangle would be $P = 2l + 2w = 2(4 \text{ m}) + 2(2 \text{ m}) = 12$ m.

The **surface area** of a three-dimensional object can be figured by adding the areas of all the sides. For example, the box below is 4 feet long, 3 feet wide, and 1 foot deep. The surface area is found by adding the areas of each face:

- top: 4 ft × 3 ft = 12 ft²
- bottom: 4 ft × 3 ft = 12 ft²
- front: 4 ft × 1 ft = 4 ft²
- back: 4 ft × 1 ft = 4 ft²
- right: 1 ft × 3 ft = 3 ft²
- left: 1 ft × 3 ft = 3 ft²

**Figure 1.8. Surface Area**

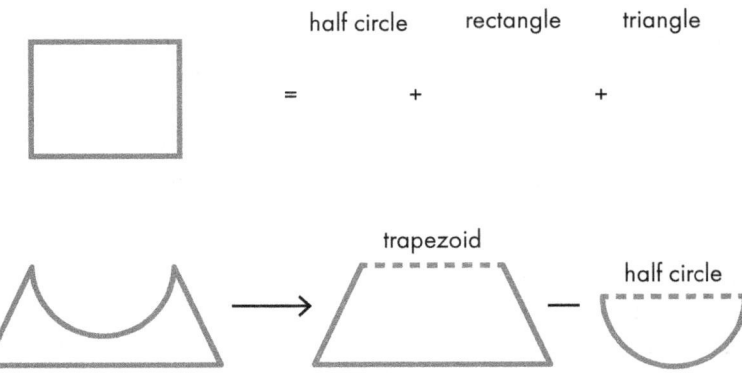

**Figure 1.9. Compound Shapes**

The HESI will also ask test takers to find the perimeter and area of compound shapes, which will include parts of circles, squares, triangles, or other polygons joined together to create an irregular shape. For these types of problems, the first step is to divide the figure into shapes whose area (or perimeter) can easily be solved for. Then, solve each part separately and add (or subtract) the parts together for the final answer.

PRACTICE QUESTIONS

**56.** What is the area of the figure shown below?

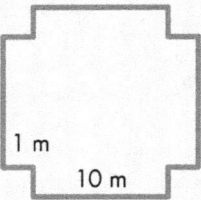

**57.** What is the area of the shaded region in the figure below?

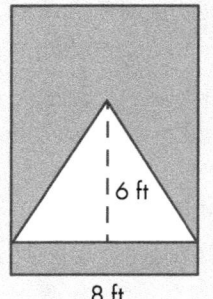

## Statistics

**Statistics** is the study of data. Analyzing data requires using **measures of central tendency** (mean, median, and mode) to identify trends or patterns.

The **mean** is the average; it is determined by adding all outcomes and then dividing by the total number of outcomes. For example, the average of the data set {16, 19, 19, 25, 27, 29, 75} is equal to $\frac{16 + 19 + 19 + 25 + 27 + 29 + 75}{7} = \frac{210}{7} = 30$.

The **median** is the number in the middle when the data set is arranged in order from least to greatest. For example, in the data set {16, 19, 19, **25**, 27, 29, 75}, the median is 25. When a data set contains an even number of values, finding the median requires averaging the two middle values. In the data set {75, 80, 82, 100}, the two numbers in the middle are 80 and 82. Consequently, the median will be the average of these two values: $\frac{80 + 82}{2} = 81$.

Finally, the **mode** is the most frequent outcome in a data set. In the set {16, 19, 19, 25, 27, 29, 75}, the mode is 19 because it occurs twice, which is more than any of the other numbers. If several values appear an equal, and most frequent, number of times, both values are considered the mode. If every value in a data set appears only once, the data set has no mode.

**HELPFUL HINT**

Mode is most common. Median is in the middle (like a median in the road). Mean is average.

Other useful indicators include range and outliers. The **range** is the difference between the highest and the lowest values in a data set. For example, the range of the set {16, 19, 19, 25, 27, 29, 75} is 75 − 16 = 59.

**Outliers**, or data points that are much different from other data points, should be noted as they can skew the central tendency. In the data set {16, 19, 19, 25, 27, 29, 75}, the value 75 is far outside the other values and raises the value of the mean. Without the outlier, the mean is much closer to the other data points.

- $\frac{16 + 19 + 19 + 25 + 27 + 29 + 75}{7} = \frac{210}{7} = 30$
- $\frac{16 + 19 + 19 + 25 + 27 + 29}{6} = \frac{135}{6} = 22.5$

Generally, the median is a better indicator of a central tendency if outliers are present to skew the mean.

Trends in a data set can also be seen by graphing the data as a dot plot. The distribution of the data can then be described based on the shape of the graph. A **symmetric** distribution looks like two mirrored halves, while a **skewed** distribution is weighted more heavily toward the right or the left. Note the direction of the skew describes the side of the graph with fewer data points. In a **uniform** data set, the points are distributed evenly along the graph.

A symmetric or skewed distribution may have peaks, or sets of data points that appear more frequently. A **unimodal** distribution has one peak while a **bimodal** distribution has two peaks. A normal (or bell-shaped) distribution is a special symmetric, unimodal graph with a specific distribution of data points.

## PRACTICE QUESTIONS

**58.** Which of the following best describes the distribution of the graph?

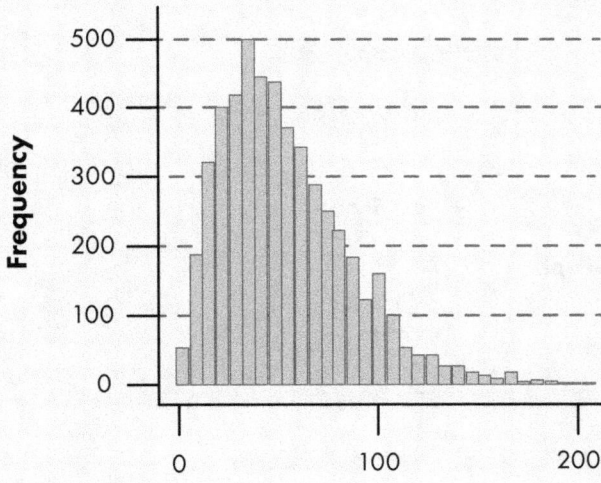

- **A)** Skewed left
- **B)** Skewed right
- **C)** Bimodal
- **D)** Uniform

**59.** Which of the following is the mean of the data set?

14, 18, 11, 28, 23, 14

- **A)** 11
- **B)** 14
- **C)** 18
- **D)** 28

## Data Presentation

Data can be presented in a variety of ways. In addition to a simple table, there are a number of different graphs and charts that can be used to visually represent data. The most appropriate type of graph or chart depends on the data being displayed.

**Box plots** (also called box and whisker plots) show data using the median, range, and outliers of a data set. They provide a helpful visual guide, showing how data is distributed around the median. In the example below, 70 is the median and the range is 0 – 100, or 100.

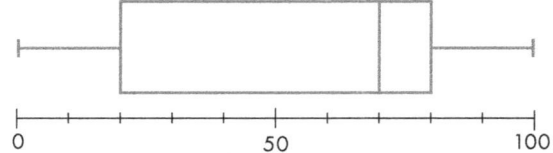

**Figure 1.10. Box Plot**

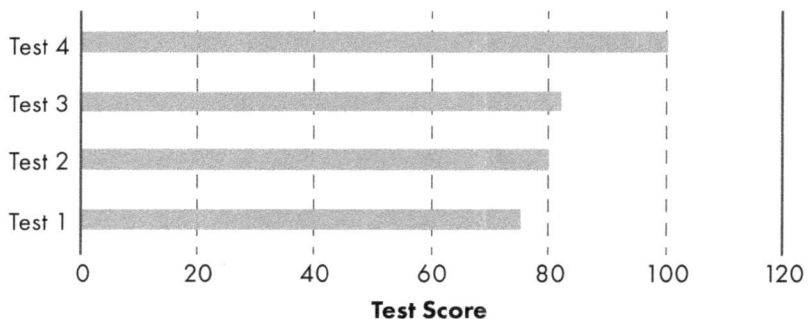

**Figure 1.11. Bar Graph**

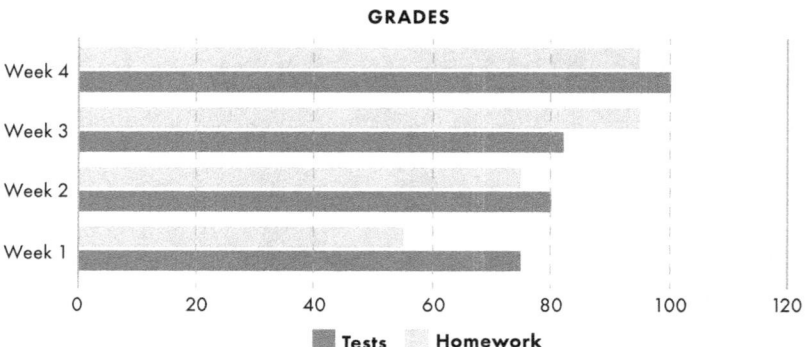

**Figure 1.12. Double Bar Graph**

**Bar graphs** use bars of different lengths to compare data. The independent variable on a bar graph is grouped into categories such as months, flavors, or locations, and the dependent variable is a quantity. Thus, comparing the length of bars provides a visual guide to the relative amounts in each category. **Double bar graphs** show more than one data set on the same set of axes.

**Histograms** similarly use bars to compare data, but the independent variable is a continuous variable that has been "binned" or divided into categories. For example, the time of day can be broken down into 8:00 a.m. to 12:00 p.m., 12:00 p.m. to 4:00 p.m., and so on. Usually (but not always), a gap is included between the bars of a bar graph but not a histogram. The bars of a bar graph show actual data, but the bars (or bins) of a histogram show the frequency of the data in various ranges.

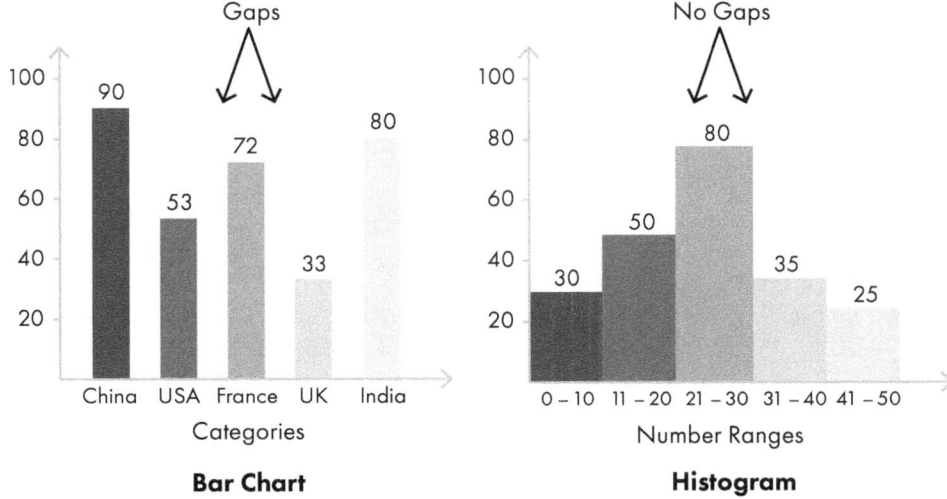

**Figure 1.13. Bar Chart vs. Histogram**

**Dot plots** display the frequency of a value or event data graphically using dots, and thus can be used to observe the distribution of a data set. Typically, a value or category is listed on the $x$-axis, and the number of times that value appears in the data set is represented by a line of vertical dots. Dot plots make it easy to see which values occur most often.

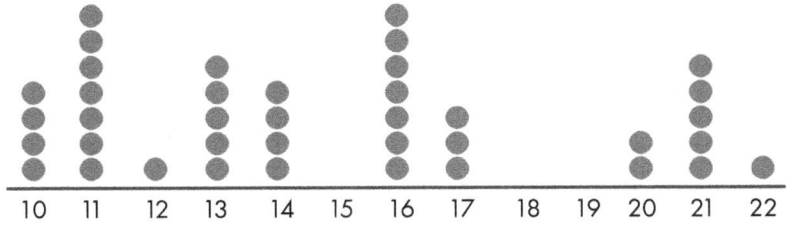

**Figure 1.14. Dot Plot**

**Scatter plots** use points to show relationships between two variables which can be plotted as coordinate points. One variable describes a position on the $x$-axis, and the other a point on the $y$-axis. Scatter plots can suggest relationships between variables. For example, both variables might increase together, or one may increase when the other decreases.

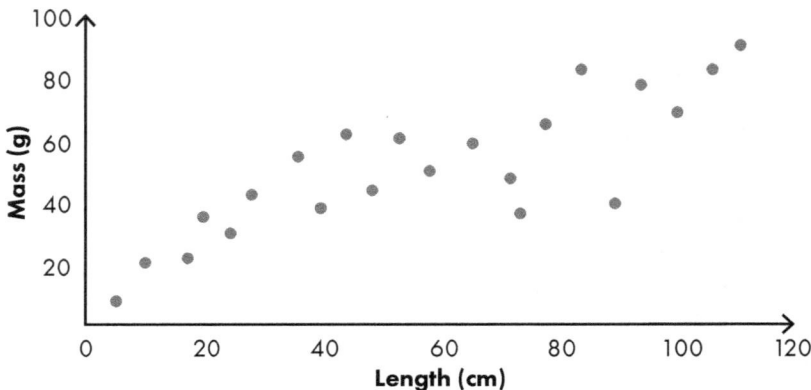

**Figure 1.15. Scatter Plot**

**Line graphs** show changes in data by connecting points on a scatter graph using a line. These graphs will often measure time on the *x*-axis and are used to show trends in the data, such as temperature changes over a day or school attendance throughout

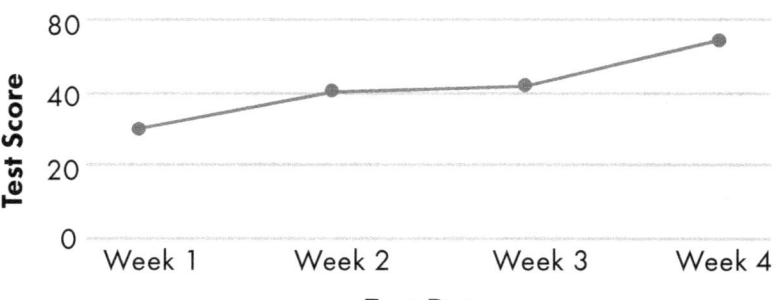

**Figure 1.16. Line Graph**

the year. **Double line graphs** present two sets of data on the same set of axes.

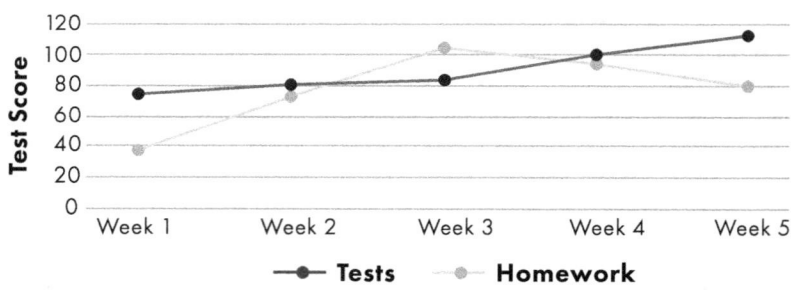

**Figure 1.17. Double Line Graph**

**Circle graphs** (also called pie charts) are used to show parts of a whole: the "pie" is the whole, and each "slice" represents a percentage or part of the whole.

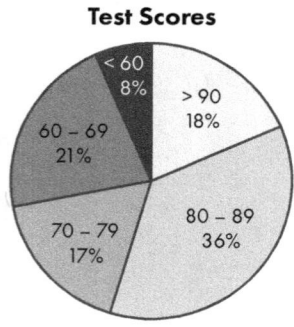

**Figure 1.18. Circle Graph**

# PRACTICE QUESTION

**60.** Students are asked if they prefer vanilla, chocolate, or strawberry ice cream. The results are tallied on the following table.

Four students display the information from the table in a bar graph. Which student completes the bar graph correctly?

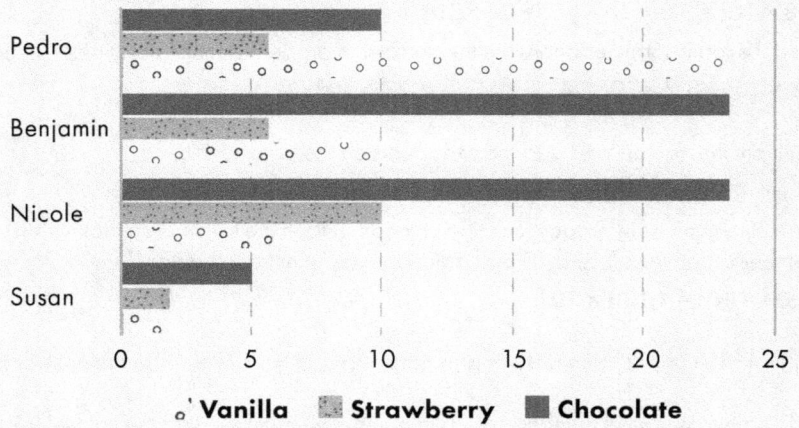

**A)** Pedro
**B)** Benjamin
**C)** Nicole
**D)** Susan

# ANSWER KEY

1. **Natural, whole, integer,** and **rational** (72 can be written as the fraction $\frac{72}{1}$).

2. **Rational** (The number is a fraction.)

3. **Irrational** (The number cannot be written as a fraction, and written as a decimal it is approximately 2.2360679... Notice this decimal does not terminate, nor does it have a repeating pattern.)

4. In order to add, the exponents of 10 must be the same. Change the first number so the power of 10 is 2:
   $3.8 \times 10^3 = 3.8 \times 10 \times 10^2 = 38 \times 10^2$
   Add the terms together and write the number in proper scientific notation:
   $38 \times 10^2 + 4.7 \times 10^2 = 42.7 \times 10^2 = \mathbf{4.27 \times 10^3}$

5. Multiply the factors and add the exponents on the base of 10:
   $(8.1 \times 1.4)(10^{-5} \times 10^7) = 11.34 \times 10^2$
   Write the number in proper scientific notation: (Place the decimal so that the first number is between 1 and 10 and adjust the exponent accordingly.)
   $11.34 \times 10^2 = \mathbf{1.134 \times 10^3}$

6. Since $|-18| > |12|$, the answer is negative. $|-18| - |12| = 6$. So the answer is **−6**.

7. Adding two negative numbers results in a negative number. Add the values: **−5.82**

8. **5.12**

9. Change the subtraction to addition, change the sign of the second number, then add:
   $86 - (-20) = 86 + (+20) = \mathbf{106}$

10. Multiply the numerators, multiply the denominators, then simplify: $-\frac{90}{15} = \mathbf{-6}$

11. A negative divided by a negative is a positive number: **6.4**

12. The parentheses indicate multiplication: **7.26**

13. A negative divided by a positive is negative: **−4**

14. Calculate the expressions inside the parenthesis:
    $2(21 - 14) + 6 \div (-2) \times 3 - 10 =$
    $2(7) + 6 \div (-2) \times 3 - 10$
    There are no exponents or radicals, so perform multiplication and division from left to right:
    $2(7) + 6 \div (-2) \times 3 - 10 =$
    $14 + 6 \div (-2) \times 3 - 10 =$
    $14 + (-3) \times 3 - 10 =$
    $14 + (-9) - 10$
    Lastly, perform addition and subtraction from left to right:
    $14 + (-9) - 10 = 5 - 10 = \mathbf{-5}$

15. Calculate the expressions inside the parentheses:

    $-(3)^2 + 4(5) + (5-6)^2 - 8 =$

    $-(3)^2 + 4(5) + (-1)^2 - 8$

    Simplify exponents and radicals:

    $-(3)^2 + 4(5) + (-1)^2 - 8 =$

    $-9 + 4(5) + 1 - 8$

    Note that $-(3)^2 = -1(3)^2 = -9$ but $(-1)^2 = (-1)(-1) = 1$

    Perform multiplication and division from left to right:

    $-9 + 4(5) + 1 - 8 =$

    $-9 + 20 + 1 - 8$

    Lastly, perform addition and subtraction from left to right:

    $-9 + 20 + 1 - 8 =$

    $11 + 1 - 8 = 12 - 8 =$ **4**

16. Simplify the top and bottom expressions separately using the same steps described above:

    $$\frac{(-2)^3 + 8(-2)}{4^2 - 5^2} = \frac{-8 + (-16)}{16 - 25} = \frac{-24}{-9} = \frac{8}{3}$$

17. Apply the order of operations left to right:

    $24.38 + 16.51 = 40.89$

    $40.89 - 29.87 =$ **11.02**

18. Multiply the numbers ignoring the decimals: $104 \times 182 = 18{,}928$

    The original problem includes two decimal places (10.4 has one place after the decimal point and 18.2 has one place after the decimal point), so place the decimal point in the answer so that there are two places after the decimal point. Estimating is a good way to check the answer ($10.4 \approx 10$, $18.2 \approx 18$, $10 \times 18 = 180$)

    $18{,}928 \rightarrow$ **189.28**

19. The divisor is 2.5. Move the decimal one place to the right (multiply 2.5 by 10) so that the divisor is a whole number. Since the decimal point of the divisor was moved one place to the right, the decimal point in the dividend must be moved one place to the right (multiplying it by 10 as well).

    $80 \rightarrow 800$ and $2.5 \rightarrow 25$

    Divide normally: $800 \div 25 =$ **32**

20. The first step is to change each fraction so it has a denominator of 20, which is the LCD of 5, 4, and 2:

    $2\frac{3}{5} + 3\frac{1}{4} - 1\frac{1}{2} = 2\frac{12}{20} + 3\frac{5}{20} - 1\frac{10}{20}$

    Next, add and subtract the whole numbers together and the fractions together:

    $2 + 3 - 1 = 4$

    $\frac{12}{20} + \frac{5}{20} - \frac{10}{20} = \frac{7}{20}$

    Lastly, combine to get the final answer (a mixed number): $\mathbf{4\frac{7}{20}}$

21. Change the mixed number to an improper fraction: $3\frac{1}{3} = \frac{10}{3}$

    Multiply the numerators together and the denominators together, and then reduce the fraction:

$$\frac{7}{8}\left(\frac{10}{3}\right) = \frac{7 \times 10}{8 \times 3} = \frac{70}{24} = \frac{35}{12} = 2\frac{11}{12}$$

22. Change the mixed number to an improper fraction. Then, multiply the first fraction by the reciprocal of the second fraction and simplify:

    $$\frac{9}{2} \div \frac{2}{3} = \frac{9}{2} \times \frac{3}{2} = \frac{27}{4} = 6\frac{3}{4}$$

23. Divide the denominator into the numerator using long division:

    ```
         0.875
    8 ) 7.0000
       -64
         60
        -56
          60
         -56
           40
          -40
            0
    ```

24. Dividing using long division yields a repeating decimal:

    ```
          0.4545
    11 ) 5.0000
        -44
          60
         -55
           50
          -44
            60
           -55
             5
    ```

25. Place the numbers to the right of the decimal (125) in the numerator. There are three numbers, so put the number 1000 in the denominator, and then reduce: $\frac{125}{1000} = \frac{1}{8}$

26. The 8 is in the thousands place, and the number to its right is a 4. Because 4 is less than 5, the 8 remains and all numbers to the right become zero:
    138,472 ≈ **138,000**

27. Round each value to the thousands place and add:
    12,341 ≈ 12,000
    8,975 ≈ 9,000
    9,431 ≈ 9,000
    10,521 ≈ 11,000
    11,427 ≈ 11,000
    12,000 + 9,000 + 9,000 + 11,000 + 11,000 = **52,000**

28. There are 22 total students in the class. The ratio can be written as $\frac{10}{22}$, and reduced to $\frac{5}{11}$. The ratio of girls to boys is **12:10 or 6:5**.

**29.** The family's total expenses for the month add up to $2,300. The ratio of the rent to total amount of expenses can be written as $\frac{600}{2300}$ and reduced to $\mathbf{\frac{6}{23}}$.

**30.** Start by cross multiplying:
$\frac{3-5}{2} = \frac{-8}{3} \rightarrow 3(3 - 5x) = 2(-8)$
Then, solve the equation:
$9 - 15x = -16$
$-15x = -25$
$x = \frac{-25}{-15} = \mathbf{\frac{5}{3}}$

**31.** Write a proportion where x equals the actual distance and each ratio is written as inches:miles.
$\frac{2.5}{40} = \frac{17.25}{x}$
Then, cross-multiply and divide to solve: $2.5x = 690$
$x = 276$
**The two cities are 276 miles apart.**

**32.** Write a proportion in which x is the number of defective parts made and both ratios are written as defective parts:total parts.
$\frac{4}{1000} = \frac{x}{125,000}$
Then, cross-multiply and divide to solve for x: $1000x = 500,000$
$x = 500$
**There are 500 defective parts for the month.**

**33.** The percent is written as a fraction over 100 and reduced: $\frac{18}{100} = \mathbf{\frac{9}{50}}$.

**34.** Dividing 5 by 3 gives the value 0.6, which is then multiplied by 100: **60%**.

**35.** The decimal point is moved two places to the right: **112.5%**.

**36.** The decimal point is moved two places to the left: 84% = **0.84**.

**37.** The first step is to find the percent of students who are girls by subtracting from 100%:
100% − 54% = 46%
Next, identify the variables and plug into the appropriate equation:
percent = 46% = 0.46
whole = 650 students
part = ?
part = whole × percent = 0.46 × 650 = 299
**There are 299 girls.**

**38.** The first step is to identify the necessary values. These can then be plugged into the appropriate equation:
original amount = 1,500
percent change = 45% = 0.45
amount of change = ?
amount of change = original amount × percent change = 1,500 × 0.45 = 675

To find the new price, subtract the amount of change from the original price:
1,500 − 675 = 825 → The final price is **$825**.

**39.** Identify the necessary values and plug into the appropriate equation:

original amount = 100,000

amount of change = 120,000 − 100,000 = 20,000

percent change = ?

percent change = $\frac{\text{amount of change}}{\text{original amount}}$

= $\frac{20,000}{100,000}$ = 0.20

To find the percent growth, multiply by 100: 0.20 × 100 = **20%**

**40.** Change each fraction to a decimal:

$-\frac{2}{3} = -0.\overline{66}$

$\frac{5}{4} = 1.25$

$\frac{1}{8} = 0.125$

Now place the decimals in order from greatest to least:

1.25, 1.2, 0.125, 0, −0.$\overline{66}$, −1, −2.1

Lastly, convert back to fractions if the problem requires it:

$\frac{5}{4}$, 1.2, $\frac{1}{8}$, 0, $-\frac{2}{3}$, −1, −2.1

**41.** Convert each value using the least common denominator value of 24:

$\frac{1}{3} = \frac{8}{24}$

$-\frac{5}{6} = -\frac{20}{24}$

$1\frac{1}{8} = \frac{9}{8} = \frac{27}{24}$

$\frac{7}{12} = \frac{14}{24}$

$-\frac{3}{4} = -\frac{18}{24}$

$-\frac{3}{2} = -\frac{36}{24}$

Next, put the fractions in order from least to greatest by comparing the numerators:

$-\frac{36}{24}, -\frac{20}{24}, -\frac{18}{24}, \frac{8}{24}, \frac{14}{24}, \frac{27}{24}$

Finally, put the fractions back in their original form if the problem requires it:

$-\frac{3}{2}, -\frac{5}{6}, -\frac{3}{4}, \frac{1}{3}, \frac{7}{12}, 1\frac{1}{8}$

**42.** First, plug the value 4 in for $m$ in the expression:

$5(m - 2)^3 + 3m^2 - \frac{m}{4} - 1$

$= 5(4 - 2)^3 + 3(4)^2 - \frac{4}{4} - 1$

Then, simplify using PEMDAS:

P: $5(2)^3 + 3(4)^2 - \frac{4}{4} - 1$

E: $5(8) + 3(16) - \frac{4}{4} - 1$

M and D, working left to right: 40 + 48 − 1 − 1

A and S, working left to right: **86**

**43.** The only like terms in both expressions are 12x and 8x, so these two terms will be added, and all other terms will remain the same:

$a + b = (12x + 8x) + 7xy - 9y - 9xz + 7z$

$= \mathbf{20x + 7xy - 9y - 9xz + 7z}$

**44.** The term outside the parentheses must be distributed and multiplied by all three terms inside the parentheses:

$(5x)(x^2) = 5x^3$

$(5x)(-2c) = -10xc$

$(5x)(10) = 50x$

$5x(x^2 - 2c + 10) \rightarrow \mathbf{5x^3 - 10xc + 50x}$

**45.** Start by distributing for each set of parentheses:

$x(5 + z) - z(4x - z^2)$

Notice that $-z$ is distributed and that $(-z)(-z^2) = +z^3$. Failing to distribute the negative is a very common error.

$5x + xz - 4zx + z^3$

Note that $xz$ is a like term with $zx$ (commutative property), and they can therefore be combined.

Now combine like terms and place terms in the appropriate order (highest exponents first): $\mathbf{z^3 - 3xz + 5x}$

**46.** To cancel out the denominator, multiply both sides by 20:

$20 \frac{100(x + 5)}{20} = 1 \times 20$

$100(x + 5) = 20$

Next, distribute 100 through the parentheses:

$100(x + 5) = 20$

$100x + 500 = 20$

"Undo" the +500 by subtracting 500 from both sides of the equation to isolate the variable term: $100x = -480$

Finally, "undo" the multiplication by 100: divide by 100 on both sides to solve for $x$:

$\mathbf{x = \frac{-480}{100} = -4.8}$

**47.** First, simplify the left-hand side of the equation using order of operations and combining like terms.

$2(x + 2)^2 - 2x^2 + 10 = 20$

Do the exponent first: $2(x + 2)(x + 2) - 2x^2 + 10 = 20$

FOIL: $2(x^2 + 4x + 4) - 2x^2 + 10 = 20$

Distribute the 2: $2x^2 + 8x + 8 - 2x^2 + 10 = 20$

Combine like terms on the left-hand side: $8x + 18 = 20$

Now, isolate the variable.

"Undo" +18 by subtracting 18 from both sides: $8x + 18 = 20$

$8x = 2$

"Undo" multiplication by 8 by dividing both sides by 8: $\mathbf{x = \frac{2}{8} \text{ or } \frac{1}{4}}$

**48.** The y-intercept can be identified on the graph as (0, 3). Thus, b = 3.

To find the slope, choose any two points and plug the values into the slope equation. The two points chosen here are (2, −1) and (3, −3).

$m = \frac{(-3) - (-1)}{3 - 2} = \frac{-2}{1} = -2$

Replace m with −2 and b with 3 in y = mx + b.

The equation of the line is **y = −2x + 3**.

**49.** Rearrange the equation into slope-intercept form by solving the equation for y. Isolate −2y by subtracting 6x and adding 8 to both sides of the equation.

−2y = −6x + 8

Divide both sides by −2:

$y = \frac{-6x + 8}{-2}$

Simplify the fraction.

y = 3x − 4

**The slope is 3, since it is the coefficient of x.**

**50.** The problem is asking for the number of tickets. First, identify the quantities:

number of tickets = x

cost per ticket = 5

cost for x tickets = 5x

total cost = 28

entry fee = 3

Now, set up an equation. The total cost for x tickets will be equal to the cost for x tickets plus the $3 entry fee: 5x + 3 = 28

Now solve the equation:

5x + 3 = 28

5x = 25

x = 5

**The student bought 5 tickets.**

**51.** The problem asks for the number of hours Abby will have to work. First, identify the quantities:

number of hours = x

amount earned per hour = 10

amount of money earned = 10x

price of bicycle = 395

money borrowed = 150

Now, set up an equation. The amount of money she has borrowed plus the money she earned as a waitress needs to equal the cost of the bicycle: 10x + 150 = 395

Now solve the equation:

10x + 150 = 395

10x = 245

x = 24.5 hours

**She will need to work 24.5 hours.**

52. Inequalities can be solved using the same steps used to solve equations. Start by subtracting 10 from both sides:

    $4x + 10 > 58$

    $4x > 48$

    Now divide by 4 to isolate $x$: **$x > 12$**

53. They have to spend less than $2,500 on uniforms, so this problem is an inequality. First, identify the quantities:

    number of t-shirts = $t$

    total cost of t-shirts = $12t$

    number of pants = $p$

    total cost of pants = $15p$

    number of pairs of shoes = $s$

    total cost of shoes = $45s$

    The cost of all the items must be less than $2,500: **$12t + 15p + 45s < 2,500$**

54. $4.25 \text{ km} \left( \frac{1000 \text{ m}}{1 \text{ km}} \right) =$ **4250 m**

55. $12 \text{ ft} \left( \frac{12 \text{ in}}{1 \text{ ft}} \right) =$ **144 in**

56. The figure can be broken apart into three rectangles:

    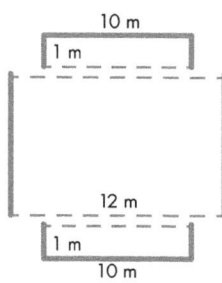

    The area of each smaller rectangle is 1 m × 10 m = 10 m². The area of the larger rectangle is 10 m × 12 m = 120 m². Together, the area of the three shapes is 10 m² + 10 m² + 120 m² = **140 m²**

57. The area of the shaded region is the area of the rectangle minus the area of the triangle:

    rectangle − triangle = (8 ft × 16 ft) − (0.5 × 8 ft × 6 ft) = 128 ft² − 24 ft² = **104 ft²**

58. **B) is correct.** The graph is skewed right because there are fewer data points on the right half.

59. **C) is correct.** The mean is the average: $\frac{14 + 18 + 11 + 28 + 23 + 14}{6} = \frac{108}{6} = 18$

60. **B) is correct.** Benjamin's bar graph indicates that ten students prefer vanilla, six students prefer strawberry, and twenty-three students prefer chocolate ice cream.

# TWO: READING

The **HESI A² Reading Comprehension** test includes questions about a wide range of media, including fiction and nonfiction passages, diagrams, graphs, sets of directions, and professional communications like emails and memos. Generally, these questions fall into three categories.

**Key ideas and details** questions test your comprehension of the text on a broad level. You will need to see the text as a whole, identify the main ideas, and explain how they lead to specific inferences and conclusions. You will also need to discern the overall theme of a text and summarize it accurately.

**Craft and structure** questions test your understanding of the craft of writing. You might see questions about the use of language, point of view, and organization. You will need to analyze the details of the passage and relate them to the overall organization and meaning of the passage.

**Integration of knowledge** questions ask you to incorporate your skills from the other categories to answer complex questions. Questions might ask you to evaluate a text, compare multiple texts, or examine other kinds of texts, such as visual media. In order to answer questions like this, you will need to synthesize the skills applied to other types of questions and go beyond analyzing texts to evaluating and judging them.

## The Main Idea

The **main idea** of a text describes the text's main topic and the author's perspective on that topic. On the HESI, you will be asked to identify the topic and main idea of a text, and you may have to use this information to concisely summarize a passage.

To find the main idea, first identify the **topic**, which is simply what the passage is about. The **topic sentence** is generally the first sentence, or very near the first sentence, in the paragraph. It introduces the reader to the topic by making a general statement about that topic so that the reader knows what to expect in the rest of the passage. Once you've identified the topic, use the text to figure out what the author wants to say about that topic.

**HELPFUL HINT**

To determine the topic, ask yourself what you're reading about. To determine the main idea, ask yourself how the author feels about that topic.

As you read the following passage, think about the topic and what the author wants to communicate about that topic.

> Swimmers and beachgoers may look nervously for the telltale fin skimming the surface of the ocean, but the reality is that shark bites are extremely rare and almost never unprovoked. Sharks attack people at very predictable times and for very predictable reasons: rough surf, poor visibility, or a swimmer sending visual and physical signals that mimic a shark's normal prey are just a few examples. The "shark mania" of recent years can be largely pinned on the sensationalistic media surrounding the animals. The release of *Jaws* in 1975 to the ultra-hyped shark feeding frenzies and "worst shark attacks" countdowns known as *Shark Week* are just some examples. Popular culture both demonizes and fetishizes sharks until the public cannot get enough.

The topic of the passage is the single thing that is discussed throughout the passage: the danger of sharks. To identify the main idea of the passage, ask yourself what the author wants to say about this topic. What does she want the reader to think about the danger of sharks after reading this passage? It's clear from the author's opening sentence that she wants the reader to understand that shark attacks are not nearly as common or dangerous as popular culture makes them seem. The author includes details about the reasons shark bites happen in the real world, then explains how this danger is exaggerated in movies and on TV.

## PRACTICE QUESTIONS

Tourists flock to Yellowstone National Park each year to view the geysers that bubble and erupt throughout it. What most of these tourists do not know is that these geysers are formed by a caldera, a hot crater in the earth's crust that was created by a series of three eruptions from an ancient supervolcano. These eruptions, which began 2.1 million years ago, spewed between 1,000 and 2,450 cubic kilometers of volcanic matter at such a rate that the volcano's magma chamber collapsed, creating the craters.

**1.** Which of the following is the topic of the passage?
   **A)** tourists
   **B)** geysers
   **C)** volcanic eruptions
   **D)** supervolcanoes

The Battle of Little Bighorn (1876), commonly called Custer's Last Stand, was a battle between the Lakota, the Northern Cheyenne, the Arapaho, and the Seventh Calvary Regiment of the US Army. Led by war leaders Crazy Horse and Chief Gall and the religious leader Sitting Bull, the allied tribes of the Plains Indians decisively defeated their US foes. Two hundred sixty-eight US soldiers were killed, including General George Armstrong Custer, two of his brothers, his nephew, his brother-in-law, and six Indian scouts.

**2.** Which of the following could be considered the main idea of the passage?
   **A)** Most of General Custer's family died in the Battle of Little Bighorn.
   **B)** During the nineteenth century, the US Army often fought with Indian tribes.
   **C)** Sitting Bull and George Custer were fierce enemies.
   **D)** The Battle of Little Bighorn was a significant victory for the Plains Indians.

## Summarizing Passages

Understanding the main idea can help you summarize a passage. A **summary** is a very brief restatement of the most important parts of an argument or text. To build a summary, start by identifying the main idea, then add the most important details that support that main idea. A good summary will address ALL the ideas contained in the passage, not just one or two specific details.

The **summary sentence** of a paragraph frequently (but not always!) comes at the end of a paragraph or passage, because it wraps up all of the ideas the passage presents. This sentence gives the reader an understanding of what the author wants to say about the topic and what conclusions can be drawn about it.

**HELPFUL HINT**

When HESI Reading questions ask about the main idea of the passage, they're asking you to summarize the passage in a sentence.

### PRACTICE QUESTION

The greatest changes in sensory, motor, and perceptual development happen in the first two years of life. When babies are first born, most of their senses operate in a similar way to those of adults. For example, babies are able to hear before they are born; studies show that babies turn toward the sound of their mother's voice just minutes after being born, indicating they recognize the mother's voice from their time in the womb.

The exception to this rule is vision. A baby's vision changes significantly in the first year of life; initially infants have a range of vision of only 8 – 12 inches and no depth perception. As a result, infants rely primarily on hearing; vision does not become the dominant sense until around the age of 12 months. Babies also prefer faces to other objects. This preference, along with their limited vision range, means that their sight is initially focused on their caregiver.

**3.** Which of the following is a concise summary of the passage?
- **A)** Babies have no depth perception until 12 months, which is why they focus only on their caregivers' faces.
- **B)** Babies can recognize their mother's voice when born, so they initially rely primarily on their sense of hearing.
- **C)** Babies have senses similar to those of adults except for their sense of sight, which doesn't fully develop until 12 months.
- **D)** Babies' senses go through many changes in the first year of their lives.

## Supporting Details

An author makes her argument using **supporting details**, which make up the majority of a text passage. Supporting details can include **facts**, which can be verified as true, and **opinions**, which are the author's personal beliefs.

Supporting details are often introduced by **signal words** that explain to the reader how one sentence or idea is connected to another and hint at supporting ideas. Signal words can indicate new information, counterarguments, or conclusions.

- adding information: additionally, also, in addition, furthermore, too
- give an example: for example, for instance, in other words, in particular
- show cause and effect: because, so, therefore, consequently
- comparing: in the same way, like, likewise, similarly
- contrasting: alternatively, conversely, instead of, otherwise, unlike
- sequence: first, second, next, after, before, then, finally

**HELPFUL HINT**

When reading a text, underline key signal words like **for example** and **because** to help you identify important points.

**READING** 35

## PRACTICE QUESTIONS

Increasingly, companies are turning to subcontracting services rather than hiring full-time employees. This provides companies with many advantages. For example, subcontractors offer greater flexibility, reduced legal responsibility to employees, and lower possibility of unionization within the company. However, it has also led to increasing confusion and uncertainty over the legal definition of employment. Recently, the courts have grappled with questions about the hiring company's responsibility in maintaining fair labor practices. Companies argue that they delegate that authority to the subcontractors, while unions and other worker advocate groups argue that companies still have a legal obligation to the workers who contribute to their business.

4. According to the passage, which of the following is NOT an advantage of using subcontracting services?
   A) greater flexibility
   B) uncertainty about the legal definition of employment
   C) reduced legal responsibility to employees
   D) lower possibility of unionization within the company

5. Which of the following statements from the passage is an opinion?
   A) Companies are turning to subcontracting services rather than hiring full-time employees.
   B) Subcontractors offer greater flexibility, reduced legal responsibility to employees, and lower possibility of unionization within the company.
   C) The courts have grappled with questions about the hiring company's responsibility in maintaining fair labor practices.
   D) Companies still have a legal obligation to the workers who contribute to their business.

After looking at five houses, Robert and I have decided to buy the one on Forest Road. The first two homes we visited didn't have the space we need—the first had only one bathroom, and the second did not have a guest bedroom. The third house, on Pine Street, had enough space inside but didn't have a big enough yard for our three dogs. The fourth house we looked at, on Rice Avenue, was stunning but well above our price range. The last home, on Forest Road, wasn't in the neighborhood we wanted to live in. However, it had the right amount of space for the right price.

6. Which of the following lists the author's actions in the correct sequence?
   A) The author looked at the house on Forest Road, then at a house with a yard that was too small, then at two houses that were too small, and then finally at a house that was too expensive.
   B) The author looked at the house on Forest Road, then at two houses that were too small, then at a house with a yard that was too small, and then finally at a house that was too expensive.
   C) The author looked at two homes with yards that were too small, then a house with only one bathroom, then a house that was too expensive, and then finally the house on Forest Road.
   D) The author looked at two homes that were too small, then a house with a yard that was too small, then a house that was too expensive, and then finally the house on Forest Road.

## Text Structure

The structure of a text describes how the author chooses to organize the supporting details in a passage. To identify the organizing structure of a passage, look at the order in which the author presents information and the transitions used to connect those pieces. Specific text structures are described in the table below.

Table 2.1. Text Structure

| Name | Structure | Words to Look For |
| --- | --- | --- |
| Cause and effect | The author describes a situation and then its effects. | because, as a result, consequently, therefore, for this reason |
| Compare and contrast | The author explores the similarities and differences between two or more things. | similarly, like, in addition, however, alternatively, unlike, but |
| Problem and solution | The author presents a problem and offers a solution. | if...then, problem, solution, answer |
| Description | The author describes a thing or process. | for example, for instance, such as, to illustrate |
| Chronological | The author lists events in the order in which they happened. | first, second, next, after, before |

Underline signal words like *first*, *after*, *then*, and *consequently* to help identify the sequence of events in a passage.

### PRACTICE QUESTION

In an effort to increase women's presence in government, several countries in Latin America, including Argentina, Brazil, and Mexico, have implemented legislated candidate quotas. These quotas require that at least 30 percent of a party's candidate list in any election cycle consists of women who have a legitimate chance at election. As a result, Latin America has the greatest number of female heads of government in the world, and the second highest percentage of female members of parliament after Nordic Europe. However, these trends do not carry over outside of politics. While 25 percent of legislators in Latin America are now women, less than 2 percent of CEOs in the region are female.

7. Which of the following best describes the organization of the passage?
   A) compare and contrast
   B) chronological
   C) cause and effect
   D) description

## Drawing Conclusions

Understanding a reading passage begins with understanding the explicit, or clearly stated, information in the text. Using that information, the reader can make conclusions or inferences about what the text suggests or implies but does not explicitly say.

To draw a **conclusion**, readers must consider the details or facts in a passage, then determine what event or idea would logically follow at the end of the passage. For example, a story describes an old man sitting alone in a café. The young waiter says that the café is closing, but the old man continues to drink. The waiter starts closing up, and the old man tries to order another drink. Based on these details, the reader might conclude that the waiter will not bring the man another drink.

An **inference** is slightly different from a conclusion. An inference is an educated guess that readers make based on details in the text as well as their own knowledge and experiences. Returning to the story about the old man, the reader might use her own experiences to infer that the old man is lonely and so is reluctant to leave the café. Note that nothing in the passage explicitly states that the man is lonely—it is simply a possible interpretation of the situation.

### PRACTICE QUESTION

Alfie closed his eyes and took several deep breaths. He was trying to ignore the sounds of the crowd, but even he had to admit that it was hard not to notice the tension in the stadium. He could feel 50,000 sets of eyes burning through his skin—this crowd expected perfection from him. He took another breath and opened his eyes, setting his sights on the soccer ball resting peacefully in the grass. One shot, just one last shot, between his team and the championship. He didn't look up at the goalie, who was jumping nervously on the goal line just a few yards away. Afterward, he would swear he didn't remember anything between the referee's whistle and the thunderous roar of the crowd.

**8.** Which of the following conclusions is BEST supported by the passage?
   **A)** Alfie passed out on the field and was unable to take the shot.
   **B)** The goalie blocked Alfie's shot.
   **C)** Alfie scored the goal and won his team the championship.
   **D)** The referee declared the game a tie.

## The Author's Purpose

Every author chooses text structure, words, and content with a specific purpose and intention. The HESI will ask several types of questions that require you to figure out what the author is trying to say and what tools she is using to send that message.

Finding the **author's purpose** requires identifying the author's main idea and intended audience: What is the author trying to accomplish by writing this text? The purpose of most text passages will fall into one of four **modes**: narrative, expository, technical, or persuasive.

In a **narrative**, the author tells the reader a story, often to illustrate a theme or idea the reader needs to consider. The author will use the characteristics of storytelling, such as chronological order, characters, and a defined setting.

In an **expository** passage, the author simply explains an idea or topic to the reader. The main idea will probably be a factual statement or a direct assertion of a broadly held opinion. Expository writing can come in many forms, but one essential feature is a fair and balanced representation of a topic: the author may explore one detailed aspect or a broad range of characteristics, but he or she intends mainly to present the details or ideas to the reader to make a decision.

Similarly, in **technical** writing, the author's purpose is to explain specific processes, techniques, or equipment so the reader can use that process, technique, or equipment to obtain the desired result. In this writing, look for chronological or spatial organization, specialized vocabulary, and imperative or directive structures.

The categories of writing discussed above mostly communicate information to a reader so that he or she can take action or make a decision. In contrast, in **persuasive** writing, the author actively sets out to convince the reader to accept an opinion or belief.

### PRACTICE QUESTION

It could be said that the great battle between the North and South we call the Civil War was a battle for individual identity. The states of the South had their own culture, one based on farming, independence, and the rights of both man and state to determine their own paths. Similarly, the North had forged its own identity as a center of centralized commerce and manufacturing. This clash of lifestyles was bound to create tension, and this tension was bound to lead to war. But people who try to sell you this narrative are wrong. The Civil War was not a battle of cultural identities—it was a battle about slavery. All other explanations for the war are either a direct consequence of the South's desire for wealth at the expense of her fellow man or a fanciful invention to cover up this sad portion of our nation's history. And it cannot be denied that this time in our past was very sad indeed.

**9.** Which of the following best describes the mode of the passage?
- **A)** expository
- **B)** narrative
- **C)** persuasive
- **D)** technical

# Words in Context

The HESI will ask you to determine the definition of words in context, meaning as they appear within the text. This can be slightly more difficult than simply knowing the definition of a word, as you may be required to figure out how the author is using the word in the specific text.

### CONTEXT CLUES

To grasp the meaning of unfamiliar words, readers may use context clues or hints in the text. Using context clues is especially helpful for determining the appropriate meaning of a word with multiple definitions.

One type of context clue is a **definition** or **description clue**. Sometimes, authors may use a difficult word and then say "that is" or "which is" to signal the reader that they are providing a definition. An author may also provide a synonym or restate the idea in familiar words:

> Teachers often prefer teaching students with <u>intrinsic</u> motivation; these students have an <u>internal</u> desire to learn.

The meaning of *intrinsic* is restated as *internal*.

**HELPFUL HINT**

Read the sentence with each answer choice plugged in for the vocabulary word to see which choice best matches the context.

Similarly, authors may include **example clues** by providing an example of the unfamiliar word close to the word:

> Teachers may view extrinsic rewards as efficacious; however, an individual student may not be interested in what the teacher offers. For example, a student who has diabetes may not feel any incentive to work when offered a sweet treat.

*Efficacious* is explained with an example demonstrating the effectiveness (and lack thereof) of extrinsic rewards.

Another commonly used context clue is the **contrast/antonym clue**. In this case, authors indicate that the unfamiliar word is the opposite of a familiar word:

> In contrast to intrinsic motivation, extrinsic motivation is contingent on teachers offering rewards that are appealing.

The phrase *in contrast* tells the reader that *extrinsic* is the opposite of *intrinsic*.

## PRACTICE QUESTIONS

10. One challenge of teaching is finding ways to incentivize, or to motivate, learning. Which of the following is the meaning of *incentivize* as used in the sentence?
    A) encourage
    B) reward
    C) challenge
    D) improve

11. If an extrinsic reward is extremely desirable, a student may become so apprehensive he or she cannot focus. That is, the student may experience such intense pressure to perform that the reward undermines its intent.
    Which of the following is the meaning of *apprehensive* as used in the sentence?
    A) uncertain
    B) distracted
    C) anxious
    D) forgetful

## FIGURATIVE LANGUAGE

**Figures of speech** are expressions that are understood to have a nonliteral meaning. Instead of meaning what is actually said, figurative language suggests meaning by speaking of a subject as if it is something else. When Shakespeare says, "All the world's a stage, / And all men and women merely players," he isn't stating that the world is literally a stage. Instead, it functions like a stage, with men and women giving performances as if they were actors on a stage.

A **metaphor** is a figure of speech that works like an analogy. It uses something familiar and obvious to help the reader understand something that is new or hard to describe. For example, the phrase "the elephant in the room" is used to describe the concept of something unspoken but obvious. The unspoken idea is abstract, but the reader can grasp the concrete idea of an elephant as something so large and imposing that everyone is aware of it.

A **simile** is figurative language that directly points to similarities between two things. Saying that someone runs "as fast as lightning" doesn't mean they're actually running at the speed of light; the simile just emphasizes that the person is very fast.

### PRACTICE QUESTION

12. The coach was thrilled his team won its final game. The fact that his son scored the winning goal was just the icing on the cake.

    In the sentence, "icing on the cake" refers to which of the following?

    **A)** an unfortunate occurrence
    **B)** an added benefit
    **C)** a surprise event
    **D)** an expected result

# ANSWER KEY

1. **B) is correct.** The topic of the passage is geysers. Tourists, volcanic eruptions, and supervolcanoes are all mentioned during the explanation of what geysers are and how they are formed.

2. **D) is correct.** The author writes, "the allied tribes decisively defeated their US foes," and the remainder of the passage provides details to support this idea. Choice A is a fact from the passage but is not general enough to be the main idea. Similarly, Choice C can be inferred from the passage but is not what the majority of the passage is about. Choice B is too general and discusses topics outside the content of the passage.

3. A) is incorrect. The passage is about babies' senses in general; therefore this answer choice is too specific.

    B) is incorrect. The passage is about babies' senses in general; therefore this answer choice is too specific.

    **C) is correct.** The passage states that babies' senses are much like those of adults with the exception of their vision, which develops later.

    D) is incorrect. The passage indicates that a baby's vision "changes significantly in the first year of life" but suggests that other senses are relatively well-developed at birth.

4. **B) is correct.** Choices A, C, and D are listed as advantages of using subcontracting services (introduced after the signal words *for example*). Uncertainly about the legal definition of employment is given later as one of the disadvantages of using subcontracting services.

5. **D) is correct.** Choices A, B, and C are all facts that can be proven with evidence. For example, employment data could show that companies now choose subcontracting services over full-time employees (Choice A). Choice D is an opinion held by unions and advocate groups.

6. **D) is correct.** Choice D correctly chronologically lists the houses the author visited in the passage.

7. **C) is correct.** The passage starts by introducing the topic of candidate quotas, then goes on to explain how these quotas have affected the number of female legislators and CEOs. The transition *as a result* links the cause to the effect.

8. **C) is correct.** The crowd's support for Alfie and the collective roar after the shot implies that Alfie scored the goal and won the championship.

9. **C) is correct.** The author of the passage is trying to persuade the reader that the "Civil War was not a battle of cultural identities—it was a battle about slavery." Phrases like "people...are wrong" and "it cannot be denied" suggest that the author is trying to convince the reader that a particular viewpoint is true.

10. **A) is correct.** The word *incentivize* is defined immediately with the synonym *motivate*, or *encourage*.

11. **C) is correct.** The reader can infer that the pressure to perform is making the student anxious.

12. **B) is correct.** The fact that the coach was already thrilled implies that "the icing on the cake" provides an extra level of enjoyment, much like icing adds to the enjoyment of cake.

HESI A² Study Guide

# THREE: VOCABULARY

**The HESI will ask you** to identify the meaning of certain words. These words will only appear in a single sentence, not in a passage, so you'll have minimal context clues. Instead, you'll need to learn how to use the word.

## Word Structure

Words consist of distinct pieces that help determine meaning; the most familiar of these pieces are root words, prefixes, and suffixes.

### ROOT WORDS

**Root words** are bases from which many words take their foundational form and meaning. The most common root words are Greek and Latin, and a broad knowledge of these roots can greatly improve your ability to determine the meaning of words in context. Knowing root words cannot always provide the exact meaning of a word, but combined with an understanding of the word's place in the sentence and the context surrounding the word, it will often be enough to answer a question about meaning or relationships.

Table 3.1. List of Common Roots

| Roots | Meaning | Examples |
| --- | --- | --- |
| alter | other | alternate, alter ego |
| ambi | both | ambidextrous |
| ami, amic | love | amiable |
| amphi | both ends or all sides | amphibian |
| anthrop | man, human, humanity | misanthrope, anthropologist |
| apert | open | aperture |
| aqua | water | aqueduct, aquarium |
| aud | to hear | audience |

Table 3.1. List of Common Roots (continued)

| Roots | Meaning | Examples |
|---|---|---|
| auto | self | autobiography |
| bell | war | belligerent, bellicose |
| bene | good | benevolent |
| bio | life | biology |
| ced | yield, go | secede, intercede |
| cent | one hundred | century |
| chron | time | chronological |
| circum | around | circumference |
| contra/counter | against | contradict |
| crac, crat | rule, ruler | autocrat, bureaucrat |
| crypt | hidden | cryptogram, cryptic |
| curr, curs, cours | to run | precursory |
| dict | to say | dictator, dictation |
| dyna | power | dynamic |
| dys | bad, hard, unlucky | dysfunctional |
| equ | equal, even | equanimity |
| fac | to make, to do | factory |
| form | shape | reform, conform |
| fort | strength | fortitude |
| fract | to break | fracture |
| grad, gress | step | progression |
| gram | thing written | epigram |
| graph | writing | graphic |
| hetero | different | heterogeneous |
| homo | same | homogenous |
| hypo | below, beneath | hypothermia |
| iso | identical | isolate |
| ject | throw | projection |
| logy | study of | biology |
| luc | light | elucidate |
| mal | bad | malevolent |
| meta, met | behind, between | metacognition-behind the thinking |
| meter/metr | measure | thermometer |
| micro | small | microbe |
| mis/miso | hate | misanthrope |

| Roots | Meaning | Examples |
|---|---|---|
| mit | to send | transmit |
| mono | one | monologue |
| morph | form, shape | morphology |
| mort | death | mortal |
| multi | many | multiple |
| phil | love | philanthropist |
| port | carry | transportation |
| pseudo | false | pseudonym |
| psycho | soul, spirit | psychic |
| rupt | to break | disruption |
| scope | viewing instrument | microscope |
| scrib/scribe | to write | inscription |
| sect/sec | to cut | section |
| sequ, secu | follow | consecutive |
| soph | wisdom, knowledge | philosophy |
| spect | to look | spectator |
| struct | to build | restructure |
| tele | far off | telephone |
| terr | earth | terrestrial |
| therm | heat | thermal |
| ven, vent | to come | convene |
| vert | turn | vertigo |
| voc | voice, call | vocalize, evocative |

## PREFIXES

In addition to understanding the root of a word, it is vital to recognize common affixes that change the meaning of words and demonstrate their relationships to other words. **Prefixes** are added to the beginning of a word and frequently change the meaning of the word itself by indicating an opposite or another specifically altered meaning.

Table 3.2. Examples of Prefixes

| Prefixes | Meaning | Examples |
|---|---|---|
| a, an | without, not | anachronism, anhydrous |
| ab, abs, a | apart, away from | abscission, abnormal |
| ad | toward | adhere |
| agere | act | agent |
| amphi, ambi | round, both sides | ambivalent |

**VOCABULARY** 45

Table 3.2. Examples of Prefixes (continued)

| Prefixes | Meaning | Examples |
| --- | --- | --- |
| ante | before | antedate, anterior |
| anti | against | antipathy |
| archos | leader, first, chief | archetype |
| bi | two | binary, bivalve |
| bene | well, favorable | benevolent, beneficent |
| corpus | body | corporeal |
| credo | belief | credible |
| demos | people | demographic |
| di | two, double | dimorphism, diatomic |
| dia | across, through | dialectic |
| dis | not, apart | disenfranchise |
| dynasthai | be able | dynamo, dynasty |
| ego | I, self | egomaniac, egocentric |
| epi | upon, over | epigram, epiphyte |
| ex | out | extraneous, extemporaneous |
| geo | earth | geocentric, geomancy |
| ideo | idea | ideology, ideation |
| in | in | induction, indigenous |
| im | not | immoral |
| inter | between | interstellar |
| lexis | word | lexicography |
| liber | free, book | liberal |
| locus | place | locality |
| macro | large | macrophage |
| micro | small | micron |
| mono | one, single | monocle, monovalent |
| mortis | death | moribund |
| olig | few | oligarchy |
| peri | around | peripatetic, perineum |
| poly | many | polygamy |
| pre | before | prescient |
| solus | alone | solitary |
| subter | under, secret | subterfuge |
| un | not | unsafe |
| utilis | useful | utilitarian |

## SUFFIXES

A **suffix**, on the other hand, is added to the end of a word and generally indicates the word's relationship to other words in the sentence. Suffixes can change the part of speech or indicate if a word is plural or related to a plural.

Table 3.3. Examples of Suffixes

| Suffixes | Meaning | Examples |
| --- | --- | --- |
| able, ible | able, capable | visible |
| age | act of, state of, result of | wreckage |
| al | relating to | gradual |
| algia | pain | myalgia |
| an, ian | native of, relating to | riparian |
| ance, ancy | action, process, state | defiance |
| ary, ery, ory | relating to, quality, place | aviary |
| cian | processing a specific skill or art | physician |
| cule, ling | very small | animalcule, sapling |
| cy | action, function | normalcy |
| dom | quality, realm | wisdom |
| ee | one who receives the action | nominee |
| en | made of, to make | silken |
| ence, ency | action, state of, quality | urgency |
| er, or | one who, that which | professor |
| escent | in the process of | adolescent, senescence |
| esis, osis | action, process, condition | genesis, neurosis |
| et, ette | small one, group | baronet, lorgnette |
| fic | making, causing | specific |
| ful | full of | frightful |
| hood | order, condition, quality | adulthood |
| ice | condition, state, quality | malice |
| id, ide | a thing connected with or belonging to | bromide |
| ile | relating to, suited for, capable of | purile, juvenile |
| ine | nature of | feminine |
| ion, sion, tion | act, result, or state of | contagion |
| ish | origin, nature, resembling | impish |
| ism | system, manner, condition, characteristic | capitalism |
| ist | one who, that which | artist, flautist |
| ite | nature of, quality of, mineral product | graphite |
| ity, ty | state of, quality | captivity |

Table 3.3. Examples of Suffixes (continued)

| Suffixes | Meaning | Examples |
| --- | --- | --- |
| ive | causing, making | exhaustive |
| ize, ise | make | idolize, bowdlerize |
| ment | act of, state or, result | containment |
| nomy | law | autonomy, taxonomy |
| oid | resembling | asteroid, anthropoid |
| some | like, apt, tending to | gruesome |
| strat | cover | strata |
| tude | state of, condition of | aptitude |
| um | forms single nouns | spectrum |
| ure | state of, act, process, rank | rapture, rupture |
| ward | in the direction of | backward |
| y | inclined to, tend to | faulty |

## PRACTICE QUESTIONS

1. Which of the following prefixes should be added to a word to indicate that something is large?
   A) micro
   B) macro
   C) anti
   D) ante

2. In the sentence below, the prefix *poly–* and the suffix *–glot* in the word *polyglot* indicate that the writer's sister does which of the following?

   My sister is a <u>polyglot</u>, and she comfortably travels all over the world.
   A) speaks many languages
   B) loves to travel
   C) finds new jobs easily
   D) is unafraid of new places

## CONTEXT CLUES

Use context to determine what a new word means. There are two types of context: situational and sentence. Both provide clues to a word's meaning; the more you know about a situation, the better your chances at guessing the meaning of an unfamiliar word. The overall setting is **situational context**: the book, the passage, even the paragraph. Some words can have more than one definition, or **denotation**. The surrounding text reveals the way the author intends the word to be understood. For instance, a *band* might be a group of musicians who play music, or a piece of jewelry worn around the finger. Similarly, some words have different **connotations**, or implications. *Cold* might be used to describe temperature, but it can also be used to describe someone's dismissive attitude or uncaring demeanor.

**Sentence context** refers to the specific sentence where the vocabulary appears.

Sentence context requires you to analyze important words or features in a sentence that reveal the meaning of vocabulary words.

- Sometimes a sentence basically defines the vocabulary word. That is a **restatement clue**.
- The tone of a sentence provides a clue to a word's meaning. This is a **positive/negative clue**.
- **Contrast clues** are when words and phrases like *however*, *but*, and *in contrast* appear, showing the opposite meaning of a word.
- Finally, details in the sentence that reveal the meaning of a word are **specific detail clues**.

### PRACTICE QUESTIONS

*Select the answer that most closely matches the definition of the underlined word or phrase as it is used in the sentence.*

3. The doctor called for a transfusion because the patient had lost a <u>copious</u> amount of blood.
   - **A)** favorable
   - **B)** aftermath
   - **C)** subsequent
   - **D)** enormous

4. The mother went into labor on the way to the hospital; her baby's birth was <u>imminent</u>.
   - **A)** about to happen
   - **B)** frequently occurring
   - **C)** at risk
   - **D)** prevented by injury

# Homophones and Homographs

**Homophones** are words that sound the same but have different meanings; **homographs** are words that are spelled the same way but have different meanings. On the HESI, you may be asked to identify which homophone is appropriate in the given context, or you may need to identify the correct definition of a homograph as it is used in a sentence.

A good knowledge of homophones is especially important as many words applicable to medicine (*heel/heal*, *tic/tick*) may be homophones. Is a patient healing, or does he or she have a heel problem? Does the patient have a tic, or has he or she been bitten by a tick?

Examples of homophones include:

- tic/tick
- gait/gate
- mail/male
- pain/pane
- oral/aural
- heel/heal

Examples of homographs include:
- tear (to rip/liquid produced by the eye)
- compound (to mix/an enclosed area that includes a building or group of buildings)
- bank (a place to store money/the side of a river/a stockpile)
- novel (a piece of fiction/something new)
- change (to make different/money left over after a transaction)
- rose (a flower/to move upward)
- die (to pass away/a six-sided, numbered cube)

### PRACTICE QUESTION

5. Which of the following is the best synonym for *proceeds* as used in the sentence?
   The proceeds from the dance will be donated to a local charity.
   - **A)** entertainment
   - **B)** movement
   - **C)** profit
   - **D)** snacks

# ANSWER KEY

1. **B) is correct.** The prefix *macro–* means *large*.

2. **A) is correct.** The prefix *poly–* means *many*, and the suffix *–glot* means *in a language or tongue*. Therefore, the writer's sister speaks many languages.

3. **D) is correct.** From context, it is clear that the patient must have lost a large, or *enormous*, amount of blood; otherwise there would be no need for a transfusion.

4. **A) is correct.** This sentence features a restatement clue; if a pregnant person is in labor, birth is *imminent*, or about to happen.

5. **C) is correct.** *Proceeds* can mean either *profit* or *moving forward*. In this sentence, it is used to mean *profit* because *profit* can be donated to charity and thus makes sense in the context of the sentence.

# FOUR: GRAMMAR

## Parts of Speech

The **parts of speech** are the building blocks of sentences, paragraphs, and entire texts. Grammarians have typically defined eight parts of speech—nouns, pronouns, verbs, adverbs, adjectives, conjunctions, prepositions, and interjections—all of which play unique roles in the context of a sentence. Though some words fall easily into one category or another, many words can function as different parts of speech based on their usage within a sentence.

### NOUNS AND PRONOUNS

**Nouns** are the words that describe people, places, things, and ideas. Most often, nouns fill the position of subject or object within a sentence. Nouns have several subcategories: common nouns (*chair, car, house*), proper nouns (*Julie, Montana*), noncountable nouns (*money, water*), and countable nouns (*dollars, cubes*), among others. There is much crossover among these subcategories (for example, *chair* is common and countable), and other subcategories do exist.

**Pronouns** replace nouns in a sentence or paragraph, allowing a writer to achieve a smooth flow throughout a text by avoiding unnecessary repetition. The unique aspect of the pronoun as a part of speech is that the list of pronouns is finite: while there are innumerable nouns in the English language, there are only a few types of pronouns. The ones important for the HESI follow:

>**Personal pronouns** act as subjects or objects in a sentence.
>
>>She received a letter; I gave the letter to her.
>
>**Possessive pronouns** indicate possession.
>
>>The apartment is hers, but the furniture is mine.
>
>**Reflexive** or **intensive pronouns** intensify a noun or reflect back on a noun.
>
>>I made the dessert myself.

**HELPFUL HINT**
The HESI will ask you to identify parts of speech by name, so make sure to memorize all eight.

**QUICK REVIEW**
Identify the pronouns in the following sentence and the word(s) they refer back to: *Marcus and Paula offered to pick up the cake because they live close to the bakery, but I told them I would do it myself.*

**Indefinite pronouns** simply replace nouns to avoid unnecessary repetition.

<u>Several</u> came to the party to see <u>both</u>.

Table 4.1. Personal, Possessive, and Reflexive Pronouns

| Case | First Person | | Second Person | | Third Person | |
| --- | --- | --- | --- | --- | --- | --- |
| | Singular | Plural | Singular | Plural | Singular | Plural |
| Subject | I | we | you | you (all) | he, she, it | they |
| Object | me | us | you | you (all) | him, her, it | them |
| Possessive | mine | ours | yours | yours | his, hers, its | theirs |
| Reflexive/ intensive | myself | ourselves | yourself | yourselves | himself, herself, itself | themselves |

## PRACTICE QUESTIONS

1. What purpose do nouns usually serve in a sentence?
   A) They indicate possession.
   B) They act as subject or object.
   C) They intensify other nouns.
   D) They clarify when an action occurs.

2. _____ baked the cookies herself and ate most of them.
   Which pronoun best completes the sentence?
   A) she
   B) you
   C) they
   D) I

## VERBS

**Verbs** express action (*run, jump, play*) or state of being (*is, seems*). Verbs that describe action are **action verbs,** and those that describe being are **linking verbs.**

Action: My brother <u>plays</u> tennis.
Linking: He <u>is</u> the best player on the team.

Verbs are conjugated to indicate **person**, which refers to the point of view of the sentence. First person is the speaker (*I, we*); second person is the person being addressed (*you*); and third person is outside the conversation (*they, them*). Verbs are also conjugated to match the **number** (singular or plural) of their subject. **Helping verbs** (*to be, to have, to do*) are used to conjugate verbs. An unconjugated verb is called an **infinitive** and includes the word *to* in front (*to be, to break*).

**Participles** are verb forms lacking number and person. The **past participle** is usually formed by adding the suffix *–ed* to the verb stem (*type* becomes *typed*; *drop* becomes *dropped*). The **present participle** is always formed by adding the suffix *–ing* to the verb stem (*typing, dropping*). Participles are used in verb conjugation to indicate the state of an action (*she is going; we had waited*).

Participles also act in *participial phrases* that serve as descriptors in sentences:

<u>Seated</u> politely, Ron listened to his friend's boring story.

Maya petted the <u>sleeping</u> cat.

When a present participle acts as a noun, it is called a **gerund**. In the following sentence, *running* is a noun and serves as the subject of the sentence:

<u>Running</u> is my favorite form of exercise.

Verbs are also conjugated to indicate **tense**, or when the action has happened. Actions can happen in the past, present, or future. Tense also describes over how long a period the action took place:

- **Simple** verbs describe something that happened once or general truths.
- **Continuous** verbs describe an ongoing action.
- **Perfect** verbs describe repeated actions or actions that started in the past and have been completed.
- **Perfect continuous** verbs describe actions that started in the past and are continuing.

Table 4.2. Verb Conjugation (Present Tense)

| Person | Singular | Plural |
|---|---|---|
| First person | I give | we give |
| Second person | you give | you (all) give |
| Third person | he/she/it gives | they give |

Table 4.3. Verb Tenses

| Tense | Past | Present | Future |
|---|---|---|---|
| Simple | I <u>gave</u> her a gift yesterday. | I <u>give</u> her a gift every day. | I <u>will give</u> her a gift on her birthday. |
| Continuous | I <u>was giving</u> her a gift when you got here. | I <u>am giving</u> her a gift; come in! | I <u>will be giving</u> her a gift at dinner. |
| Perfect | I <u>had given</u> her a gift before you got there. | I <u>have given</u> her a gift already. | I <u>will have given</u> her a gift by midnight. |
| Perfect continuous | Her friends <u>had been giving</u> her gifts all night when I arrived. | I <u>have been giving</u> her gifts every year for nine years. | I <u>will have been giving</u> her gifts on holidays for ten years next year. |

Verbs that follow the standard rules of conjugation are called **regular** verbs. **Irregular** verbs do not follow these rules, and their conjugations must be memorized. Some examples of irregular verbs are given in Table 4.4.

Table 4.4. Irregular Verbs

| Present | Past | Past Participle |
|---|---|---|
| am | was | been |
| do | did | done |
| see | saw | seen |
| write | wrote | written |
| break | broke | broken |
| grow | grew | grown |
| speak | spoke | spoken |
| begin | began | begun |
| run | ran | run |
| buy | bought | bought |

**Transitive verbs** take a **direct object**, which receives the action of the verb. Intransitive verbs have no object. The person or thing that receives the direct object is the **indirect object**.

Transitive: Alex <u>gave</u> his brother the ball. (*The ball* is the direct object; *his brother* is the indirect object.)

Intransitive: She <u>jumped</u> over the fence.

## PRACTICE QUESTIONS

3. Which verb phrase correctly completes the following sentence?
   By this time tomorrow, we _____ in New York.
   A) have been landing
   B) will have landed
   C) have landed
   D) are landing

4. Identify the direct object in the following sentence.
   My friends brought me a package of souvenirs from their trip to Spain.
   A) friends
   B) me
   C) package
   D) trip

## ADJECTIVES AND ADVERBS

**Adjectives** modify or describe nouns and pronouns. In English, adjectives are usually placed before the word being modified, although they can also appear after a linking verb such as *is* or *smells*.

> The beautiful blue jade necklace will go perfectly with my dress.
> I think that lasagna smells delicious.

When multiple adjectives are used, they should be listed in the following order:

1. determiners: articles (*a*, *an*, and *the*), possessive adjectives (e.g., *my*, *her*), and descriptors of quantity (e.g., *three*, *several*)
2. opinions: modifiers that imply a value (e.g., *beautiful*, *perfect*, *ugly*)
3. size: descriptions of size (e.g., *small*, *massive*)
4. age: descriptions of age (e.g., *young*, *five-year-old*)
5. shape: descriptions of appearance or character (e.g., *smooth*, *loud*)
6. color: descriptions of color (e.g., *blue*, *dark*)
7. origin: modifiers that describe where something came from (e.g., *American*, *homemade*)
8. material: modifiers that describe what something is made from (e.g., *cotton*, *metallic*)
9. purpose: adjectives that function as part of the noun to describe its purpose (e.g., *sewing machine*, *rocking chair*)

**Adverbs**, which are often formed by adding the suffix *–ly*, modify any word or set of words that is not a noun or pronoun. They can modify verbs, adjectives, other adverbs, phrases, or clauses.

> He quickly ran to the house next door. (*Quickly* modifies the verb *ran*.)
> Her very effective speech earned her a promotion. (*Very* modifies the adjective *effective*.)
> Finally, the table was set and dinner was ready. (*Finally* modifies the clause *the table was set and dinner was ready*.)

**Comparative** adjectives and adverbs compare two items. For most one- or two-syllable words, the suffix *–er* is added to make it comparative; the word may be followed by *than*.

**Superlative** adjectives and adverbs compare three or more items. Most one- or two-syllable words are made superlative by adding a suffix, *–est*.

> My brother is tall.
> Comparative: My brother is taller than my sister.
> Superlative: My brother is the tallest of all my siblings.

**HELPFUL HINT**
Adjectives answer the questions *what kind? how many?* or *which one?*
Adverbs answer the questions *how? when? where? why?* or *to what extent?*

Longer adjectives and adverbs must be preceded by *more* to form the comparative and *most* to form the superlative.

My bed is comfortable.

Comparative: My bed at home is more comfortable than the one at the hotel.

Superlative: The bed in your guestroom is the most comfortable bed I've ever slept in!

Some adjectives and adverbs form irregular comparatives and superlatives (see Table 2.5).

The weather is bad.

Comparative: The weather is worse than yesterday.

Superlative: The weather was the worst on Monday when it rained.

Table 4.5. Some Irregular Comparative and Superlative Adjectives and Adverbs

| Adjective/Adverb | Comparative | Superlative |
| --- | --- | --- |
| much | more | most |
| bad | worse | worst |
| good | better | best |
| little | less | least |
| far | further/farther | furthest/farthest |

## PRACTICE QUESTIONS

5. Which of the following sentences is correctly constructed?
    A) Between my mom and dad, my father is the oldest.
    B) I ran less than usual today.
    C) Henry's cat is more fat than mine.
    D) After taking medicine, she felt worser.

6. Which is the adverb in the following sentence?
   He carelessly sped around the flashing yellow light.
    A) flashing
    B) yellow
    C) around
    D) carelessly

## CONJUNCTIONS

**Conjunctions** join words into phrases, clauses, and sentences. The **coordinating conjunctions** (FANBOYS) join two independent clauses: For, And, Nor, But, Or, Yet, So. They are always preceded by a comma.

Marta went to the pool, <u>and</u> Alex decided to go shopping.

Annie didn't want to eat tacos for dinner, <u>so</u> she picked up a pizza on her way home.

**Subordinating conjunctions** join dependent clauses to the independent clauses to which they are related.

We chose that restaurant <u>because</u> Juan loves pizza.

Table 4.6. Subordinating Conjunctions

| | |
|---|---|
| **Time** | after, as, as long as, as soon as, before, since, until, when, whenever, while |
| **Manner** | as, as if, as though |
| **Cause** | because |
| **Condition** | although, as long as, even if, even though, if, provided that, though, unless, while |
| **Purpose** | in order that, so that, that |
| **Comparison** | as, than |

## PRACTICE QUESTIONS

**7.** The following sentence contains an error. How should it be rewritten?

He liked to cook and baking was his specialty.

I. He liked to cook, and baking was his specialty.

II. He liked to cook so baking was his specialty.

III. He liked to cook, baking was his specialty.

**A)** I only

**B)** I and II only

**C)** I and III only

**D)** I, II, and IIII

**8.** Which of the following parts of speech is *while* as used in the sentence below?

Anne and Peter drank their coffee languidly while they read the paper.

**A)** subordinating conjunction

**B)** coordinating conjunction

**C)** irregular verb

**D)** adverb

## PREPOSITIONS

**Prepositions** set up relationships in time (*<u>after</u> the party*) or space (*<u>under</u> the cushions*) within a sentence. A preposition will always function as part of a prepositional phrase—the preposition along with the object of the preposition.

Table 4.7. Common Prepositions

**Prepositions**

| | | | |
|---|---|---|---|
| about | by | off | toward |
| among | despite | on | under |
| around | down | onto | underneath |
| at | during | out | until |
| before | except | outside | up |
| behind | for | over | upon |
| below | from | past | with |
| beneath | in | since | within |
| beside | into | through | |
| between | near | till | |
| beyond | of | to | |

**Compound Prepositions**

| | | | |
|---|---|---|---|
| according to | because of | in place of | on account of |
| aside from | by means of | in respect to | out of |
| as of | in addition to | in spite of | prior to |
| as well as | in front of | instead of | with regard to |

## PRACTICE QUESTION

9. Identify the prepositional phrase in the following sentence.

    Tran and Carol must drive through the tunnel, but Carol is claustrophobic.

    **A)** must drive

    **B)** through the tunnel

    **C)** drive through

    **D)** but Carol is

## INTERJECTIONS

**Interjections** have no grammatical attachment to the sentence itself other than to add expressions of emotion. These parts of speech may be punctuated with commas or exclamation points and may fall anywhere within the sentence.

<u>Ouch</u>! He stepped on my toe.

## PRACTICE QUESTION

10. Identify the interjection in the following sentence.

    "Come here! Look! Our team won the Super Bowl! Yay!"

    **A)** Come here!

    **B)** Our team won

    **C)** Look!

    **D)** Yay!

# Constructing Sentences

## PHRASES

A **phrase** is a group of words that communicates a partial idea and lacks either a subject or a predicate. Several phrases may be strung together, one after another, to add detail and interest to a sentence.

Phrases are categorized based on the main word in the phrase. A **prepositional phrase** begins with a preposition and ends with an object of the preposition; a **verb phrase** is composed of the main verb along with its helping verbs; and a **noun phrase** consists of a noun and its modifiers.

> Prepositional phrase: The dog is hiding under the porch.
> Verb phrase: The chef wanted to cook a different dish.
> Noun phrase: The big, red barn rests beside the vacant chicken house.

An **appositive phrase** is a particular type of noun phrase that renames the word or group of words that precedes it. Appositive phrases usually follow the noun they describe and are set apart by commas.

> My dad, a clock maker, loved antiques.

**Verbal phrases** begin with a word that would normally act as a verb but is instead filling another role within the sentence. These phrases can act as nouns, adjectives, or adverbs.

> Noun: To visit Europe had always been her dream.
> Adjective: Enjoying the stars that filled the sky, Dave lingered outside for quite a while.

**HELPFUL HINT**

A command may look like a phrase because it lacks a subject, but it's actually a complete sentence. The subject of the sentence is assumed to be you: Try it. → (You) try it.

## PRACTICE QUESTION

11. What type of phrase is underlined in the following sentence?

    Dodging traffic, Rachel drove to work on back roads.

    **A)** prepositional phrase
    **B)** noun phrase
    **C)** verb phrase
    **D)** verbal phrase

## CLAUSES AND TYPES OF SENTENCES

**Clauses** contain both a subject and a predicate. They can be either independent or dependent. An **independent** (or main) **clause** can stand alone as its own sentence:

> The dog ate her homework.

Dependent (or subordinate) clauses cannot stand alone as their own sentences. They start with a subordinating conjunction, relative pronoun, or relative adjective, which will make them sound incomplete:

<u>Because</u> the dog ate her homework

Table 4.8. Words That Begin Dependent Clauses

| Subordinating Conjunctions | Relative Pronouns and Adjectives |
|---|---|
| after, although, as, because, before, even if, even though, if, in order that, once, provided that, since, so, so that, than, that, though, unless, until, when, whenever, where, whereas, wherever, whether, while | how, that, when, where, which, who, whoever, whom, whomever, whose, why |

Sentences can be classified based on the number and type of clauses they contain. A **simple sentence** will have only one independent clause and no dependent clauses. The sentence may contain phrases, complements, and modifiers, but it will comprise only one independent clause, one complete idea.

The cat ran under the porch.

Just because a sentence is simple doesn't mean it has to be short! A simple sentence has only one subject and one verb, but can have lots of modifying phrases. To help identify the type of sentence, cross out modifiers, objects, and prepositional phrases:

~~The new~~ car ~~that I bought with the money I earned at my summer job already~~ needs ~~new tires and new brake pads~~.

A **compound sentence** has two or more independent clauses and no dependent clauses.

The cat ran under the porch, and the dog ran after him.

A **complex sentence** has only one independent clause and one or more dependent clauses.

The cat, who is scared of the dog, ran under the porch.

A **compound-complex sentence** has two or more independent clauses and one or more dependent clauses.

The cat, who is scared of the dog, ran under the porch, and the dog ran after him.

Table 4.9. Sentence Structure and Clauses

| Sentence Structure | Independent Clauses | Dependent Clauses |
|---|---|---|
| Simple | 1 | 0 |
| Compound | 2 + | 0 |
| Complex | 1 | 1 + |
| Compound-complex | 2 + | 1 + |

**HELPFUL HINT**
The HESI may ask you to identify types of sentences by name, so make sure to memorize the four types and how to identify them.

## PRACTICE QUESTION

**12.** Which of the following is a compound sentence?
- **A)** The turtle swam slowly around the pond.
- **B)** Alligators generally lie still, but they can move with lightning speed.
- **C)** Mice are most likely to come out at night after other animals have gone to sleep.
- **D)** Squirrels, to prepare for winter, gather and hide seeds and nuts underground.

## PUNCTUATION

Terminal punctuation marks are used to end sentences. The **period** (.) ends declarative (statement) and imperative (command) sentences. The **question mark** (?) terminates interrogative sentences (questions). Lastly, **exclamation points** end exclamatory sentences, in which the writer or speaker is exhibiting intense emotion or energy.

> Kwame and I are attending a concert.
> How many people are attending the concert?
> What a great show that was!

The colon and the semicolon, though often confused, each have a unique set of rules for their use. While both punctuation marks are used to join clauses, the construction of the clauses and the relationship between them is different. The **semicolon** (;) is used to join two independent clauses (IC; IC) that are closely related. It can also be used to join items in a list when those items already include a comma.

> I need to buy a new car soon; my old car broke down last month.
> The guests at the party included Mrs. Green, my third-grade teacher; Mr. Doakes, my neighbor; and Dr. Kayani, our school principal.

The **colon** (:) is used to introduce a list, definition, or clarification. The clause preceding the colon has to be independent, but what follows the colon can be an independent clause, a dependent clause, or a phrase.

> The buffet offers three choices: ham, turkey, or roast beef.
> He decided to drive instead of taking the train: he didn't think the train would arrive in time.

**Commas** show pauses in the text or set information apart from the main text. There are lots of rules for comma usage, so only the most common are summarized here.

1. Commas separate two independent clauses along with a coordinating conjunction: George ordered the steak<u>, but</u> Bruce preferred the ham.
2. Commas separate coordinate adjectives: She made herself a big bowl of <u>cold, delicious</u> ice cream.
3. Commas separate items in a series: The list of groceries included <u>cream, coffee, donuts, and tea</u>.
4. Commas separate introductory words and phrases from the rest of the sentence: <u>For example,</u> we have thirty students who demand a change.

5. Commas set off nonessential information and appositives: Estelle, our newly elected chairperson, will be in attendance.
6. Commas set off the day and month of a date within a text: I was born on February 16, 1958.
7. Commas set up numbers in a text of more than four digits: We expect 25,000 visitors to the new museum.
8. Commas set off the names of cities from their states, territories, or provinces: She lives in Houston, Texas.

**Quotation marks** have a number of different purposes. They enclose titles of short, or relatively short, literary works such as short stories, chapters, and poems. (The titles of longer works, like novels and anthologies, are italicized.) Additionally, quotation marks are used to enclose direct quotations within the text of a document where the quotation is integrated into the text. Writers also use quotation marks to set off dialogue.

> We will be reading the poem "Bright Star" in class today.
> The poem opens with the line "Bright star, would I were steadfast as thou art."

**Apostrophes**, sometimes referred to as single quotation marks, have several different purposes.
1. They show possession: boy's watch, John and Mary's house
2. They replace missing letters, numerals, and signs: do not = don't, 1989 = '89
3. They form plurals of letters, numerals, and signs: A's, 10's

Less commonly used punctuation marks include:
- **en dash** (–): indicates a range
- **em dash** (—): shows an abrupt break in a sentence and emphasizes the words within the em dashes
- **parentheses** ( ): enclose nonessential information
- **brackets** [ ]: enclose added words to a quotation and add insignificant information within parentheses
- **slash** (/): separates lines of poetry within a text or indicates interchangeable terminology
- **ellipses** (...): indicates that information has been removed from a quotation or creates a reflective pause

## PRACTICE QUESTIONS

13. Which sentence includes an improperly placed comma?
    A) Ella, Cassie, and Cameron drove to South Carolina together.
    B) Trying to impress his friends, Carl ended up totaling his car.
    C) Ice cream is my favorite food, it is so cold and creamy.
    D) Mowing the lawn, Amari discovered a family of baby rabbits.

**14.** The following sentence contains an error. How can the writer fix it?

Oak trees—with proper care—can grow upwards of thirty feet; providing shade for people, shelter for animals, and perches for birds.

- **A)** replace the em dashes with commas
- **B)** remove the comma after *people*
- **C)** insert an apostrophe at the end of *animals*
- **D)** replace the semicolon with a comma

## Capitalization

**Capitalization** is writing the first letter of a word in uppercase and the remaining letters in lowercase. The table below shows the most important rules for capitalization.

Table 4.10. Capitalization Rules

| Rule | Example |
| --- | --- |
| Words that begin sentences should be capitalized. | The patient's vitals are normal. |
| Proper nouns, including names of people and specific places, should be capitalized. The names of general locations (river, school) are not capitalized. | My sister Maria moved to Florida so she could live near the ocean. |
| The names of holidays are capitalized. Do not capitalize the word *day* unless it's part of the holiday's official name. | We will be opening presents on Christmas day; on Memorial Day we'll go to the parade. |
| Titles should be capitalized when used as a part of a person's name, but not when they stand alone. | Richard Atwell, the governor of Virginia, will be hosting a dinner to honor President Green. |
| Titles of works of art, including books, movies, and songs, should be capitalized. Do not capitalize prepositions or conjunctions. | She went to the store to buy a copy of the book *The Comfort Garden: Tales from the Trauma Unit*. |
| The pronoun *I* should always be capitalized. | He and I have never understood one another. |

### PRACTICE QUESTION

**15.** Which of the following sentences does NOT contain an error in capitalization?
- **A)** Robert and Kelly raced across the River in their small boats.
- **B)** ducks flying in a V-formation cross the Midwest in the fall.
- **C)** The chairman of the board, Rashida Smith, will lead today's meeting.
- **D)** The Senators from Virginia and Louisiana strongly favor the bill.

# Common Language Errors

## SUBJECT-VERB AGREEMENT

Verbs must agree in number with their subjects. Common rules for subject-verb agreement are given next.

1. Single subjects agree with single verbs; plural subjects agree with plural verbs.

   The girl walks her dog.
   The girls walk their dogs.

2. Compound subjects joined by *and* typically take a plural verb unless considered one item.

   Correctness and precision are required for all good writing.
   Macaroni and cheese makes a great snack for children.

3. The linking verbs agree with the subject and not the subject complement (predicate nominative).

   My favorite is strawberries and apples.
   My favorites are strawberries and apples.

4. When a relative pronoun (*who, whom, which, that*) is used as the subject of the clause, the verb will agree with the antecedent of the relative pronoun.

   This is the student who is receiving an award.
   These are the students who are receiving awards.

5. All single, indefinite pronouns agree with single verbs.

   Neither of the students is happy about the play.
   Each of the many cars is on the grass.
   Every one of the administrators speaks highly of Amir.

To make conjugating verbs easier, cross out words that appear between the subject and the verb:

The new library ~~with its many books and rooms~~ fills a long-felt need.

### PRACTICE QUESTION

16. Which sentence in the following list is correct in its subject-verb agreement?
    A) My sister and my best friend lives in Chicago.
    B) My parents or my brother is going to pick me up from the airport.
    C) Neither of the students refuse to take the exam.
    D) The team were playing a great game until the rain started.

## PRONOUN-ANTECEDENT AGREEMENT

Similarly, pronouns must agree with their antecedents (the words they replaced) in number; however, some pronouns also require gender agreement (*him, her*). **Pronoun-antecedent agreement** rules can be found next:

1. Antecedents joined by *and* typically require a plural pronoun.

   The <u>children and their dogs</u> enjoyed <u>their</u> day at the beach.

   If the two nouns refer to the same person, a singular pronoun is preferable.

   My <u>best friend and confidant</u> still lives in <u>her</u> log cabin.

2. For compound antecedents joined by *or*, the pronoun agrees with the nearer or nearest antecedent.

   Either the resident mice <u>or the manager's cat</u> gets <u>itself</u> a meal of good leftovers.

3. When indefinite pronouns are used in a sentence, the pronoun must agree with the number of the indefinite pronoun.

   <u>Neither</u> student finished <u>his or her</u> assignment.

   <u>Both</u> students finished <u>their</u> assignments.

4. When collective nouns function as antecedents, the pronoun choice will be singular or plural depending on the function of the collective.

   The <u>audience</u> was cheering as <u>it</u> rose to <u>its</u> feet in unison.

   Our <u>family</u> are spending <u>their</u> vacations in Maine, Hawaii, and Rome.

5. When *each* and *every* precede the antecedent, the pronoun agreement will be singular.

   <u>Each and every man, woman, and child</u> brings unique qualities to <u>his or her</u> family.

   <u>Every creative writer, technical writer, and research writer</u> is attending <u>his or her</u> assigned lecture.

Because English does not have a nongendered singular pronoun, it's common in everyday speech to treat *they* or *their* as singular:

   Common usage: <u>Every student</u> should check <u>their</u> homework before turning it in.

Because this usage is controversial, on tests it's important to use the technically correct response:

   Technically correct: <u>Every student</u> should check <u>his or her</u> homework before turning it in.

## PRACTICE QUESTIONS

**17.** Which sentence in the following list is correct in its pronoun-antecedent agreement?
- **A)** The grandchildren and their cousins enjoyed their day at the park.
- **B)** Most of the grass has lost their deep color.
- **C)** The jury was relieved as their commitment came to a close.
- **D)** Every boy and girl must learn to behave themselves in school.

**18.** Which sentence in the following list is correct in its pronoun and antecedent agreement?
- **A)** Either my brother or my dad will bring their van to pick us up.
- **B)** The university is having their tenth fundraiser tonight.
- **C)** Alyssa and Jacqueline bought herself a big lunch today.
- **D)** Each dog, cat, and rabbit has its own bowl and blanket.

## VERB TENSE AGREEMENT

In any passage, verb tense should be consistent and make sense in the context of other verbs, adverbs, and general meaning.

> Incorrect: Deborah was speaking with her colleague when her boss will appear, demanding a meeting.

The first part of the sentence states that Deborah *was speaking* with her colleagues, an action occurring in the past. Thus, it would make no sense for her boss to interrupt her in the future (*will appear*). The sentence can be corrected by putting her boss's action in the past tense as well:

> Correct: Deborah was speaking with her colleague when her boss appeared, demanding a meeting.

Pay attention to how verbs are conjugated in the beginning of a sentence or passage, and look for adverbial clues to spot any errors in verb tense agreement.

## PRACTICE QUESTION

**19.** Which of the following sentences has correct verb tense agreement?
- **A)** Veronica attends cooking classes, and she went to yoga classes too.
- **B)** Veronica attended cooking classes, and she went to yoga classes too.
- **C)** Veronica attended cooking classes, and she goes to yoga classes too.
- **D)** Veronica attended cooking classes, and she will go to yoga classes too.

## PARALLELISM

Errors in **parallelism** prevent a writer from creating a smooth flow, or coherence, from word to word and sentence to sentence. Writers should create parallel structure in words, phrases, and clauses wherever two or more similar and equally important ideas exist next to each other in a sentence.

Incorrect: Amanda could program computers, repair cars, and knew how to bake croissants.

Correct: Amanda could program computers, repair cars, and bake croissants.

Looking at each part of the list individually helps highlight the error: the final item reads "Amanda could knew how to make croissants." This error is fixed by writing the verbs in parallel structure: *program*, *repair*, and *bake*.

In sentences with multiple prepositional phrases in a parallel series, the preposition must be repeated unless the same preposition begins each phrase.

Incorrect: You can park your car in the garage, the carport, or on the street.

Correct: You can park your car in the garage, in the carport, or on the street.

## PRACTICE QUESTION

**20.** Which word or phrase best completes the following sentence?

Shelly achieved more at nursing school because she was going to bed earlier, eating healthy food, and _____ home to study more.

**A)** staying

**B)** to stay

**C)** will be staying

**D)** stays

## SENTENCE CONSTRUCTION ERRORS

There are three main types of sentence construction errors: fragments, comma splices (comma fault), and fused sentences (run-on). A **fragment** occurs when a group of words is not a complete sentence but is punctuated like one. The fragment might be a phrase or a dependent clause. To fix a fragment, an independent clause needs to be created.

Fragment (phrase): The girl in my class who asks a lot of questions.

Correct: The girl in my class who asks a lot of questions sits in the back row.

Fragment (dependent clause): Because of the big storm we had last weekend.

Correct: Because of the big storm we had last weekend, the park will be closed.

A **comma splice** (comma fault) occurs when two independent clauses are joined together in a paragraph with only a comma to "splice" them together. **Fused** (run-on) sentences occur when two independent clauses are joined with no punctuation whatsoever. To fix a comma splice or fused sentence, add the correct punctuation and/or conjunction.

Comma splice: My family eats turkey at Thanksgiving,
we eat ham at Christmas.

Correct: My family eats turkey at Thanksgiving,
and we eat ham at Christmas.

Correct: My family eats turkey at Thanksgiving. We eat ham at Christmas.

Correct: My family eats turkey at Thanksgiving; we eat ham at Christmas.

Fused sentence: I bought a chocolate pie from the bakery it was delicious.

Correct: I bought a chocolate pie from the bakery. It was delicious.

Correct: I bought a chocolate pie from the bakery, and it was delicious.

Correct: I bought a chocolate pie from the bakery; it was delicious.

Another common error that can occur in sentence structure is a dangling modifier, which occurs when a modifying phrase is separated from the word it describes. The sentence itself is still grammatically correct but can be confusing.

Incorrect: Discussing the state of the nation,
I listened to the president's speech.

Here, the president, not the narrator, is discussing the state of the nation; the narrator is simply *listening*. However, the participial phrase "Discussing the state of the nation" is disconnected from the word it modifies, *president*. Thus it is *dangling* in the sentence, creating confusion. The sentence needs to be rewritten to move the phrase next to the word it modifies.

Correct: I listened to the president's speech discussing
the state of the nation.

## PRACTICE QUESTION

**21.** Which of the following is correctly punctuated?
- **A)** Since she went to the store.
- **B)** The football game ended in a tie, the underdog caught up in the fourth quarter.
- **C)** The mall is closing early today so we'll have to go shopping tomorrow.
- **D)** When the players dropped their gloves, a fight broke out on the ice hockey rink floor.

## EASILY CONFUSED WORDS

- **a, an**: *A* precedes words beginning with consonants or consonant sounds; *an* precedes words beginning with vowels or vowel sounds.
- **affect, effect**: *Affect* is most often a verb; *effect* is usually a noun. (*The experience affected me significantly* OR *The experience had a significant effect on me.*)
- **amount, number**: *Amount* is used for noncountable sums; *number* is used with countable nouns.
- **cite, site**: The verb *cite* credits an author of a quotation, paraphrase, or summary; the noun *site* is a location.

- **every day, everyday:** *Every day* is an indefinite adjective modifying a noun; *everyday* is a one-word adjective implying frequent occurrence. (*Our visit to the Minnesota State Fair is an everyday activity during August.*)
- **fewer, less:** *Fewer* is used with a countable noun; *less* is used with a noncountable noun. (*Fewer parents are experiencing stress since the new teacher was hired. Parents are experiencing less stress since the new teacher was hired.*)
- **good, well:** *Good* is always the adjective; *well* is always the adverb except in cases of health. (*She felt well after the surgery.*)
- **implied, inferred:** *Implied* is something a speaker does; *inferred* is something the listener does after assessing the speaker's message. (*The speaker implied something mysterious, but I inferred the wrong thing.*)
- **irregardless, regardless:** *Irregardless* is nonstandard usage and should be avoided; *regardless* is the proper usage of the transitional statement.
- **its, it's:** *Its* is a possessive case pronoun; *it's* is a contraction for *it is*.
- **principal, principle:** As a noun, *principal* is an authority figure, often the head of a school; as an adjective, *principal* means *main*; the noun *principle* means idea or tenet. (*The principal of the school spoke on the principal meaning of the main principles of the school.*)
- **quote, quotation:** *Quote* is a verb; *quotation* is a noun.
- **should of, should have:** *Should of* is improper usage—*of* is not a helping verb and therefore cannot complete the verb phrase; *should have* is the proper usage. (*He should have driven.*)
- **than, then:** *Than* sets up a comparison; *then* indicates a reference to a point in time. (*When I said that I liked the hat better than the gloves, my sister laughed; then she bought both for me.*)
- **their, there, they're:** *Their* is the possessive case of the pronoun *they*; *there* is the demonstrative pronoun indicating location or place; *they're* is a contraction of the words *they are*.
- **to lie (to recline), to lay (to place):** *To lie* is the intransitive verb meaning *to recline*; *to lay* is the transitive verb meaning *to place something*. (*I lie out in the sun; I lay my towel on the beach.*)
- **unique:** *Unique* is an ultimate superlative; it should not be preceded by adverbs like *very* or *extremely*. (*The experience was unique.*)
- **who, whom:** *Who* is the subject relative pronoun. (*My son, who is a good student, studies hard.*) Here, the son is carrying out the action of studying, so the pronoun is a subject pronoun (*who*). *Whom* is the object relative pronoun. (*My son, whom the other students admire, studies hard.*) Here, *son* is the object of the other students' admiration, so the pronoun standing in for him, *whom*, is an object pronoun.
- **your, you're:** *Your* is the possessive case of the pronoun *you*; *you're* is a contraction of the words *you are*.

## PRACTICE QUESTION

**22.** The below passage has an error. How should it be fixed?

My dad, who is a car fanatic, has a very unique way of celebrating the holiday season. He decorates his Ford Mustang with Christmas lights, which have a striking effect when the car cruises down the street. Then he drives to the homes of our relatives to drop off holiday gifts.

- **A)** change *who* to *whom*
- **B)** delete *very* before the adjective *unique*
- **C)** change *effect* to *affect*
- **D)** change *Then* to *Than*

# ANSWER KEY

1.  A) is incorrect. Possessive pronouns and other conventions of Standard English indicate possession.

    **B) is correct.** Nouns are people, places, things, or ideas; they usually act as the subject or object in a sentence.

    C) is incorrect. Reflexive pronouns intensify other nouns and pronouns.

    D) is incorrect. Verb tense explains when actions occur in time.

2.  **A) is correct.** The subject of the sentence is female (as shown by the reflexive pronoun *herself*), so the female subject pronoun *she* should be used.

3.  **B) is correct.** The phrase "by this time tomorrow" indicates an action that will take place and be completed in the future at a set time. This is the future perfect tense: "will have landed."

4.  A) is incorrect. *Friends* is the subject of the sentence.

    B) is incorrect. *Me* is the recipient of the package, so it is an indirect object.

    **C) is correct.** *Package* is the direct object of the verb *brought*.

    D) is incorrect. *Trip* is not related to the verb in the sentence; it is part of the prepositional phrase *from their trip to Spain*.

5.  A) is incorrect. The speaker has two parents and is comparing their father to their mother. Thus *older*, not *oldest*, should be used.

    **B) is correct.** The speaker is comparing today's run to the norm, not to any additional instances, so the comparative is acceptable here. Furthermore, the word *than* appears, a clue that the comparative is appropriate. *Less* is the irregular comparative form of *little*.

    C) is incorrect. *Fat* is a one-syllable adjective, so it should be written *fatter* in the comparative form. In general, only three-syllable adjectives (or longer) are preceded by *more* to form the comparative.

    D) is incorrect. While the comparative could be appropriate here, *worser* is not a word; *worse* is already in the comparative form.

6.  A) is incorrect. *Flashing* is an adjective describing *light*.

    B) is incorrect. *Yellow* is an adjective describing *light*.

    C) is incorrect. *Around* is a preposition working with the verb *sped* to explain the relationship between the subject and the light.

    **D) is correct.** *Carelessly* is an adverb modifying *sped* and explaining *how* the driving occurred. The subject was not mindful as he drove; he raced through a yellow light when he should have exercised caution.

7.  **A) is correct.** This sentence includes two independent clauses: "He liked to cook" and "baking was his specialty." They should be joined by a comma and coordinating conjunction (here, *and* is a reasonable choice).

8.  **A) is correct.** "While they read the paper" is a dependent clause; the subordinating conjunction *while* connects it to the independent clause "Anne and Peter drank their coffee languidly."

    B) is incorrect. Coordinating conjunctions connect two independent clauses using a comma and a FANBOY conjunction.

C) is incorrect. An irregular verb is a verb that does not follow the standard rules of conjugation.

D) is incorrect. An adverb is a descriptor.

9. A) is incorrect. *Must drive* is a verb phrase.

    **B) is correct.** "Through the tunnel" is a prepositional phrase explaining the relationship between the subjects and the tunnel using the preposition *through* and the object *the tunnel*.

    C) is incorrect. While *through* is a preposition, *drive through* is not a prepositional phrase. It does not contain an object.

    D) is incorrect. "But Carol is" is the beginning of a second independent clause connected to the first by a coordinating conjunction (*but*). The clause *Carol is* consists of a noun and verb only.

10. A) is incorrect. *Come here* is a command; the speaker is instructing another person to perform an action using the verb *to come*. The second person *you* is the implied subject.

    B) is incorrect. *Our team won* is an independent clause and the beginning of the sentence "Our team won the Super Bowl."

    C) is incorrect. *Look* is a command; the speaker is instructing another person to perform an action using the verb *to look*. The second person *you* is the implied subject.

    **D) is correct.** *Yay* is an expression of emotion.

11. A) is incorrect. A prepositional phrase must start with a preposition.

    B) is incorrect. A noun phrase includes only the noun and its modifiers. C) is incorrect. A verb phrase is composed of the main verb and its helping verbs, if any.

    **D) is correct.** The phrase is a verbal phrase modifying the noun *Rachel*. It begins with the word *dodging*, derived from the verb *to dodge*.

12. A) is incorrect. This is a simple sentence.

    **B) is correct.** "Alligators…still" and "they…speed" are two independent clauses connected by a comma and the coordinating conjunction *but*.

    C) is incorrect. This is a complex sentence, as "after other animals…" is a dependent clause beginning with the subordinating conjunction *after*.

    D) is incorrect. This is a simple sentence although it contains both a prepositional and a verb phrase.

13. A) is incorrect. The commas separate items in a series (in this case, the three friends).

    B) is incorrect. The comma correctly follows the verbal phrase "trying to impress his friends," which modifies *Carl*.

    **C) is correct.** "Ice cream…food" and "it…creamy" are two independent clauses. The writer should include a coordinating conjunction like *for* or separate the clauses with a semicolon.

    D) is incorrect. The comma correctly follows the verbal phrase "mowing the lawn," which modifies *Amari*.

14. A) is incorrect. Both em dashes and commas are appropriate here.

    B) is incorrect. The comma is properly used in a list of items.

    C) is incorrect. *Animals* is acting as a plural noun with no possession indicated.

**D) is correct.** "Providing shade..." is not an independent clause; therefore, it cannot be preceded by a semicolon.

15. A) is incorrect. *River* should not be capitalized. In this sentence, it is a common noun.

    B) is incorrect. As the first word in a sentence, *ducks* should be capitalized.

    **C) is correct.** *Rashida Smith*, as a proper noun, should be capitalized, but "chairman of the board" should not because it is separated from the name by a comma.

    D) is incorrect. *Senators* should not be capitalized because this word replaces a name in this sentence.

16. A) is incorrect. Because the sentence reads "<u>My</u> sister and <u>my</u> best friend," the subject is plural and needs a plural verb (*live*).

    **B) is correct.** The verb agrees with the closest subject—in this case, the singular *brother*.

    C) is incorrect. *Neither* is a singular, indefinite pronoun, so the agreement is singular. *Neither refuses...*

    D) is incorrect. In the context of a game, the team is functioning as a singular, so it should take a singular verb. *The team was...*

17. **A) is correct.** The plural antecedents *Grandchildren* and *cousins* match the plural possessive pronoun *their*.

    B) is incorrect. The antecedent *grass* is singular; therefore its matching pronoun should also be the singular *its*, not *their*. The sentence should read, "Most of the grass has lost <u>its</u> deep color."

    C) is incorrect. Here, the collective noun *jury* is functioning as a singular body and thus takes a singular pronoun. The sentence should read, "The jury was relieved as <u>its</u> commitment came to a close."

    D) is incorrect. When *every* precedes the antecedent, the pronoun agreement is singular. The technically correct sentence should read, "Every boy and girl must learn to behave <u>himself or herself</u> in school."

18. A) is incorrect. In sentences with correlative conjunctions like *either...or*, pronouns (and verbs) agree with the nearest antecedent. Technically this sentence should read, "Either my brother or my dad will bring <u>his</u> van to pick us up."

    B) is incorrect. The antecedent *university* is a singular noun—an institution. Its pronoun should also be singular. The sentence should read, "The university is having <u>its</u> tenth fundraiser tomorrow night."

    C) is incorrect. Antecedents joined by *and* typically require a plural pronoun. The sentence should read, "Alyssa and Jacqueline bought <u>themselves</u> a big lunch today."

    **D) is correct.** When *each* precedes the antecedent, the pronoun agreement is singular. The pronoun *its* therefore agrees with the antecedents *Each dog, cat, and rabbit*.

19. **B) is correct.** The use of *too* suggests that both Veronica's activities are occurring at the same time. Only choice B has the two verbs in the same tense: *attended* and *went* are both past tense.

20. **A) is correct.** The other verbs in the series are *going* and *eating*, so *staying* is the only verb that fits in the series.

**21.** A) is incorrect. This is a dependent clause and needs an independent clause to be complete.

B) is incorrect. This is a comma splice.

C) is incorrect. This is a fused sentence.

**D) is correct.** This is a complete sentence that is punctuated properly with a comma between the dependent and independent clauses.

**22.** A) is incorrect. The relative pronoun *who* is acting as the subject of the subordinate clause "who is a car fanatic," so it is correct. *Whom* is the object pronoun.

**B) is correct.** *Unique* is an ultimate superlative, meaning it cannot be modified by adverbs like *very*. If something is unique, it cannot be more or less unique than something else.

C) is incorrect. Here, *effect* is a noun meaning *impression*. It is used correctly in this passage. *Affect* is generally used as a verb meaning "to act upon."

D) is incorrect. *Then* refers to a point in time; here, when the narrator's father drives to deliver holiday gifts. It is used correctly in this passage. *Than* sets up a comparison and would not make sense here.

# FIVE: BIOLOGY

## Biological Macromolecules

There are four basic biological macromolecules that are common between all organisms: carbohydrates, lipids, nucleic acids, and proteins. These molecules make life possible by performing basic cellular functions.

Macromolecules are **polymers**, which are large molecules comprised of smaller molecules called **monomers**. The monomers are joined together in an endothermic (energy requiring) dehydration reaction, so-called because it releases a molecule of water. Conversely, the bonds in polymers can be broken by an exothermic (energy-releasing) reaction that requires water.

### CARBOHYDRATES

**Carbohydrates**, commonly known as sugars, are made up of carbon, hydrogen, and oxygen. The monomers of carbohydrates, called **monosaccharides**, have these elements in the ratio $C_nH_{2n}O_n$. Common monosaccharides include glucose and fructose.

Monosaccharides bond together to build larger carbohydrate molecules. Two monosaccharides bond together to form **disaccharides** such as sucrose and lactose. **Oligosaccharides** are formed when small numbers of monosaccharies (usually between two and ten) bond together, and **polysaccharides** can include hundreds or even thousands of monosaccharides.

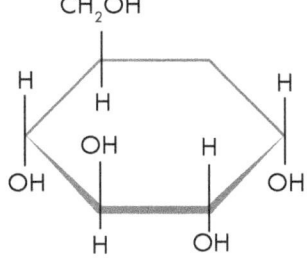

**Figure 5.1. Glucose**

Carbohydrates are often taken into the body through ingestion of food and serve a number of purposes, acting as:

- fuel sources (glycogen, amylose)
- means of communication between cells (glycoproteins)
- cell structure support (cellulose, chitin)

Carbohydrates are broken down to their constituent parts for fuel and other biological functions. Inability to process sugars can lead to health issues; for example, inability to break down lactose (often due to problems with the enzyme **lactase**, which serves this function) leads to lactose intolerance, and problems with insulin not working properly in the breakdown of sugars can lead to diabetes.

## LIPIDS

**Lipids**, commonly known as fats, are composed mainly of hydrogen and carbon. They serve a number of functions depending on their particular structure: they make up the outer structure of cells, and can act as fuel, as steroids, and as hormones. Lipids are hydrophobic, meaning they repel water.

Cholesterol is one example of a lipid, and is essential for normal functioning, although excessive accumulation can cause inflammation issues and high blood pressure. There are two types of cholesterol: **high-density lipoprotein (HDL)** and **low-density lipoprotein (LDL)**, with HDL commonly referred to as "good" cholesterol and LDL as "bad" cholesterol, as high levels of LDL in particular can cause health problems.

## PROTEINS

**Proteins** serve an incredibly wide variety of purposes within the body. As enzymes, they play key roles in important processes like DNA replication, cellular division, and cellular metabolism. Structural proteins provide rigidity to cartilage, hair, nails, and the cytoskeletons (the network of molecules that holds the parts of a cell in place). They are also involved in communication between cells and in the transportation of molecules.

Proteins are composed of individual **amino acids**, each of which has an amino group and carboxylic acid group, along with other side groups. Amino acids are joined together by **peptide bonds** to form polypeptides. There are twenty amino acids, and the order of the amino acids in the polypeptide determines the shape and function of the molecule.

## NUCLEIC ACIDS

**Nucleic acids** store hereditary information and are composed of monomers called **nucleotides**. Each nucleotide includes a sugar, a phosphate group, and a nitrogenous base.

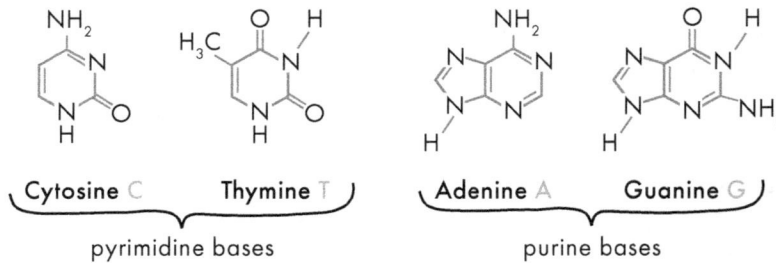

**Figure 5.2. DNA Nucleotides**

**HELPFUL HINT**

There are three main differences between DNA and RNA:
1. DNA contains the nucleotide thymine; RNA contains the nucleotide uracil.
2. DNA is double stranded; RNA is single stranded.
3. DNA is made from the sugar deoxyribose; RNA is made from the sugar ribose.

There are two types of nucleic acids. **Deoxyribonucleic acid (DNA)** contains the genetic instructions to produce proteins. It is composed of two strings of nucleotides wound into a double helix shape. The backbone of the helix is made from the nucleotide's sugar (deoxyribose) and phosphate groups. The "rungs" of the ladder are made from one of four nitrogenous bases: adenine, thymine, cytosine, and guanine. These bases bond together in specific pairs: adenine with thymine and cytosine with guanine.

**Ribonucleic acid (RNA)** transcribes information from DNA and plays several vital roles in the replication of DNA and the manufacturing of proteins. RNA nucleotides contain a sugar (ribose), a phosphate group, and one of four nitrogenous bases: adenine, uracil, cytosine, and guanine. It is usually found as a single stranded molecule.

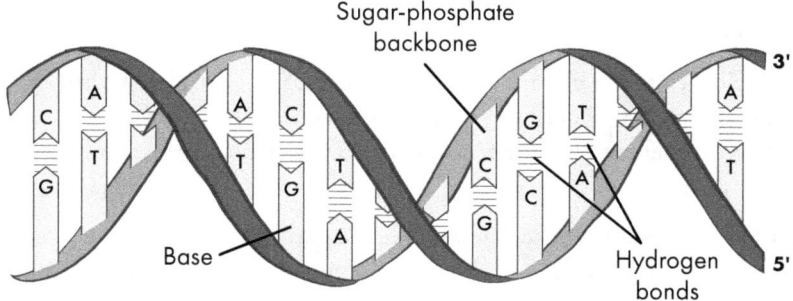

**Figure 5.3. DNA**

## THE STRUCTURE AND ROLE OF DNA

DNA stores information by coding for proteins using blocks of three nucleotides called **codons**. Each codon codes for a specific amino acid; together, all the codons needed to make a specific protein are called a **gene**. In addition to codons for specific amino acids, there are also codons that signal "start" and "stop."

The production of a protein starts with **transcription**. During transcription, the two sides of the DNA helix unwind and a complementary strand of messenger RNA (mRNA) is manufactured using the DNA as a template.

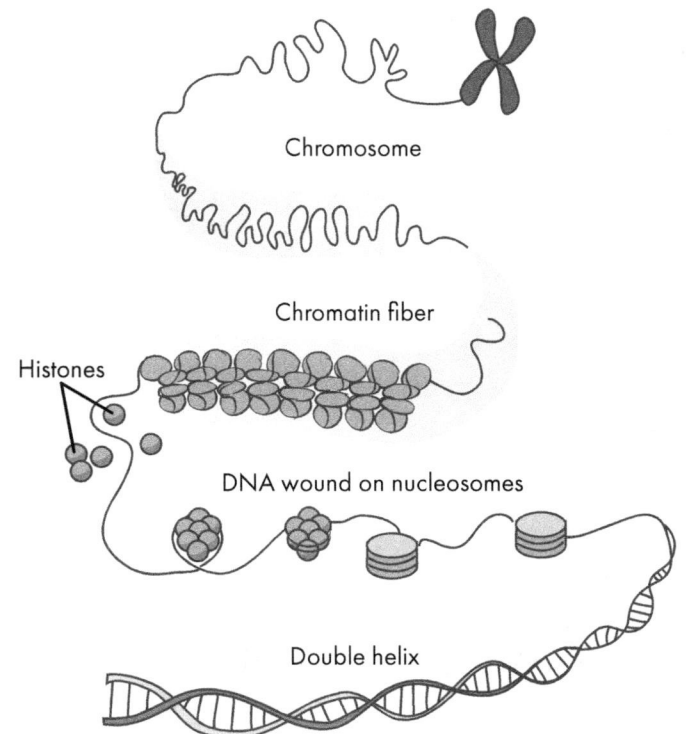

**Figure 5.4. DNA, Chromatin, and Chromosomes**

**BIOLOGY**

**QUICK REVIEW**

How might a mutation in a single codon affect the finished protein?

This mRNA then travels outside the nucleus where it is "read" by a ribosome during **translation**. Each codon on the mRNA is matched to an **anti-codon** on a strand of tRNA, which carries a specific amino acid. The amino acids bond as they are lined up next to each other, forming a polypeptide.

A **mutation** causes a change in the sequence of nucleotides within DNA. For example, the codon GAC codes for the amino acid aspartic acid. However, if the cytosine is swapped for an adenine, the codon now reads GAA, which corresponds to the amino acid glutamic acid.

When it is not being transcribed, DNA is tightly wound around proteins called **histones** to create **nucleosomes**, which are in turn packaged into **chromatin**. The structure of chromatin allows large amounts of DNA to be stored in a very small space and helps regulate transcription by controlling access to specific sections of DNA. Tightly folding the DNA also helps prevent damage to the genetic code. Chromatin is further bundled into packages of DNA called **chromosomes**. During cell division, DNA is replicated to create two identical copies of each chromosome called **chromatids**.

### PRACTICE QUESTIONS

1. Which of the following is NOT an amino acid found in DNA?
    A) adenine
    B) guanine
    C) uracil
    D) thymine

2. Which of the following processes uses the information stored in RNA to produce a protein?
    A) replication
    B) translation
    C) transcription
    D) mutation

3. Which of the following is a monomer used to build carbohydrates?
    A) glucose
    B) thymine
    C) aspartic acid
    D) histone

## The Cell

A **cell** is the smallest unit of life that can reproduce on its own. Unicellular organisms, such as amoebae, are made up of only one cell, while multicellular organisms are comprised of many cells. Cells consist of many different parts that work together to maintain the life of the cell.

## CELL MEMBRANES

The outer surface of human cells is made up of a **plasma membrane**, which gives the cell its shape. This membrane is primarily composed of a **phospholipid bilayer**, which itself is made up of two layers of lipids facing in opposing directions. This functions to separate the inner cellular environment from the **extracellular space**, the space between cells.

Molecules travel through the cell membrane using a number of different methods. During **diffusion**, molecules pass through the membrane from areas of high to low concentration. (When that molecule is water, the process is called **osmosis**.) **Facilitated diffusion** occurs with the assistance of proteins embedded in the membrane. Diffusion is known as **passive transport** because it does not require energy.

During **active transport**, proteins in the membrane use energy (in the form of ATP) to move molecules across the membrane. Usually these molecules are large or are being moved against their concentration gradient (from areas of low to high concentration).

## CELL ORGANELLES

Within the cell, specialized parts known as **organelles** serve individual functions to support the cell. The inside of the cell (excluding the nucleus) is the **cytoplasm**, which includes both organelles and **cytosol**, a fluid that aids in molecular transport and reactions.

The function of individual organelles can be compared to the functions of components in a city. The "power plant" for the cell is its mitochondria, which produce energy for the cell in the form of **adenosine triphosphate** (**ATP**). This process is known as **cellular respiration**, as it requires oxygen that is taken in from the lungs and supplied in blood. Byproducts of cellular respiration are water and carbon dioxide, the latter of which is transported into blood and then to the lungs, where it is exhaled.

The "city hall" of the cell is the cell **nucleus**, which is where the cell's "instructions" governing its functions originate. The nucleus contains the cell's DNA and is surrounded by a **nuclear membrane**. Only eukaryotic cells have nuclei; prokaryotic nucleic acids are not contained with a membrane-bound organelle.

The transporting "railway" function is largely served by **endoplasmic reticulum**. Proteins and lipids travel along endoplasmic reticulum as they are constructed and transported within the cell. There are two types of endoplasmic reticulum, **smooth** and **rough**, which are distinguished by the fact that the latter is embedded with **ribosomes**. Also, smooth endoplasmic reticulum are associated with the production and transport of lipids, whereas rough endoplasmic reticulum are associated with the production and transport of proteins. Ribosomes themselves are sites of protein production; here, molecules produced from the nucleus-encoding proteins guide the assembly of proteins from amino acids.

The **Golgi apparatus** is another organelle involved in protein synthesis and transport. After a new protein is synthesized at the ribosome and travels along the endoplasmic reticulum, the Golgi apparatus packages it into a **vesicle** (essentially a plasma membrane "bubble"), which can then be transported within the cell or secreted outside of the cell, as needed.

Plant cells include a number of structures not found in animal cells. These include the **cell wall**, which provides the cell with a hard outer structure, and **chloroplasts**, where photosynthesis occurs. During **photosynthesis**, plants store energy from sunlight as sugars, which serve as the main source of energy for cell functions.

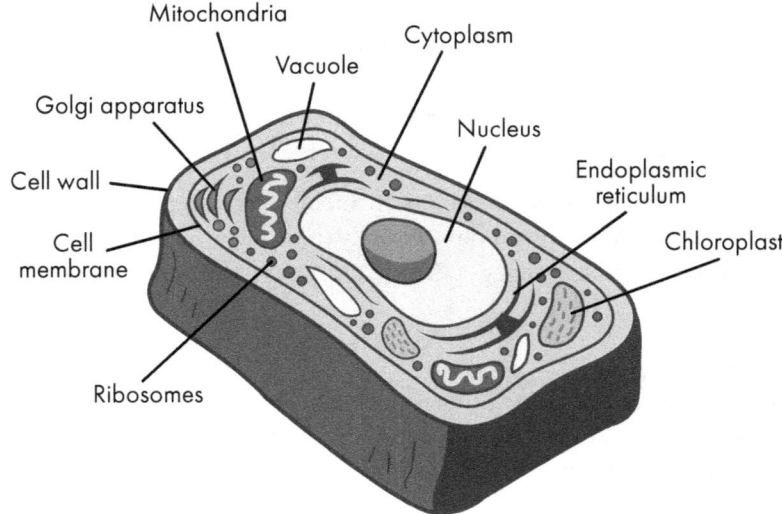

**Figure 5.5. Plant Cell**

## THE CELL CYCLE

From the very earliest moments of life throughout adulthood, cell division is a critical function of cell biology. The rate of division differs between cell types; hair and skin cells divide relatively rapidly (which is why chemotherapy drugs, which target rapidly-dividing cells in an effort to destroy cancerous cells, often cause hair loss), whereas liver cells rarely divide, except in response to injury. Regardless of cell type (with the exception of reproductive cells), the process of cell division follows consistent stages, which make up the **cell cycle**.

The cell cycle is made up of five stages. Cells at rest, which are not dividing, are considered to be at the $G_0$ (**growth phase 0**) stage of the cell cycle. Once cell division is triggered (for example, by extracellular signals in response to nearby damage, requiring new cells to replace the damaged cells), cells enter stage $G_1$. In this stage, the organelles of the soon-to-be-dividing cell are duplicated, in order to support both daughter cells upon division. Similarly, in the next stage, **S** (**DNA synthesis**) **phase**, the genetic material of the cell (DNA) is duplicated, to ensure that each cell has the full complement of genetic instructions. Additional growth and protein production occurs in the subsequent stage, $G_2$ **phase**.

$G_1$, S, and $G_2$ are collectively known as **interphase**, in which the cell is growing and preparing to divide; the subsequent stages in which the cell is actively dividing are stages of **mitosis**. The first mitotic stage is **prophase**, in which the newly replicated DNA condenses into chromosomes. These chromosomes are in pairs (humans have twenty-three pairs of chromosomes), with each pair joined together at the **centromere**.

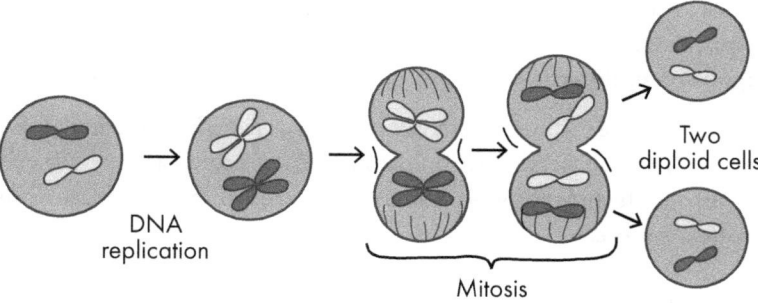

**Figure 5.6. Mitosis**

Next, in **prometaphase**, the nuclear membrane breaks down. **Kinetochores** form on chromosomes, which are proteins that attach to kinetochore **microtubules** (cellular filaments) anchored at opposite ends of the cell. In **metaphase**, the chromosomes align along the center of the cell, perpendicular to the poles anchoring the microtubules. The alignment is such that one of each chromosome duplicates is attached to each pole by these microtubules.

In **anaphase**, the microtubules pull the duplicates apart from each other toward each of the poles. In the final stage of mitosis, **telophase**, nuclei reform in each pole of the cell, and cellular filaments contract. The process of **cytokinesis** divides the cell into two daughter cells, both with a full complement of genetic material and organelles.

Following mitosis, both daughter cells return to the $G_1$ phase, either to begin the process of division once again or to rest without dividing ($G_0$).

The process of producing sex cells (**gametes: ovum** for women and **spermatozoa** for men) is similar to mitosis, except that it produces cells with only half the normal number of chromosomes. Thus, when two sex cells fuse, the resulting **zygote** has the proper amount of chromosomes (and genetic information from both parents). This process is known as **meiosis**.

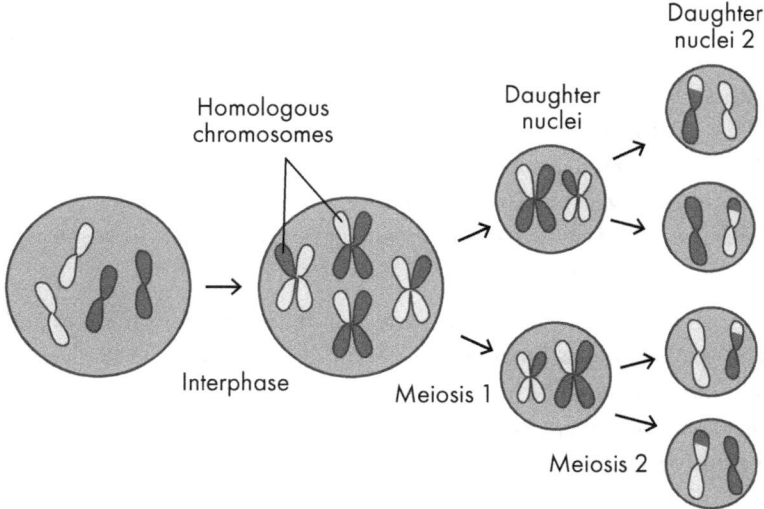

**Figure 5.7. Meiosis**

In the prophase of meiosis, chromosome pairs align next to each other. At this stage, transfer of genetic material can occur between members of each pair, in a process known as **homologous recombination**, which can increase the genetic diversity of offspring.

In meiotic metaphase, these chromosomes align as pairs in the center of the cell, and the chromosomes are separated during anaphase. As a result, each gamete cell ends up with one copy of each chromosome pair, and thus one half of the genetic complement necessary for the zygote.

## PRACTICE QUESTIONS

4. Cellular respiration produces which of the following molecules?
   A) oxygen
   B) DNA
   C) ATP
   D) glucose

5. Which of the following houses the cell's DNA?
   A) rough endoplasmic reticulum
   B) smooth endoplasmic reticulum
   C) mitochondrion
   D) nucleus

6. Which of the following processes creates daughter cells with half the number of chromosomes contained in somatic (body) cells?
   A) mitosis
   B) meiosis
   C) recombination
   D) the cell cycle

# Genetics

## HEREDITY

When organisms reproduce, **genetic** information is passed to the next generation through DNA. Within DNA are blocks of nucleotides called genes, each of which contains the code needed to produce a specific protein. Genes are responsible for **traits**, or characteristics, in organisms such as eye color, height, and flower color. The sequence of nucleotides in DNA is called an organism's **genotype**, while the resulting physical traits are the organism's **phenotype**.

Different versions of the same gene (e.g., one that codes for blue eyes and one for green eyes) are called **alleles**. During sexual reproduction, the child receives two alleles of each gene—one each on the mother's chromosomes and the father's chromosomes. These alleles can be **homozygous** (identical) or **heterozygous** (different). If the organism is heterozygous for a particular gene, which allele is expressed is determined by which alleles are dominant and/or recessive. According to the rules of Mendelian heredity, **dominant** alleles will always be expressed, while **recessive** alleles are only expressed if the organism has no dominant alleles for that gene.

**HELPFUL HINT**
Many of the rules of genetics were discovered by Gregor Mendel, a nineteenth century abbot who used pea plants to show how traits are passed down through generations.

The genotype, and resulting phenotype, of sexually reproducing organisms can be tracked using Punnett squares, which show the alleles of the **parent generation** on each of two axes. (Note that dominant alleles are always depicted using capital letters while recessive alleles are written in lower case.) The possible phenotype of the resulting offspring, called the **F1 generation**, are then shown in the body of the square. The squares do not show the phenotypes of any one offspring; instead, they show the ratio of phenotypes found across the generation. In Figure 5.8, two heterozygous parents for trait R are mated, resulting in a ratio of 1:2:1 for homozygous dominant, heterozygous, and homozygous recessive. Note that this creates a 3:1 ratio of dominant to recessive phenotypes.

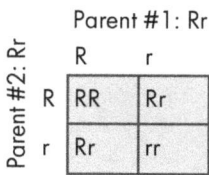

**Figure 5.8. Punnett Square**

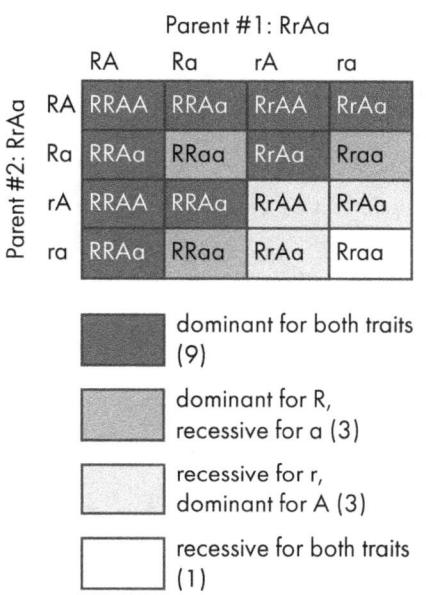

**Figure 5.9. Dihybrid Cross**

Similarly, crossing two parents that are heterozygous for two traits (dihybrids) results in a phenotypic ratio of 9:3:3:1, as shown below. This ratio is known as the **dihybrid ratio**.

Non-Mendelian inheritance describes patterns in inheritance that do not follow the ratios described above. The patterns can occur for a number of reasons. Alleles might show **incomplete dominance**, where one allele is not fully expressed over the other, resulting in a third phenotype (for example, a red flower and white flower cross to create a pink flower). Alleles can also be **codominant**, meaning both are fully expressed (such as the AB blood type).

The expression of genes can also be regulated by mechanisms other than the dominant/recessive relationship. For example, some genes may inhibit the expression of other genes, a process called **epistasis**. The environment can also impact gene expression. For example, organisms with the same genotype may grow to different sizes depending on the nutrients available to them.

When a person's genetic code is damaged, that organism may have a **genetic disorder**. For example, cystic fibrosis, which causes difficulty with basic bodily functions such as breathing and eating, results from damage to the gene which codes for a protein called CFTR. Down syndrome, which causes developmental delays, occurs when a person has three copies of chromosome 21 (meaning they received two copies from a parent as a result of an error in meiosis).

## NATURAL SELECTION AND EVOLUTION

Genes are not static. Over time, **mutations**, or changes in the genetic code, occur that can affect an organism's ability to survive. Harmful mutations will appear less often in a population or be removed entirely because those organisms will be less likely to reproduce (and thus will not pass on that trait). Beneficial mutations may help an organism reproduce, and thus that trait will appear more often. Over time, this process, called **natural selection**, results in the evolution of new species. The theory of evolution

**HELPFUL HINT**

When the F1 generation is mated together, the resulting offspring are called the F2 generation.

**QUICK REVIEW**

Why might a harmful mutation continue to exist in a population?

was developed by naturalist Charles Darwin based in part on his observations of finches on the Galapagos Islands. These finches had a variety of beak shapes and sizes that allowed them to coexist by using different food sources.

As a result of these processes, all organisms share a distant evolutionary predecessor. As evolution progressed, species subsequently split off as different branches of the phylogenetic (evolutionary) tree of species diversity, leading to the complexity of life seen today. For example, humans share a recent evolutionary ancestor with other primates (but did not evolve directly from any of these species).

## PRACTICE QUESTIONS

7. If a plant that is homozygous dominant (**T**) for a trait is crossed with a plant that is homozygous recessive (**t**) for the same trait, what will be the phenotype of the offspring if the trait follows Mendelian patterns of inheritance?
   A) All offspring will show the dominant phenotype.
   B) All offspring will show the recessive phenotype.
   C) Half the offspring will show the dominant trait, and the other half will show the recessive phenotype.
   D) All the offspring will show a mix of the dominant and recessive phenotypes.

8. Which of the following mutations would most likely be passed on to an organism's offspring?
   A) a mutation that prevents the production of functioning sperm cells
   B) a mutation that causes the deterioration of nerve cells in mature adults
   C) a mutation that does not cause any changes to the organism's phenotype
   D) a mutation that limits the growth of bone cells in children

# ANSWER KEY

1. **C) is correct.** Uracil is found only in RNA.

2. **B) is correct.** Translation is the process of matching codons in RNA to the correct anti-codon to manufacture a protein.

3. **A) is correct.** Glucose is a monosaccharide that can be used to build larger polysaccharides.

4. **C) is correct.** Cellular respiration uses glucose and oxygen to produce ATP.

5. **D) is correct.** Smooth and rough endoplasmic reticula process and transport lipids and proteins, and mitochondria produce the cell's chemical energy.

6. **B) is correct.** Meiosis produces sex cells, which have half the number of chromosomes that somatic cells contain.

7. **A) is correct.** Because each offspring will inherit the dominant allele, all the offspring will show the dominant phenotype. The offspring would only show a mix of the two phenotypes if they did not follow Mendelian inheritance patterns.

8. **B) is correct.** Because this mutation presents in older adults who have likely already reproduced, it is likely to have been passed on to the next generation. Mutations that affect reproduction and children are much less likely to be passed on. A mutation that causes no changes in phenotype may either disappear or spread as a result of random fluctuations in the gene pool.

# SIX: CHEMISTRY

## Properties of Atoms

An **atom** is defined as the smallest constituent unit of an element that still retains all of the original properties of the element, and all matter is composed of atoms. Atoms are not irreducible, however, and may be broken into further components: protons, neutrons, and electrons. All atomic nuclei are comprised of positively charged **protons** and neutrally charged **neutrons**, meaning nuclei have an overall positive charge.

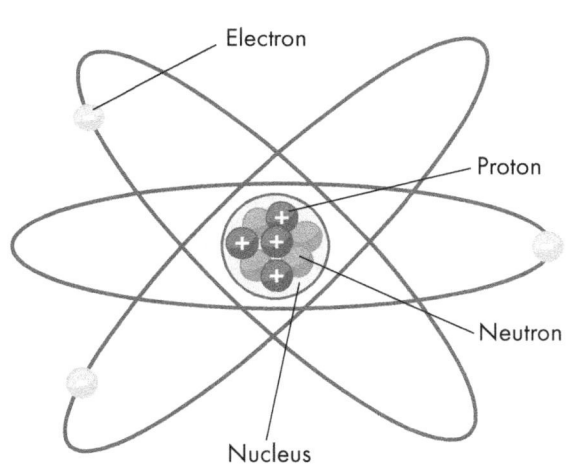

**Figure 6.1. Structure of an Atom**

Negatively charged **electrons** orbit the nucleus in orbitals, with the orbitals closer to the nucleus having less energy than those farther away. Thus, overall atomic charge is determined by the number of positively charged protons and negatively charged electrons in an atom.

Every atom of an element has the same number of protons, which is that element's **atomic number**. Elements are arranged on the Periodic Table of the Elements by their atomic number which increases from top to bottom and left to right on the table. Hydrogen, the first element on the periodic table, has one proton while helium, the second element, has two, and so on.

Along with atomic charge, atoms have measurable mass. Protons and neutrons are significantly more massive than electrons (about 1,800 times), so the mass of electrons is not considered when calculating the mass of an atom. Thus, an element's **mass number** is the number of protons and neutrons present in its atoms. The number of neutrons in an atom can be found by subtracting the atomic number from the mass number.

**HELPFUL HINT**

The attractive and repulsive forces in an atom follow the universal law that "like charges repel and opposite charges attract."

While atoms of the same element have the same number of protons, their number of neutrons may vary. Atoms which differ in their number of neutrons but have equal numbers of protons are **isotopes** of the same element.

**HELPFUL HINT**

*atomic number* = number of protons

*mass number* = number of protons + number of neutrons

*atomic mass* = average mass of all isotopes

When writing the atomic symbol of an element, isotopes are differentiated by writing the mass number in the upper left-hand corner of the symbol. The atomic symbol for ordinary hydrogen is written as $^1H$, to signify that it has no neutrons and 1 proton, while deuterium, which is a hydrogen isotope with 1 neutron, is written as $^2H$.

The **atomic mass** of an atom, which is different from the mass number, is the average mass of all known isotopes of an element. For each element on the Periodic Table, the atomic number is listed above the symbol of the element and the atomic mass (measured in atomic mass units, or AMU) is listed underneath the symbol.

Atoms may lose or gain electrons, creating charged particles called **ions**. Ions are called **cations** if they are positively charged (due to the loss of electrons) or **anions** if they are negatively charged (due to the gaining of electrons). Ionic charges are denoted by adding a plus or minus sign onto the elemental symbol; for example, a sodium ion with a charge of +1 would be written as $Na^+$.

Ions may be composed of two or more atoms known as molecular ions or **polyatomic ions**. The overall charge of a polyatomic ion is equal to the sum of the charges of all constituent atoms.

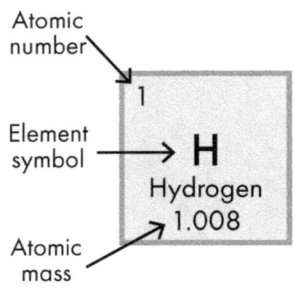

**Figure 6.2. Reading the Periodic Table**

| Table 6.1. Common Polyatomic Ions | |
|---|---|
| $NH_4^+$ | ammonium |
| $H_3O^+$ | hydronium |
| $PO_4^{3-}$ | phosphate |
| $SO_4^{2-}$ | sulfate |
| $MnO_4^{2-}$ | manganate |
| $OH^-$ | hydroxide |
| $CN^-$ | cyanide |
| $CO_3^{2-}$ | carbonate |
| $HCO_3^{1-}$ | hydrogen carbonate |
| $ClO^{2-}$ | chlorite |

## THE PERIODIC TABLE OF THE ELEMENTS

There are many useful physical and chemical patterns represented in the Periodic Table of the Elements. The periodic table is organized into rows called **periods** and columns called **groups**. The position of an element's symbol on the periodic table indicates its electron configuration. The elements in each group on the table all contain the same amount of electrons in their valence shell, which results in all elements in a group having similar chemical properties.

The majority of the elements in the periodic table are metals. **Metals** have the following properties:

- They are ductile and malleable.

| 1 | 2 | 3 | 4 | 5 | 6 | 7 | 8 | 9 | 10 | 11 | 12 | 13 | 14 | 15 | 16 | 17 | 18 |
|---|---|---|---|---|---|---|---|---|---|---|---|---|---|---|---|---|---|
| 1 H Hydrogen 1.008 | | | | | | | | | | | | | | | | | 2 He Helium 4.0026 |
| 3 Li Lithium 6.941 | 4 Be Beryllium 9.0122 | | | | | | | | | | | 5 B Boron 10.81 | 6 C Carbon 12.011 | 7 N Nitrogen 14.007 | 8 O Oxygen 15.999 | 9 F Fluorine 18.998 | 10 Ne Neon 20.180 |
| 11 Na Sodium 22.990 | 12 Mg Magnesium 24.305 | | | | | | | | | | | 13 Al Aluminum 26.982 | 14 Si Silicon 28.085 | 15 P Phosphorus 30.974 | 16 S Sulfur 32.06 | 17 Cl Chlorine 35.45 | 18 Ar Argon 39.948 |
| 19 K Potassium 39.098 | 20 Ca Calcium 40.078 | 21 Sc Scandium 44.956 | 22 Ti Titanium 47.867 | 23 V Vanadium 50.942 | 24 Cr Chromium 51.996 | 25 Mn Maganese 54.938 | 26 Fe Iron 55.845 | 27 Co Cobalt 58.933 | 28 Ni Nickel 58.963 | 29 Cu Copper 63.546 | 30 Zn Zinc 65.38 | 31 Ga Gallium 69.723 | 32 Ge Germanium 72.64 | 33 Es Arsenic 74.922 | 34 Se Selenium 78.971 | 35 Br Bromine 79.904 | 36 Kr Krypton 83.798 |
| 37 Rb Rubidium 85.468 | 38 Sr Strontium 87.62 | 39 Y Yttrium 88.906 | 40 Zr Zirconium 91.224 | 41 Nb Niobium 92.906 | 42 Mo Molybdenum 254 | 43 Tc Technetium 98 | 44 Ru Ruthenium 101.07 | 45 Rh Rhodium 102.91 | 46 Pd Palladium 106.42 | 47 Ag Silver 107.87 | 48 Cd Cadmium 112.41 | 49 In Indium 114.82 | 50 Sn Tin 118.71 | 51 Sb Antimony 121.76 | 52 Te Tellurium 127.60 | 53 I Iodine 126.90 | 54 Xe Xenon 121.29 |
| 55 Cs Caesium 132.91 | 56 Ba Barium 137.33 | 57-71 | 72 Hf Hafnium 178.49 | 73 Ta Tantalum 183.84 | 74 W Tungsten 183.84 | 75 Re Rhenium 186.21 | 76 Os Osmium 190.23 | 77 Ir Iridium 192.22 | 78 Pt Platinum 195.08 | 79 Au Gold 196.97 | 80 Hg Mercury 200.59 | 81 Tl Thallium 204.38 | 82 Pb Lead 207.2 | 83 Bi Bismuth 208.98 | 84 Po Polonium 209 | 85 At Astatine 210 | 86 Rn Radon 222 |
| 87 Fr Francium 223.020 | 88 Ra Radium 226 | 89-103 | 104 Rf Rutherfordium 267 | 105 Db Dubnium 268 | 106 Sg Seaborgium 271 | 107 Bh Bohrium 272 | 108 Hs Hassium 277 | 109 Mt Meitnerium 276 | 110 Ds Darmstadtium 281 | 111 Rg Roentgenium 280 | 112 Cn Copernicium 285 | 113 Uut Ununtrium Unknown | 114 Fl Flerovium 254 | 115 Uup Ununpentium Unknown | 116 Lv Livermorium 291 | 117 Uus Ununseptium Unknown | 118 Uuo Ununoctium Unknown |

| |
|---|
| Atomic Number |
| Symbol |
| Name |
| Atomic Mass |

| | | | | | | | | | | | | | | | |
|---|---|---|---|---|---|---|---|---|---|---|---|---|---|---|---|
| Lanthanide | 57 La Lanthanium 138.905 | 58 Ce Cerium 140.12 | 59 Pr Praseodymium 140.91 | 60 Nd Neodymium 144.24 | 61 Pm Promethium 144.913 | 62 Sm Samarium 150.36 | 63 Eu Europium 151.96 | 64 Gd Gadolinium 157.25 | 65 Tb Terbium 158.93 | 66 Dy Dysprosium 152.50 | 67 Ho Holmium 154.930 | 68 Er Erbium 167.259 | 69 Tm Thulium 168.934 | 70 Yb Ytterbium 173.065 | 71 Lu Lutetium 174.967 |
| Actinide | 89 Ac Actinium 227.028 | 90 Th Thorium 232.038 | 91 Pa Protactinuim 231.036 | 92 U Uranium 238.029 | 93 Np Neptunium 237.048 | 94 Pu Plutonium 244.064 | 95 Am Americium 243.061 | 96 Cm Curium 247.070 | 97 Bk Berkelium 247.070 | 98 Cf Californium 251.080 | 99 Es Einsteinium 254 | 100 Fm Fermium 257.095 | 101 Md Mendelevium 258.1 | 102 No Nobelium 259.101 | 103 Lr Lawrencium 262 |

| | | | | | | | | | |
|---|---|---|---|---|---|---|---|---|---|
| Alkaline Metal | Alkaline Earth Metals | Transition Metal | Basic Metal | Metalloid | Nonmetal | Halogen | Noble Gas | Lanthanide | Actinide |

**Figure 6.3. Periodic Table of the Elements**

- They conduct electricity.
- They can form alloys.
- They are thermally conductive.
- They are hard, opaque, and shiny.
- With the exception of mercury, they are solids.

Solid metals usually consist of tightly packed atoms, resulting in fairly high densities. Metals begin on the left side of the periodic table and span across the middle of the table, almost all the way to the right side. Examples of metals include gold (Au), tin (Sn), and lead (Pb).

**Nonmetals** are elements that do not conduct electricity and tend to be more volatile than metals. They can be solids, liquids, or gases. The nonmetals are located on the right side of the periodic table. Examples of nonmetals include sulfur (S), hydrogen (H), and oxygen (O).

**Metalloids**, or semimetals, are elements that possess both metal and nonmetal characteristics. For example, some metalloids are shiny but do not conduct electricity well. Many metalloids are semiconductors. Metalloids are located between the metals and nonmetals on the periodic table. Some examples of metalloids are boron (B), silicon (Si), and arsenic (As).

Specific names are given to certain groups on the periodic table. Group 1 elements (belonging to the leftmost column) are known as the **alkali metals** and are characterized by the fact that they are very unstable and react violently with water. Other notably reactive elements are in Group 17, the **halogens**. In contrast to both of these groups, Group 18 contains the **noble gases**, which are inert and very non-reactive because they have a full outer shell of electrons.

There are two periods below and separated from the main periodic table. These are called **lanthanides** and **actinides**. They are set apart from the other elements for two reasons: first, to consolidate the periodic table, and second, because they are more complicated chemically than the rest of the elements—which means that they do not follow any of the trends outlined below.

The periodic table is organized so that elements show trends across periods and groups. Some of these trends are summarized below.

- **Atomic Number:** The atomic number (equal to the number of protons) of an element increases from left to right and top to bottom on the Periodic Table of the Elements. This means that hydrogen, with the lowest atomic number, is located at the upper left corner of the table.
- **Atomic Radius:** Atomic radius (the distance from the center of the atom to its outermost electron shell) increases from right to left and top to bottom on the periodic table, with the largest elements residing in the lower left corner.
- **Electron Affinity:** An atom's electron affinity describes the amount of energy released or gained when an electron is added to the atom. On the periodic table, electron affinity increases from left to right and bottom to top, with the highest electron affinities belonging to elements residing in the upper right corner.

- **Electronegativity**: Electronegativity measures how easily an atom can attract electrons and form chemical bonds. In general, electronegativity increases from left to right and bottom to top on the Periodic Table of the Elements, with fluorine being the most electronegative element. Electronegativity decreases from top to bottom of a group on the periodic table because of the increasing atomic radius, which corresponds with a greater distance between the electron orbital shells. One notable exception to these electronegativity trends is Group 18, the noble gases, since they possess a complete valence shell in their ground state and generally do not attract electrons.
- **Ionization Energy**: The ionization energy of an element is defined as the energy necessary to remove an electron from a neutral atom in its gaseous phase. In other words, the lower this energy is, the more likely an atom is to lose an electron and become a cation. Ionization energies increase from left to right and bottom to top on the periodic table, meaning that the lowest ionization energies are in the lower left corner and the highest are in the upper right corner. This is because elements to the right on the periodic table are unlikely to lose electrons and become cations since their outer valence shells are nearly full.

**HELPFUL HINT**

Electronegativity and ionization energy follow the same periodic trends. These two properties are simply different ways of describing the same basic property: the strength with which an atom holds electrons.

## ELECTRON CONFIGURATION

An atom's **electron configuration**—the location of its electrons—influences its physical and chemical properties, including boiling point, conductivity, and its tendency to engage in chemical reactions (also called the atom's stability). The chemical reactivity of an atom is determined by the electrons in the outermost shell, as they are first to interact with neighboring atoms.

Conventionally, electrons are depicted as orbiting a nucleus in defined pathways, much like a planet orbits the sun. In reality, electrons move in clouds surrounding the nucleus known as **orbitals**. Each orbital in an atom holds two electrons.

Orbitals are grouped into four types of **subshells** labeled with the letters $s$, $p$, $d$, and $f$. Each subshell has a specific number of orbitals:
- $s$ has 1 orbital and holds $1 \times 2 = 2$ electrons
- $p$ has 3 orbitals and holds $3 \times 2 = 6$ electrons
- $d$ has 5 orbitals and holds $5 \times 2 = 10$ electrons
- $f$ has 7 orbitals and holds $7 \times 2 = 14$ electrons

The orbitals in each type of subshell have a particular shape. For example, the $s$ subshell is spherical, while the $p$ subshell is shaped like a bow tie.

Subshells are further grouped into **shells**, which are labeled with integers (1, 2, 3, ...). The shell numbered 1 is closest to the nucleus, and the energy of the electrons in shells increases the further the shell is from the nucleus.

The location of a electron is described by its shell number and subshell letter, with the number of electrons in that orbital given as a superscript. The one electron in hydrogen, for example, is written as $1s^1$.

**HELPFUL HINT**

You can use the periodic table to remember the order in which orbitals are filled: start at the upper left corner and move from left to right, then move down to the next row.

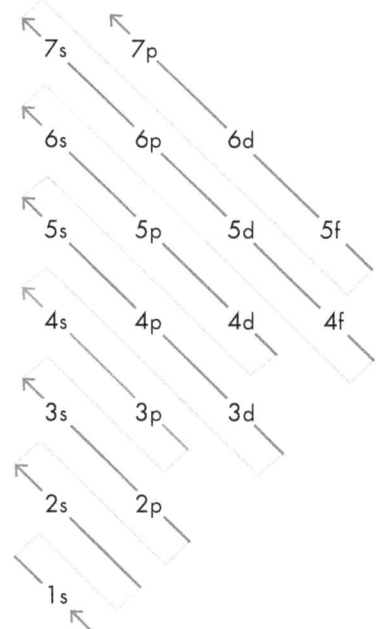

increasing energy →
1s 2s 2p 3s 3p 4s 3d 4p 5s 4d 5p 6s ...

**Figure 6.4. Electron Configuration**

The orbtials for the first four shells are described in the table below.

Table 6.2. Electron Configuration Notation

| Shell | Subshell | No. of Orbitals | No. of Electrons in Subshell | Notation for Full Subshell |
|---|---|---|---|---|
| 1 | s | 1 | 2 | $1s^2$ |
| 2 | s | 1 | 2 | $2s^2$ |
|   | p | 3 | 6 | $2p^6$ |
| 3 | s | 1 | 2 | $3s^2$ |
|   | p | 3 | 6 | $3p^6$ |
|   | d | 5 | 10 | $3d^{10}$ |
| 4 | s | 1 | 2 | $4s^2$ |
|   | p | 3 | 6 | $4p^6$ |
|   | d | 5 | 10 | $4d^{10}$ |
|   | f | 7 | 14 | $4f^{14}$ |

Electrons fill orbitals in order of increasing energy, meaning they fill orbitals close to the nucleus before filling in outer orbitals. The order in which orbitals are filled is shown in Figure 6.4.

The electrons in an atom's outermost shell are its **valence electrons**. Most elements require eight electrons to fill their outermost shell (2 in s and 6 in p). So, elements with six or seven valence electrons are likely to gain electrons (and become cations). Conversely, elements with one or two electrons are very likely to lose electrons (and become anions). Elements with exactly eight electrons (the noble gases), are almost completely unreactive.

The electron configuration of each element correlates to its position on the periodic table: Group 1 and Group 2 (defined as the **s-block**) have valence electrons in s-orbitals. Elements in Groups 13 to 18 (defined as the **p-block**) have valence electrons in their p-orbitals. These groups (with the exception of the noble gases) are very reactive.

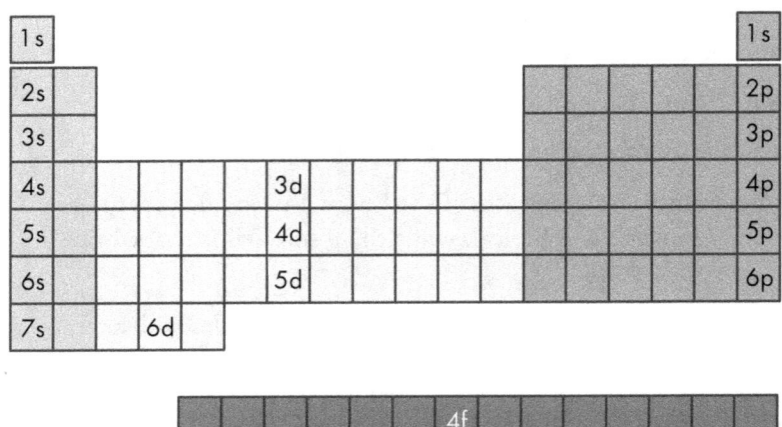

**Figure 6.5. Electron Orbitals on the Periodic Table**

Group 3 through Group 12 elements (defined as the **d-block**) have valence electrons in *d*-orbitals. The lanthanides and actinides have valence electrons in their *f*-orbitals (and are called the **f-block**). The properties of these elements are less predictable because atoms' *d* and *f* orbitals do not fill in a straightforward order.

## PRACTICE QUESTIONS

1. Rank the following in order of increasing atomic radius: xenon (Xe), barium (Ba), cesium (Cs).
    A) Xe < Cs < Ba
    B) Cs < Xe < Ba
    C) Ba < Cs < Xe
    D) Xe < Ba < Cs

2. What is the electron configuration of ground-state neutral magnesium (Mg)?
    A) $1s^2 2s^2 2p^6 3s^2$
    B) $1s^2 2s^2 2p^2 3s^2$
    C) $1s^2 2s^6 2p^2 3s^2$
    D) $1s^2 2s^2 2p^2 3s^3$

3. List the following in order of decreasing electronegativity: fluorine (F), bromine (Br), magnesium (Mg), strontium (Sr).
    A) F > Mg > Br < Sr
    B) F > Br > Mg > Sr
    C) Br > Mg > Sr > F
    D) Sr > Mg > Br > F

# Intramolecular Bonds

Chemical bonds, also called intramolecular bonds, are attractions between atoms that allow for the creation of substances consisting of more than one atom. When all the chemically bonded atoms are the same element, the substance is known as a **molecule**. When two or more different elements bond together, the result is called a **compound**. (However, the word *molecule* is often used colloquially to refer to both types of substances.)

**HELPFUL HINT**

All compounds are molecules but not all molecules are compounds.

Table 6.3. Common Molecules and Compounds

| | |
|---|---|
| $H_2O$ | water |
| NaCl | table salt |
| $CO_2$ | carbon dioxide |
| HCl | hydrochloric acid |
| $O_3$ | ozone |
| $C_6H_{12}O_6$ | glucose (sugar) |
| $H_2$ | hydrogen gas |

**CHEMISTRY**

## TYPES OF BONDS

Not all chemical bonds are alike. Their causes vary, and thus the strength of those bonds also varies widely. There are two major types of bonds, distinguished from one another based on whether electrons are shared or transferred between the atoms. A **covalent bond** involves a pair of atoms sharing electrons from their outer orbitals to fill their valence shells. These bonds form between non-metals with similar electronegativities.

In an **ionic bond**, one atom "gives" its electrons to the other, resulting in one positively and one negatively charged atom. The bond is a result of the attraction between ions. Ionic bonds form between atoms with very different electronegativities.

Metals can form tightly packed arrays in which each atom is in close contact with many neighbors. So many atomic orbitals overlap with each atom that they form very large molecular orbitals that in turn overlap with each other creating a continuous band in which electrons can move. Any excitation, such as an electrical current, can cause the electrons to move throughout the array. The high electrical and thermal conductivity of metals is due to this ability of electrons to move throughout the lattice. This type of delocalized bonding is called **metallic bonding**. Metals are ductile or can be bent without breaking because the atoms can slide past each other without breaking the delocalized bonds.

**HELPFUL HINT**

In a covalent bond, two atoms share electrons. In an ionic bond, one atom gives electrons to the other.

## POLARITY

Polarity is the difference in charge across a compound caused by the uneven partial charge distribution between the atoms. Ionic bonds have higher polarity than covalent bonds because they consist of ions of full opposite charges, meaning one side of the compound is very positive and one very negative. The charge distribution in covalent bonds is more variable, resulting in either polar covalent bonds or non-polar covalent bonds.

**Non-polar covalent bonds** have no uneven distribution of charge. This is because electrons are completely shared between the two atoms, meaning neither has a strong hold on the shared electrons. Non-polar covalent bonds generally arise between two non-metal atoms with equal electronegativity, for example, two hydrogen atoms.

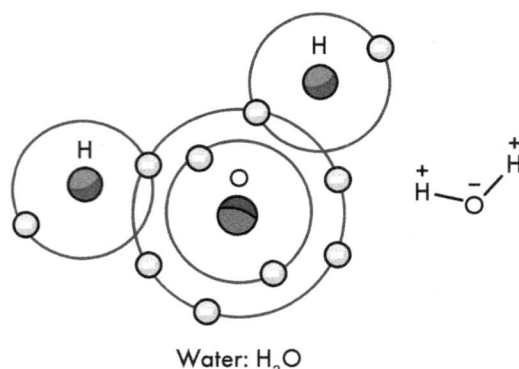

Water: $H_2O$

**Figure 6.6. Polar Covalent Bond**

**Polar covalent bonds** arise between two non-metal atoms with different electronegativities. In these bonds, electrons are shared unequally. Neither atom is a completely charged ion; instead, the more electronegative atom will hold onto the electron more often, creating a slightly negative charge. The other atom will thus have a slightly positive charge. These slight charges are called **dipoles**.

A **dipole moment** is a measure of the unequal charge distribution in a polar bond. It is possible for a polar molecule to have no net dipole moment if the dipole moments of each bond are equal in magnitude and opposing in direction. These covalent compounds have a symmetrical molecular geometry, meaning that the dipoles created by the polar bond cancel each other out.

## PRACTICE QUESTIONS

4. Which of the following bonds would have the largest dipole moment?
   A) C—H
   B) C—F
   C) C—O
   D) C—N

5. Which group on the periodic table will typically adopt a charge of +1 when forming ionic compounds?
   A) alkaline earth metals
   B) lanthanides
   C) halogens
   D) alkali metals

# Intermolecular Bonds

While intramolecular bonds occur within compounds to hold atoms together, it is also possible for bonds to exist between compounds. These intermolecular bonds do not result from the transfer or sharing of electrons. Rather, they are caused by the attraction between the positive and negative parts of separate compounds.

The force of attraction between hydrogen and an extremely electronegative atom, such as oxygen or nitrogen, is known as a **hydrogen bond**. For example, in water ($H_2O$), oxygen atoms are attracted to the hydrogen atoms in nearby molecules, creating hydrogen bonds. These bonds are significantly weaker than the chemical bonds that involve sharing or transfer of electrons, and have only 5 to 10 percent of the strength of a covalent bond. Despite its relative weakness, hydrogen bonding is quite important in the natural world; it has major effects on the properties of water and ice and is important biologically with regard to proteins and nucleic acids as well as the DNA double helix structure.

**Van der Waals forces** are electrical interactions between two or more molecules or atoms. They are the weakest type of intermolecular attraction, but if substantial amounts of these forces are present, their net effect can be quite strong.

There are two major types of van der Waals forces. The **London dispersion force** is a temporary force that occurs when electrons in two adjacent atoms form spontaneous, temporary dipoles due to the positions the atoms are occupying. This is the weakest intermolecular force and it does not exert a force over long distances. Interestingly,

**QUICK REVIEW**
Why would molecules with large dipole moments be more likely to interact than non-polar molecules?

London dispersion forces are the only forces that exist between noble gas atoms; without these forces, noble gases would not be able to liquefy.

The second type of van der Waals force is **dipole-dipole interactions**, which are the result of two dipolar molecules interacting with each other. This interaction occurs when the partial positive dipole in one molecule is attracted to the partial negative dipole in the other molecule.

### PRACTICE QUESTION

**6.** Which intermolecular forces would need to be considered in predicting the relative physical properties of $CH_3F$, $CH_3Cl$, $CH_3Br$, and $CH_3I$?
   - **A)** London force only
   - **B)** dipole-dipole and London force only
   - **C)** dipole-dipole and hydrogen bonding only
   - **D)** dipole-dipole, hydrogen bonding, and London force

## Properties of Substances
### CHEMICAL AND PHYSICAL PROPERTIES

Properties of substances are divided into two categories: physical and chemical. **Physical properties** are those which are measurable and can be seen without changing the chemical makeup of a substance. In contrast, **chemical properties** are those that determine how a substance will behave in a chemical reaction. These two categories differ in that a physical property may be identified just by observing, touching, or measuring the substance in some way; however, chemical properties cannot be identified simply by observing a material. Rather, the material must be engaged in a chemical reaction in order to identify its chemical properties.

**HELPFUL HINT**
In both physical and chemical changes, matter is always conserved, meaning it can never be created or destroyed.

Table 6.4. Physical and Chemical Properties

| Physical Properties | Chemical Properties |
| --- | --- |
| temperature | heat of combustion |
| color | flammability |
| mass | toxicity |
| viscosity | chemical stability |
| density | enthalpy of formation |

### MIXTURES

When substances are combined without a chemical reaction to bond them, the resulting substance is called a **mixture**. Physical changes can be used to separate mixtures. For example, heating salt water until the water evaporates, leaving the salt behind, will separate a salt water solution.

In a mixture, the components can be unevenly distributed, such as in trail mix or soil. These mixtures are described at **heterogeneous**. Alternatively, the components can be **homogeneously**, or uniformly, distributed, as in salt water.

**HELPFUL HINT**
Mixtures can exist as solids, liquids, or gases.

A **solution** is a special type of stable homogenous mixture. The components of a solution will not separate on their own, and cannot be separated using a filter. The substance being dissolved is the **solute**, and the substance acting on the solute, or doing the dissolving, is the **solvent**.

## CHEMICAL PROPERTIES OF WATER

Though it is one of the most common and biologically essential compounds on Earth, water is chemically abnormal. Its chemical formula is $H_2O$, which means that water consists of one oxygen atom bound to two hydrogen atoms. The shape of this molecule is often described as looking like Mickey Mouse, with the oxygen atom in the middle as Mickey's face and the two hydrogen atoms as his ears.

This imbalanced shape means that oxygen has a slightly positive charge localized on the two hydrogen atoms, and a slightly negative charge on the lone oxygen. Because of this polarity, water molecules attract each other and tend to clump together, a property called **cohesion**. Water is also extremely **adhesive**, meaning it clings to other substances. These attractive forces account for a number of water's unique properties.

Water has a high **surface tension**, meaning the bonds between water molecules on the surface of a liquid are stronger than those beneath the surface. Surface tension makes it more difficult to puncture the surface of water. Combined with adhesion, it also helps cause **capillary action**, which is the ability of water to travel against gravity. Capillary action moves blood through vessels in the body and water from the roots to the leaves of plants.

Water is an efficient solvent for ionic compounds because of its hydrogen bonds and associated polarity. When ionic compounds like NaCl are placed in water, the individual ions are attracted to the opposite ends of the dipole moment in water. But water is stronger than the average solvent. In fact, it is known as the "universal solvent," because it is able to dissolve more substances than any other known liquid. The readiness with which ionic compounds dissolve in water is why so many minerals and nutrients are found naturally in water.

Water also has a low molecular weight. Most low-weight compounds exist in a gaseous form at room temperature, but water is a liquid at room temperature. Though water molecules have a relatively low weight, the boiling point and freezing point of water are abnormally high. This is because water's strong hydrogen bonds require high amounts of heat to break. These properties of water make it the only compound found naturally in all three phases—solid, liquid, and gas—on Earth.

Consistent with its high boiling point, water also has an unusually high specific heat index, meaning that water needs to absorb a lot of heat before it actually gets hot. This property allows the oceans to regulate global temperature, as they can absorb a large amount of energy.

Ice, or frozen water, is also abnormal. Normally molecules are tightly packed in the solid state, but water's hydrogen bonds form a crystalline lattice structure, placing molecules far apart. This extra space makes ice less dense than liquid water, which is why ice floats.

## OSMOSIS, DIFFUSION, AND TONICITY

Molecules and atoms have a tendency to spread out in space, moving from areas of high concentration to areas of lower concentration. This net movement is called **diffusion**. When solutions of differing concentrations are separated from each other by a porous membrane, the solvent molecules will flow across the membrane in order to equalize these different concentrations. This net movement of solvent particles is called **osmosis**. Osmosis is especially important in biological contexts, as cell and organelle membranes are semipermeable. Osmosis provides the main means by which water is transported in and out of cells.

**HELPFUL HINT**

An important characteristic of osmosis is that the solvent molecules are free to move across the membrane, but the solute cannot cross the membrane.

When two solutions are separated by a semipermeable membrane, their relative concentrations (which determine the direction of the movement of solute molecules) are called **tonicity**. This chemical property is typically used to describe the response of a cell when placed in a solvent.

Three types of tonicity are relevant in biological situations. **Hypertonic** solutions are those which have a higher concentration of a given solute than the interior of the cell. When placed in such solutions, the cell will lose solvent (water) as it travels to areas of higher solute concentration.

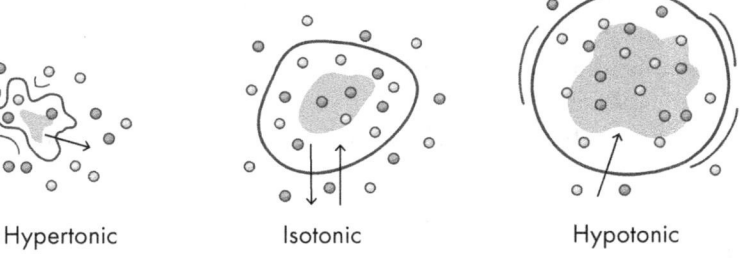

**Figure 6.7. Tonicity**

**Hypotonicity** refers to a solution that has a lower concentration of a given solute than the cell. Water will enter the cell, causing it to swell in response to hypotonic solutions.

**Isotonic** solutions are those in which solute concentration equals solute concentration inside the cell, and no net flux of solvent will occur between the cell and an isotonic solution.

## PRACTICE QUESTIONS

**7.** Which of the following is a chemical property?
- **A)** area
- **B)** boiling point
- **C)** solubility
- **D)** preferred oxidation state

**8.** The water glider is an insect that can walk on water. What property of water facilitates this ability?
- **A)** high surface tension
- **B)** osmosis
- **C)** tonicity
- **D)** ability of ice to float in water

## States of Matter

All matter exists in one of four **states**: solid, liquid, gas, or plasma. **Solid** matter has densely packed molecules and does not change volume or shape. **Liquids** have more loosely packed molecules and can change shape but not volume. **Gas** molecules are widely dispersed, and gases can change both shape and volume. **Plasma** is similar to a gas but contains free-moving charged particles (although its overall charge is neutral).

Particles in gases, liquids, and solids all vibrate. Those in gases vibrate and move at high speeds; those in liquids vibrate and move slightly; those in solids vibrate yet stay packed in place in their rigid structure.

Changes in temperature and pressure can cause matter to change states. Generally, adding energy (in the form of heat) changes a substance to a higher energy state (e.g., solid to liquid). Transitions from a high to lower energy state (e.g., liquid to solid) release energy. Each of these changes has a specific name:

- solid to liquid: melting
- liquid to solid: freezing
- liquid to gas: evaporation
- gas to liquid: condensation
- solid to gas: sublimation
- gas to solid: deposition

> **HELPFUL HINT**
> A **crystal** is a specific type of solid where atoms are arranged in a regular, repeating, geometric pattern known as a crystal lattice.

The occurrence of these processes depends on the amount of energy in individual molecules, rather than the collective energy of the system. For example, in a pool of water outside on a hot day, the whole pool does not evaporate at once; evaporation occurs incrementally in molecules with a high enough energy. Evaporation is also more likely to occur in conjunction with a decrease in the gas pressure around a liquid, since molecules tend to move from areas of high pressure to areas of low pressure.

**Phase diagrams** are used to indicate the phase in which a substance is found at a given pressure and temperature. Phase diagrams are constructed on an $x$, $y$-coordinate system where temperature is plotted along the $x$-axis and pressure is plotted along the $y$-axis. Phase regions are areas on a phase diagram (corresponding to specific temperature and pressure combinations) at which the substance will exist in a particular physical phase. Lines called phase boundaries separate these phase regions, representing pressure and temperature combinations at which the substance undergoes phase transitions.

Every phase diagram includes two important points. The **triple point** is the point at which the lines of equilibrium intersect and all three phases (solid, liquid, and gas) exist in equilibrium. The second special point on a phase diagram is the **critical point**. This point is found along the phase boundary between liquid and gas, and is the point at which the phase boundary terminates. This represents the fact that at very high temperature and pressure, liquid and gas phases become indistinguishable. This is known as a supercritical fluid.

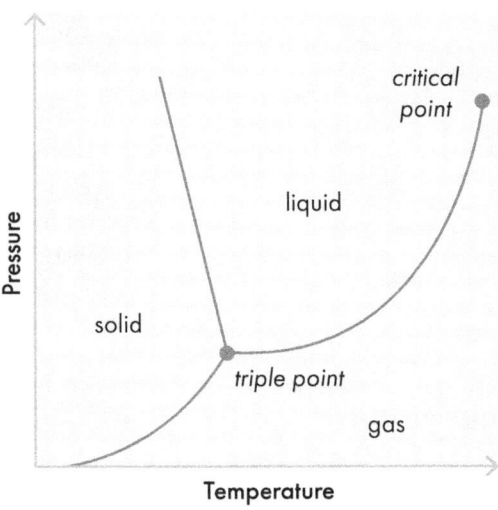

**Figure 6.8. Phase Diagram**

## PRACTICE QUESTIONS

**9.** Sublimation is the change from
   **A)** gas to solid.
   **B)** liquid to solid.
   **C)** gas to liquid.
   **D)** solid to gas.

**10.** The process that takes place when water reaches its boiling point is called
   **A)** condensation.
   **B)** evaporation.
   **C)** melting.
   **D)** sublimation.

# Chemical Reactions

A **chemical reaction** involves some sort of chemical change in molecules, atoms, or ions when two or more of these interact. It is important to note that chemical reactions are not the same as state changes. For example, liquid water changing to ice is not a chemical reaction because water and ice have the same chemical properties, just different physical ones. A chemical reaction occurs between two reactants (substances) that form a new substance with different chemical properties than either of the two initial reactants.

**Reactants** are the substances that are consumed or altered in the chemical reaction, while **products** are substances formed as a result of the chemical reaction. Equations are usually written with the reactants on the left, the products on the right, and an arrow between them. The state of the chemical compounds are sometimes noted using the labels *s* (solid), *l* (liquid), *g* (gas), or *aq* (aqueous, meaning a solution).

Chemical reactions generally occur in two directions. A reaction can move "forward" (from reactants to products), and in "reverse" (from products to reactants). To describe this, chemists say that the reaction occurs in two directions. Oftentimes, the arrow in a chemical equation has a head on each side, signifying that the reaction occurs in both directions.

The equilibrium point of a reaction is defined as the point where both the forward and reverse reactions are occurring at equal rates simultaneously—products are turning into reactants and reactants back into products. This produces a state in which, while the reaction is still taking place, no net change in concentration of reactants or products is occurring.

### BALANCING CHEMICAL REACTIONS

**HELPFUL HINT**

When balancing chemical equations containing atoms of elements in addition to hydrogen and oxygen, wait until the end to balance hydrogen and oxygen atoms.

In the equation below, $H_2$ and $O_2$ are the reactants, while water ($H_2O$) is the product.

$$2H_2 + O_2 \rightarrow 2H_2O$$

In this equation, the number 2 is called a coefficient, and it describes the number of atoms or molecules involved in the reaction. In this reaction, four hydrogen atoms (two molecules of $H_2$) react with two oxygen atoms. Note that the products also contain four hydrogen and two oxygen molecules. When chemical equations are written, they must include the same number of each atom on both the reactant and product side of the arrow. This is an important step because chemical reactions adhere to the **law of conservation of matter**, which states that matter is neither created nor destroyed in a chemical reaction.

In order to balance the equation above, first examine the initial equation without coefficients, which looks like this:

$$H_2 + O_2 \rightarrow H_2O$$

This equation is unbalanced: there are two H atoms on each side, but the reactant side has two O atoms while the product side only has one. To fix this discrepancy, a coefficient of 2 is added in front of the product, $H_2O$, making the number of O atoms equal on both sides of the equation:

$$H_2 + O_2 \rightarrow 2H_2O$$

Now there are four H atoms on the product side while there are only 2 on the reactant side. This means that in order to finish balancing the equation, a coefficient of 2 must be added in front of $H_2$, so that there are four H atoms on the reactant side as well:

$$2H_2 + O_2 \rightarrow 2H_2O$$

Remember that in a chemical reaction, only the coefficients may be changed in order to balance it; the subscripts must not be changed. This would be like changing the actual chemical in the equation.

## TYPES OF REACTIONS

There are several common types of chemical reactions, including decomposition, substitution, and combustion reactions.

**Decomposition** reactions are a common class of reaction, consisting of the separation of a compound into atoms or simpler molecules:

$$\text{General Reaction: } AB \rightarrow A + B$$
$$2H_2O_2 \rightarrow 2H_2O + O_2$$

**Single replacement** reactions are those in which a part of one molecule is replaced by another atom or molecule. Reactivity in single substitutions is determined by the **activity series**: elements on the list will replace any element that is below it on the list (Table 6.5).

$$\text{General Reaction: } AB + C \rightarrow AC + B$$
$$CH_4 + Cl_2 \rightarrow CH_3Cl + HCl$$

In a **double replacement** reaction, two parts of two different molecules swap places:

$$\text{General Reaction: } AB + CD \rightarrow CB + AD$$
$$CuCl_2 + 2AgNO_3 \rightarrow Cu(NO_3)_2 + 2AgCl$$

Table 6.5. Activity Series

| Li | Ca | Mn | Ni | Cu |
| K | Na | Zn | Sn | Hg |
| Ba | Mg | Cr | Pb | Ag |
| Sr | Al | Fe | $H_2$ | Pd |
| Pt | Au | | | |

**Combustion** or burning reactions are high-temperature reactions in which a great deal of heat is released. In combustion reactions, oxygen is a reactant and carbon dioxide and water are produced. Because of the substantial amount of heat energy produced by combustion reactions, they have been important means of generating energy throughout human history, including combustion of fossil fuels, coal, and oil.

$$\text{General Reaction: } C_xH_x + O_2 \rightarrow CO_2 + H_2O$$
$$2C_8H_{18} + 25O_2 \rightarrow 16CO_2 + 18H_2O$$

## REACTION RATES

**Exothermic reactions** are defined as those which produce energy, whereas **endothermic reactions** need energy in order to occur. Regardless of whether energy is absorbed or released overall, every chemical reaction requires a certain amount of energy in order to begin. This amount is referred to as the **activation energy**.

Collisions of reactant particles supply the activation energy for a reaction. The more particles collide, the more energy will be produced. Thus, the more often particles collide, the more likely a reaction is to occur. However, it is quite possible that though some particles collide, not enough energy is generated for an actual reaction to occur.

Given the variability in activation energies of a reaction, as well as variation in the frequency of reactant particle collisions, not all chemical reactions occur at the same rate. A number of variables affect the rate of reaction, including temperature, pressure, concentration, and surface area. The higher the temperature, pressure and concentration, the more likely particles are to collide and thus the reaction rate will be higher. The same is true of surface area for a reaction between a solid and a liquid in which it is immersed. The larger the surface area, the more solid reactant particles are in contact with liquid particles, and the faster the reaction occurs.

## PRACTICE QUESTIONS

**11.** When the following chemical equation for the combustion of methanol ($CH_3OH$) is balanced, what is the coefficient of $H_2O$?

__$CH_3OH$ + __$O_2$ → __$CO_2$ + __$H_2O$

**A)** 3
**B)** 2
**C)** 1
**D)** 4

**12.** How is the following reaction classified?

$2KClO_3 \rightarrow 2KCl + 3O_2$

**A)** decomposition

**B)** combustion

**C)** substitution

**D)** double displacement

**13.** What is the missing product in the following combustion reaction?

$C_{10}H_8 + 12O_2 \rightarrow H_2O +$ ____

**A)** $CO$

**B)** $CH_4$

**C)** $CO_2$

**D)** $C_2H_3O_2$

# Catalysts

**Catalysts** reduce the amount of energy that a chemical reaction needs in order to happen, so that the reaction can occur more easily. However, the catalyst itself remains chemically unchanged and is not consumed at all in the reaction. A catalyst lowers the **activation energy** needed for a reaction to take place, and it will change the rate of both directions of the reaction.

Catalysts function by one of two main methods. The first is **adsorption**, where particles stick to the surface of the catalyst and move around, increasing their likelihood of collision. A more complicated method is the creation of **intermediate compounds** which are unstable and then break down into other substances, leaving the catalyst in its original state. Many enzymes (proteins which function as catalysts), which are discussed below, work via the creation of intermediate compounds.

If the rate of a chemical reaction can be increased, it can also be decreased. **Inhibitors** are essentially the opposite of catalysts, and they act to slow down the reaction rate or even stop the reaction altogether. Inhibitors are used for various reasons, including giving scientists more control over reactions. Both inhibitors and catalysts naturally play significant roles in the chemical reactions that occur in human bodies.

### ENZYMES

**Enzymes** are efficient catalysts functioning in biochemical reactions. They are large, soluble protein molecules that serve to speed up chemical reactions in cells. Cellular respiration, DNA replication, digestion, protein synthesis, and photosynthesis are common processes, all essential for life, that are catalyzed with enzymes.

Like other types of catalysts, enzymes take part in a reaction to provide an alternative pathway with a smaller activation energy, but they remain unchanged themselves. However, enzymes only alter the reaction rate; they do not actually change the equilibrium point of a reaction. Also, unlike most chemical catalysts, enzymes are very selective, which means that they only catalyze certain reactions. (Many other types of catalysts catalyze a variety of reactions.)

**HELPFUL HINT**

Enzyme inhibitors will typically function by binding to an enzyme and thereby preventing it from functioning.

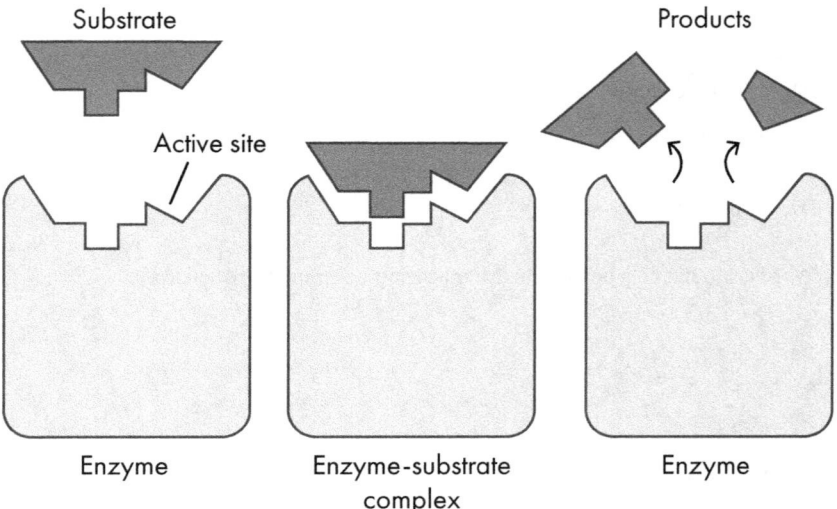

**Figure 6.9. Lock and Key Model of Enzymes**

This particular aspect of enzyme behavior is referred to as the **lock and key model**. This alludes to the fact that not all keys can open all locks; most keys can only open specific locks. Similarly, the shape of any one enzyme only matches the shape of the molecule it reacts with, called a **substrate**. The **active site** is the place on the enzyme that directly contacts the substrate, or the place where the two "puzzle pieces" fit together facilitating the actual reaction.

Enzymes have a characteristic optimum temperature at which they function best and require a sufficient substrate concentration. The reason for these restrictions is that variables like temperature and pH affect the shape of an enzyme's active site. In fact, if the temperature is increased too much, usually past 60 degrees Celsius, an enzyme can become **denatured**. This means that the active site has undergone a permanent change in shape, so it can no longer serve its purpose as a catalyst.

**HELPFUL HINT**

As suggested by the lock and key model, enzymes are typically highly specific to the reaction they catalyze. In a cellular context, why would it be detrimental if enzymes universally catalyzed any reaction?

PRACTICE QUESTION

**14.** A catalyst increases a reaction rate by
   **A)** increasing the activation energy.
   **B)** increasing the concentration of the reactants.
   **C)** changing the relative partial pressures of the reactants.
   **D)** changing the reaction mechanism.

## Acids and Bases

Many scientists have attempted to define and differentiate the properties of acids and bases throughout the centuries. As far back as the sixteenth century, Robert Boyle noted that acids are corrosive, sour, and change the color of vegetable dyes like litmus from blue to red. On the other hand, bases, or alkaline solutions are slippery, bitter, and change the color of litmus from red to blue. The litmus test is still used today to determine whether a solution is acidic or basic.

Later, Svante Arrhenius gave an even more specific definition of acids and bases. He defined **acids** as compounds that ionize when they dissolve in water, releasing $H^+$ ions along with a negative ion called a **counterion**. For example, the well-known acid HCl (hydrochloric acid) dissolves into $H^+$ and $Cl^-$ ions in water.

Similarly, Arrhenius defined bases as substances which release $OH^-$ ions (hydroxide) and a positive ion when dissolved in water. For example, the compound NaOH dissolves into $Na^+$ (the counterion) and $OH^-$ ions in water. His theory also explains why acids and bases neutralize each other. If acids have an $H^+$ ion and bases have an $OH^-$ ion, when combined the ions will form water. Along with the water, the counterions usually combine to form a salt. For example, when HCl and NaOH are combined, the result is water and table salt ($H_2O$ and NaCl).

Thomas Lowry and J.N. Bronsted later presented a revised theory of acids and bases. In the Bronsted-Lowry definition of acids and bases, acids are defined as proton donors and bases as proton acceptors. An acid and base are always paired as reactants. The base reactant produces a **conjugate acid** as a product, paired with a **conjugate base** produced from the reactant acid. Water, often involved in these reactions, can either accept or donate a proton, meaning that it can act as either an acid or a base, depending on the particular equation.

In the example below, acetic acid ($CH_3CO_2H$) is dissolved in water, producing a conjugate base ($CH_3CO_2^-$). Water acts as the base, and its conjugate acid is the hydronium ion ($H_3O^+$).

$$CH_3CO_2H + H_2O \rightarrow CH_3CO_2^- + H_3O^+$$

acid + base → conjugate base + conjugate acid

This is perhaps easiest to understand when considering the definition of hydrogen cations. $H^+$ is essentially a lone proton, and may act as an acid, being donated to another molecule. If it is in a solution of water, it can combine with water to form hydronium, $H_3O^+$, which is always an acid as it is a proton acceptor.

The strength of an acid or base is measured on the pH scale, which ranges from 1 – 14, with 1 being the strongest acid, 14 the strongest base, and 7 being neutral. A substance's pH value is a measure of how many hydrogen ions are in the solution. The scale is exponential, meaning an acid with a pH of 3 has ten times as many hydrogen ions as an acid with a pH of 4. Water, which separates into equal numbers of hydrogen and hydroxide ions, has a neutral pH of 7.

**Strong acids and bases** are defined as those that completely ionize in water. Other acids and bases are considered weak, which means that they only partially ionize in water.

**HELPFUL HINT**

Any base containing a Group 1 or Group 2 metal is a strong base.

Table 6.6. Strong Acids and Bases

| Strong Acids | Strong Bases |
| --- | --- |
| HI | NaOH |
| HBr | KOH |
| $HClO_4$ | LiOH |
| $HClO_3$ | RbOH |

Table 6.6. Strong Acids and Bases (continued)

| Strong Acids | Strong Bases |
|---|---|
| HCl | CsOH |
| $HNO_3$ | $Ca(OH)_2$ |
| $H_2SO_4$ | $Ba(OH)_2$ |
| $HIO_4$ | $Sr(OH)_2$ |

## PRACTICE QUESTIONS

15. Which is NOT a definition of an acid?
    A) A substance that contains hydrogen and produces H+ in water.
    B) A substance that donates protons to a base.
    C) A substance that reacts with a base to form a salt and water.
    D) A substance that accepts protons.

16. Which of the following is NOT a strong acid?
    A) $HClO_3$
    B) $HClO_4$
    C) $HNO_3$
    D) $HNO_2$

# ANSWER KEY

1. **D) is correct.** Atomic radius increases from the top of the periodic table to the bottom and also from right to left. This means that the largest atoms are found in the lower left-hand corner of the periodic table while the smallest are found in the upper right-hand corner. Of the three elements listed, xenon has the smallest radius, barium is larger as it is further down and to the left, and cesium is the largest as it is furthest to the left of the three: Xe < Ba < Cs.

2. **A) is correct.** Mg has an atomic number of 12 on the periodic table, meaning it has 12 protons and 12 electrons. These 12 electrons are assigned to orbitals in the order shown in Figure 6.4: $1s^2 2s^2 2p^6 3s^2$.

3. **B) is correct.** Electronegativity generally increases from bottom to top and from right to left on the periodic table. This means that the most electronegative atoms are at the top right of the table. Thus, of the elements listed, F is the most electronegative, followed by Br, Mg, and then Sr with the lowest electronegativity: F > Br > Mg > Sr.

4. **B) is correct.** The difference in electronegativity is the greatest between carbon and fluorine, so the C—F bond will have the largest dipole moment.

5. **D) is correct.** The alkali metals have a full valence shell when they lose one electron, so they easily form ions of +1.

6. **B) is correct.** These molecules are polar and so are subject to both dipole-dipole and London forces. There are no hydrogen atoms bound to high electronegative atoms, so there will be no hydrogen bonding.

7. **D) is correct.** Area, boiling point, and solubility are all physical properties that can be measured without undergoing a chemical reaction. The preferred oxidation state of a metal cannot be identified in any way except through a chemical reaction, and is thus a chemical property.

8. **A) is correct.** The high surface tension of water, which is a byproduct of hydrogen bonding, allows the water glider to walk on water.

9. **D) is correct.** Sublimation is when matter changes from a solid to a gas.

10. **B) is correct.** Evaporation is the process of conversion from liquid to gas that occurs at the boiling point.

11. **D) is correct.** The same number of C and O atoms appear on both sides, so start by balancing for H: __$CH_3OH$ + __$O_2$ → __$CO_2$ + $2H_2O$

    Next, add a coefficient on the left to balance O: $2CH_3OH$ + __$O_2$ → __$CO_2$ + $2H_2O$

    Next, add or change coefficients to balance C and H: $2CH_3OH$ + __$O_2$ → $2CO_2$ + $4H_2O$

    Finally, add coefficients to balance O: $2CH_3OH$ + $3O_2$ → $2CO_2$ + $4H_2O$

12. **A) is correct.** This reaction has a single reactant compound and produces simpler molecules. It is therefore a decomposition reaction.

13. **C) is correct.** All combustion reactions produce $H_2O$ and $CO_2$, so the missing product is $CO_2$.

14. **D) is correct.** A catalyst reduces the activation energy by creating an alternative reaction mechanism for the reaction.

15. **D) is correct.** Acids increase the concentration of hydrogen ions in solution and do not accept protons.

16. **D) is correct.** $HNO_2$ is not a strong acid. All the other choices are strong acids.

# SEVEN: ANATOMY and PHYSIOLOGY

## Anatomical Terminology

### THE BIOLOGICAL HIERARCHY

Organisms are living things consisting of at least one cell, which is the smallest unit of life that can reproduce on its own. Unicellular organisms, such as the amoeba, are made up of only one cell, while multicellular organisms are comprised of many cells. In a multicellular organism, the cells are grouped together into **tissues**, and these tissues are grouped into **organs**, which perform a specific function. The heart, for example, is the organ that pumps blood throughout the body. Organs are further grouped into **organ systems**, such as the digestive or respiratory systems.

A system is a collection of interconnected parts that make up a complex whole with defined boundaries. Systems may be closed, meaning nothing passes in or out of them, or open, meaning they have inputs and outputs. Organ systems are open and will have a number of inputs and outputs.

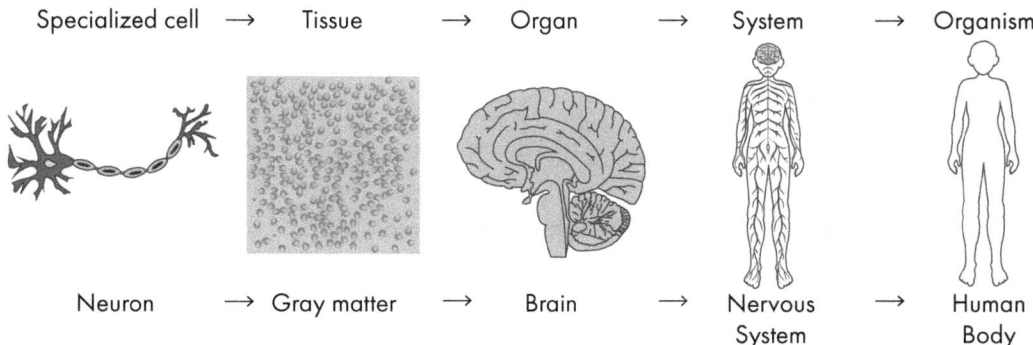

**Figure 7.1. The Biological Hierarchy**

### DIRECTIONAL TERMS

Learning anatomy requires an understanding of the terminology used to describe the location of a particular structure. Anatomical science uses common terms to describe spatial relationships, often in pairs of opposites. These terms usually refer to the position of a structure in an organism that is upright with respect to its environment (e.g., in its typical orientation while moving forward).

Table 7.1. Directional Terms

| Term | Meaning | Example |
| --- | --- | --- |
| inferior | away from the head | The pelvis is inferior to the head. |
| superior | closer to the head | The head is superior to the pelvis. |
| anterior | toward the front | The eyes are anterior to the ears. |
| posterior | toward the back | The ears are posterior to the eyes. |
| ventral | toward the front | The stomach is ventral to the spine. |
| dorsal | toward the back | The spine is dorsal to the stomach. |
| medial | toward the midline of the body | The heart is medial to the arm. |
| lateral | further from the midline of the body | The arm is lateral to the chest. |
| proximal | closer to the trunk | The knee is proximal to the ankle. |
| distal | away from the trunk | The ankle is distal to the knee. |

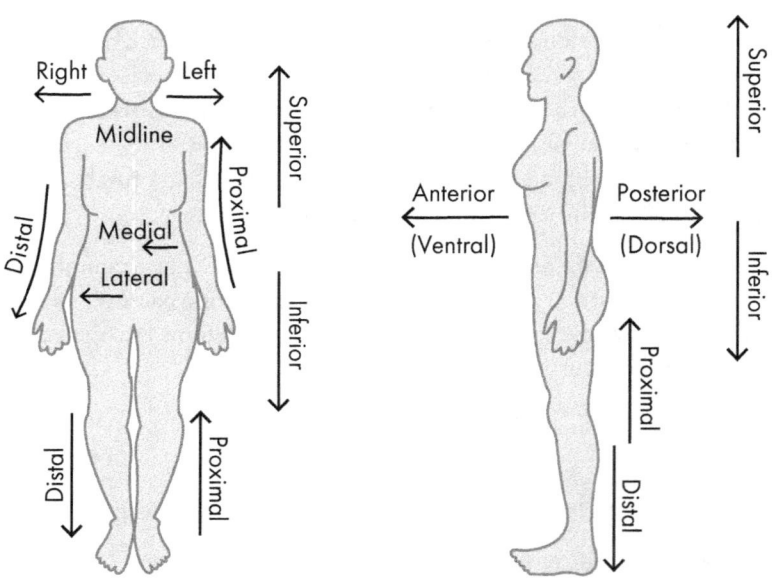

**Figure 7.2. Anatomical Terms (Directional)**

## BODY CAVITIES

The internal structure of the human body is organized into compartments called **cavities**, which are separated by membranes. There are two main cavities in the human body: the dorsal cavity and the ventral cavity (both named for their relative positions).

The **dorsal cavity** is further divided into the **cranial cavity**, which holds the brain, and the **spinal cavity**, which surrounds the spine. The two sections of the dorsal cavity are continuous with each other. Both sections are lined by the **meninges**, a three-layered membrane that protects the brain and spinal cord.

The **ventral cavity** houses the majority of the body's organs. It also can be further divided into smaller cavities. The **thoracic cavity** holds the heart and lungs, the **abdominal cavity** holds the digestive organs and kidneys, and the **pelvic cavity** holds the bladder and reproductive organs. Both the abdominal and pelvic cavities are enclosed by a membrane called the **peritoneum**.

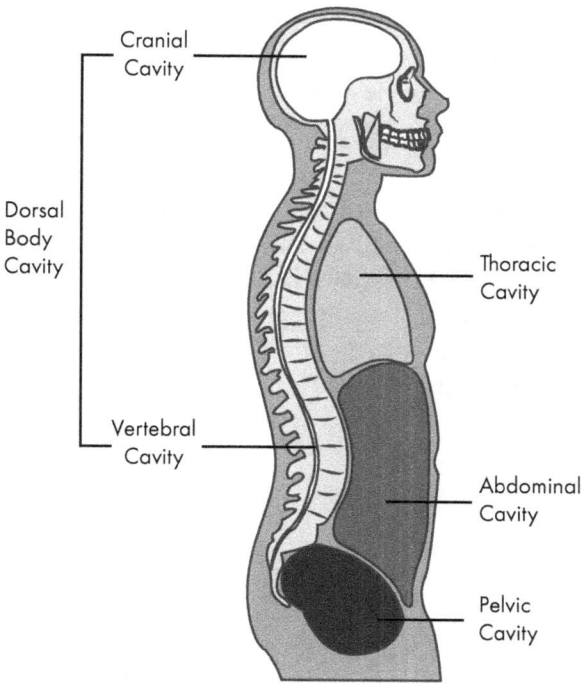

**Figure 7.3. Body Cavities**

PRACTICE QUESTIONS

1. Which term means *above*?
    A) anterior
    B) posterior
    C) superior
    D) medial

2. Where is the wrist located relative to the elbow?
    A) distal
    B) proximal
    C) anterior
    D) posterior

# The Respiratory System
## STRUCTURE AND FUNCTION OF THE RESPIRATORY SYSTEM

Mammalian cells require oxygen for glucose metabolism and release carbon dioxide as a byproduct. This process requires constant gas exchange between the human body and the environment to replenish the oxygen supply and remove carbon dioxide. This exchange is accomplished through the efforts of the **respiratory system**, in which powerful muscles force oxygen-rich air into the lungs and carbon dioxide-rich air out of the body.

Gas exchange takes place in the **lungs**. Humans have two lungs, a right and a left, with the right being slightly larger than the left due to the heart's placement in the left side of the chest cavity. The right lung has three **lobes**, and the left has two. The lungs are surrounded by a thick membrane called the **pleura**.

Air enters the body through the mouth or nasal cavity and passes through the **trachea** (sometimes called the windpipe) and into the two bronchi, each of which leads to one lung. Within the lung, the bronchi branch into smaller passageways called **bronchioles** and then terminate in sac-like structures called **alveoli**, which is where gas exchange between the air and the capillaries occurs. The large surface area of the alveoli allows for efficient exchange of gases through diffusion (movement of particles from areas of high to low concentration). Alveoli are covered in a layer of **surfactant**, which lubricates the sacs and prevents the lungs from collapsing.

> **HELPFUL HINT**
> In anatomy, the terms *right* and *left* are used with respect to the subject, not the observer.

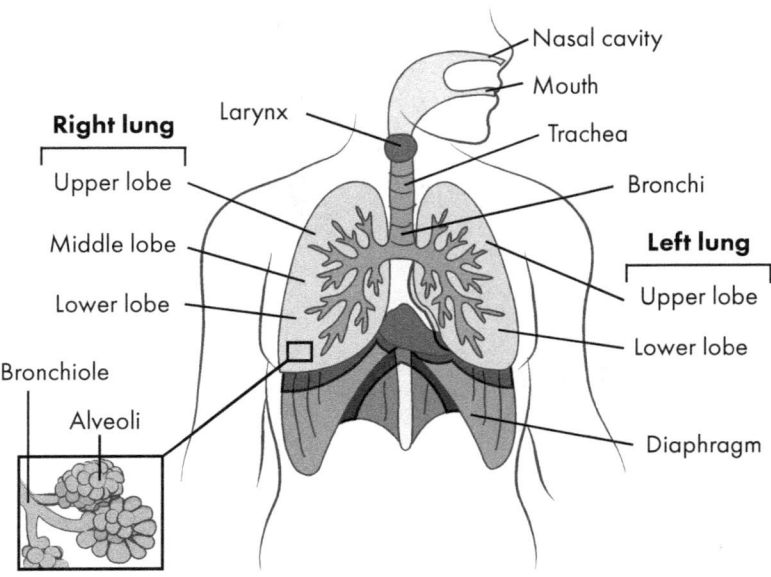

**Figure 7.4. The Respiratory System**

The heart pumps deoxygenated blood into the lungs via the **pulmonary artery**. This blood is oxygenated in the alveoli and then delivered back into the heart by the **pulmonary veins** for distribution to the body.

The **diaphragm** contributes to the activity of ventilation—the process of inhalation and exhalation. The contraction of the diaphragm creates a vacuum, forcing air into the lungs. Relaxation of the diaphragm compresses the lungs, forcing carbon dioxide-enriched gas out in exhalation. The amount of air breathed in and out is the **tidal volume**, and the **residual capacity** is the small volume of air left in the lungs after exhalation.

> **QUICK REVIEW**
> How might measuring tidal volume and residual capacity help evaluate respiratory health?

## PATHOLOGIES OF THE RESPIRATORY SYSTEM

The body's critical and constant need for the exchange of carbon dioxide for oxygen makes the pulmonary system a locus of many serious diseases. Lung diseases that result in the continual restriction of airflow are known as **chronic obstructive pulmonary disease (COPD)**. These include **emphysema**, which is the destruction of lung tissues, and **asthma**, in which the airways are compromised due to a dysfunctional immune response. The main causes of COPD are smoking and air pollution, but genetic factors can also influence the severity of the disease.

The system is also prone to **respiratory tract infections**, with upper respiratory tract infections affecting air inputs in the nose and throat and lower respiratory tract infections affecting the lungs and their immediate pulmonary inputs. Viral infections of the respiratory system include influenza and the common cold; bacterial infections include tuberculosis and pertussis (whooping cough). **Pneumonia**, which affects alveoli, is a bacterial or viral infection that is often seen in people whose respiratory system has been weakened by other conditions.

### PRACTICE QUESTIONS

3. Which of the following structures are small air sacs that function as the site of gas exchange in the lungs?
   - **A)** capillaries
   - **B)** bronchi
   - **C)** alveoli
   - **D)** cilia

4. Which of the following conditions is caused by an immune response?
   - **A)** COPD
   - **B)** influenza
   - **C)** asthma
   - **D)** emphysema

# The Cardiovascular System

## STRUCTURE AND FUNCTION OF THE CARDIOVASCULAR SYSTEM

The cardiovascular system circulates blood throughout the body. Blood carries a wide range of molecules necessary for the body to function, including nutrients, wastes, hormones, and gases. Blood is broken into a number of different parts. Red blood cells, which contain the protein **hemoglobin**, transport oxygen, and white blood cells circulate as part of the immune system. Both red and white blood cells are suspended in a fluid called **plasma**, which the other molecules transported by the blood are dissolved in.

Blood is circulated by a muscular organ called the **heart**. The circulatory system includes two closed loops. In the pulmonary loop, deoxygenated blood leaves the heart and travels to the lungs, where it loses carbon dioxide and becomes rich in oxygen. The oxygenated blood then returns to the heart, which pumps it through the systemic loop. The systemic loop delivers oxygen to the rest of the body and returns deoxygenated blood to the heart. The pumping action of the heart is regulated primarily by two neurological nodes, the **sinoatrial** and **atrioventricular nodes**, whose electrical activity sets the rhythm of the heart.

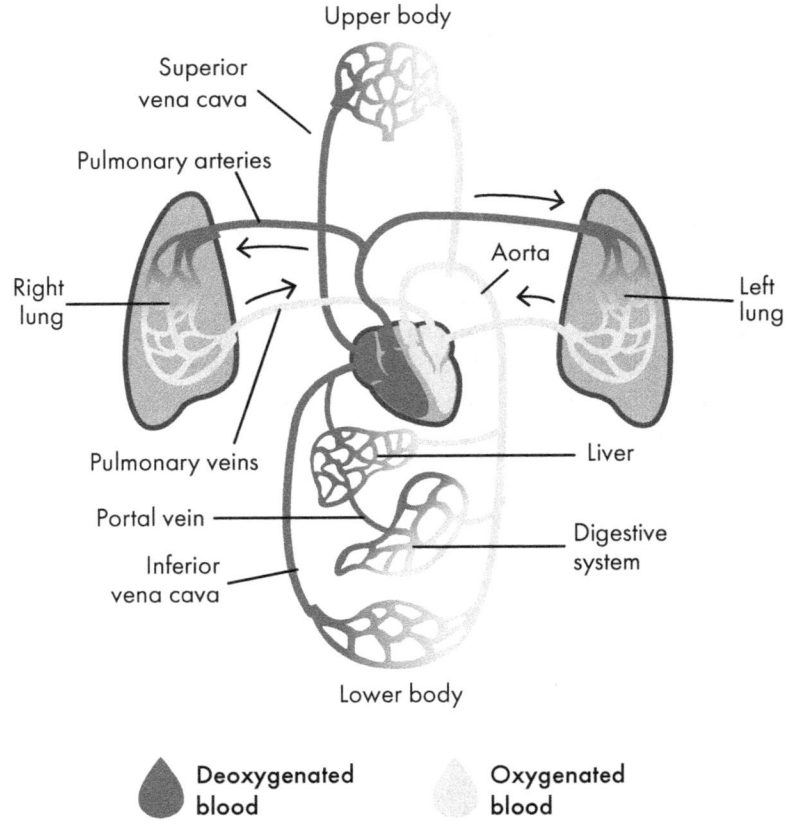

**Figure 7.5. Circulatory System**

Deoxygenated blood from the body enters the heart via the **right atrium**. It then passes through the **tricuspid** valve into the **right ventricle** and is pumped out to the lungs. Oxygenated blood returns from the lungs into the **left atrium**. It then passes through the **mitral valve** into the **left ventricle** and is pumped out to the body through the **aorta**. The contraction of the heart during this process is called **systole**, and the relaxation of the heart is **diastole**.

Blood is carried through the body in a system of blood vessels. Oxygenated blood leaves the heart in large vessels called **arteries**, which branch into smaller and smaller vessels. The smallest vessels, **capillaries**, are where the exchange of molecules between blood and cells takes place. Deoxygenated blood returns to the heart in **veins**.

Blood leaves the heart to travel to the body through the **aorta**; in the lower body, the aorta branches into the **iliac arteries**. Deoxygenated blood returns to the heart from the body via the **superior vena cava** (upper body) and **inferior vena cava** (lower body). Blood then leaves the heart again to travel to the lungs through the **pulmonary arteries**, and returns from the lungs via the **pulmonary veins**.

**HELPFUL HINT**

The pulmonary veins are the only veins in the human body that carry oxygenated blood.

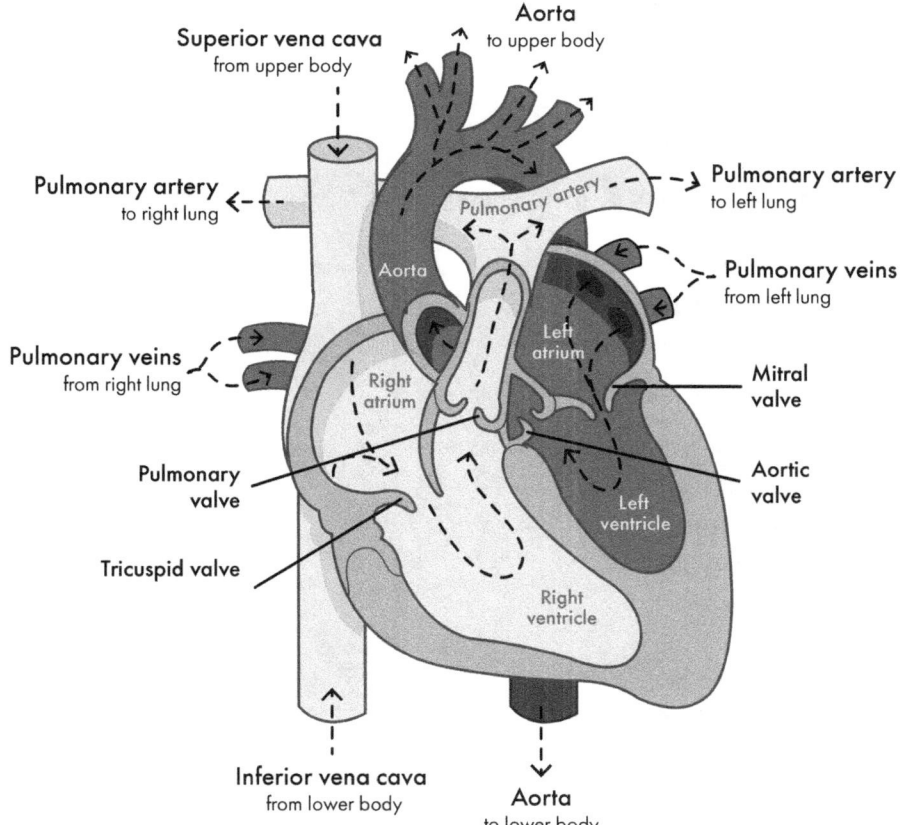

**Figure 7.6. The Heart**

## THE LYMPHATIC SYSTEM

The **lymphatic system** is an open circulatory system that functions alongside the cardiovascular system. It facilitates the movement of substances between cells and the blood by removing interstitial fluid (the fluid between cells). It also plays an important role in the immune system by circulating white blood cells. The system is composed of **lymphatic vessels** that carry **lymph**, a clear fluid containing lymphocytes and waste products. Lymph passes through **lymph nodes**, which are collections of tissue rich in white blood cells that filter out harmful substances such as pathogens and cell waste. The lymph is then returned to the circulatory system through the veins near the heart.

**HELPFUL HINT**

Lymph nodes can become inflamed during infections when they contain a higher than normal number of lymphocytes.

## PATHOLOGIES OF THE CARDIOVASCULAR SYSTEM

The cardiovascular system is subject to a number of pathologies. In a **heart attack**, blood flow to part of the heart is stopped, causing damage to the heart muscle. An irregular heartbeat, called an **arrhythmia**, is caused by disruptions with the electrical signals in the heart. Many arrhythmias can be treated—with a pacemaker, for example—or do not cause any symptoms.

Problems with blood vessels include **atherosclerosis**, in which white blood cells and plaque build up in arteries, and **hypertension**, or high blood pressure. In a stroke, blood flow is blocked in the brain, resulting in damage to brain cells.

## PRACTICE QUESTIONS

5. The mitral valve transports blood between which of the following two regions of the heart?
    - A) aorta and left atrium
    - B) aorta and right atrium
    - C) right atrium and right ventricle
    - D) left atrium and left ventricle

6. Which of the following supplies blood to the lower body?
    - A) superior vena cava
    - B) inferior vena cava
    - C) iliac artery
    - D) aortic arch

7. Which of the following electrically signals the heart to pump?
    - A) sinoatrial node
    - B) aorta
    - C) mitral valve
    - D) left ventricle

# The Nervous System

The nervous system is made up of two distinct parts: the central nervous system (brain and spinal cord) and the peripheral nervous system. However, the fundamental physiological principles underlying both systems are similar. In both systems, **neurons** communicate electrically and chemically with one another along pathways. These pathways allow the nervous system as a whole to conduct its incredibly broad array of functions, from motor control and sensory perception to complex thinking and emotions.

## NERVE CELLS

**HELPFUL HINT**

Nerve cell signaling is controlled by moving ions across the cell membrane to maintain an action potential. Depolarizing the cell, or lowering the action potential, triggers the release of neurotransmitters.

Neurons, a.k.a. nerve cells, have several key anatomical features that contribute to their specialized functions. These cells typically contain an **axon**, a long projection from the cell that sends information over a distance. These cells also have **dendrites**, which are long, branching extensions of the cell that receive information from neighboring cells. The number of dendrites and the extent of their branching varies widely, distinguishing the various types of these cells.

Neurons and nerve cells do not touch; instead, communication occurs across a specialized gap called a **synapse**. The chemicals that facilitate communication across synapses are known as **neurotransmitters**, and include serotonin and dopamine. Communication occurs when electrical signals cause the **axon terminal** to release neurotransmitters.

Nerve cells are accompanied by glia, or supporting cells, that surround the cell and provide support, protection, and nutrients. In the peripheral nervous system, the primary glial cell is a **Schwann cell**. Schwann cells secrete a fatty substance called **myelin** that wraps around the neuron and allows much faster transmission of the electrical signal the neuron is sending. Gaps in the myelin sheath are called nodes of Ranvier.

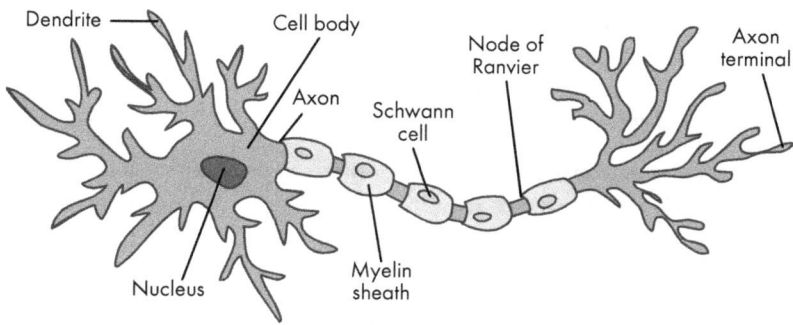

**Figure 7.7. Nerve Cell**

## THE CENTRAL NERVOUS SYSTEM

The central nervous system (CNS), which includes the brain and spinal cord, is responsible for arguably the body's most complex and abstract functions, including cognition, emotion, and behavioral regulation. The brain is divided into six general regions:

- **cerebrum**: the largest part of the brain; responsible for voluntary movement, language, learning, and memory
- **diencephalon**: includes the thalamus, hypothalamus, and pineal body; relays sensory information and controls some automatic functions of the peripheral nervous system
- **mesencephalon** (midbrain): processes hearing and visual information; maintains sleep/wake cycles and temperature
- **pons**: controls many involuntary processes, including respiration, bladder control, and sleep; also responsible for facial movements and eye movement
- **cerebellum**: responsible for motor control and motor learning
- **medulla oblongata**: controls involuntary processes of the cardiac and respiratory systems; responsible for reflexes such as sneezing and vomiting

The cerebrum and cerebellum are further broken down into **lobes** that each carry out a broad common function. For example, in the cerebrum, the processing of visual information occurs in the **occipital lobe,** and the **temporal lobe** is involved in language comprehension and emotional associations.

In addition to its organization by lobes and structures, regions of the brain are also designated by myelination status: **white matter** regions are myelinated and **gray matter** regions are unmyelinated. Brain structures in the cerebral cortex (the outermost brain layer) form a convoluted pattern of **gyri** (ridges) and **sulci** (valleys) that maximize the ratio of surface area to volume.

**HELPFUL HINT**

Alzheimer's disease, which causes dementia, is the result of damaged neurons in the cerebral cortex, the area of the brain responsible for higher order functions like information processing and language.

**ANATOMY AND PHYSIOLOGY**

## THE PERIPHERAL NERVOUS SYSTEM

The peripheral nervous system, which includes all the nerve cells outside the brain and spinal cord, has one main function and that is to communicate between the CNS and the rest of the body.

The peripheral nervous system is further divided into two systems. The **automatic nervous system** (ANS) is the part of the peripheral nervous system that controls involuntary bodily functions such as digestion, respiration, and heart rate. The autonomic nervous system is further broken down into the sympathetic nervous system and parasympathetic nervous system.

The **sympathetic nervous system** is responsible for the body's reaction to stress and induces a "fight or flight" response to stimuli. For instance, if an individual is frightened, the sympathetic nervous system increases the person's heart rate and blood pressure to prepare that person to either fight or flee.

In contrast, the **parasympathetic nervous system** is stimulated by the body's need for rest or recovery. The parasympathetic nervous system responds by decreasing heart rate, blood pressure, and muscular activation when a person is getting ready for activities such as sleeping or digesting food. For example, the body activates the parasympathetic nervous system after a person eats a large meal, which is why that individual may then feel sluggish.

> **HELPFUL HINT**
> The "fight or flight" reaction includes accelerated breathing and heart rate, dilation of blood vessels in muscles, release of energy molecules for use by muscles, relaxation of the bladder, and slowing or stopping movement in the upper digestive tract.

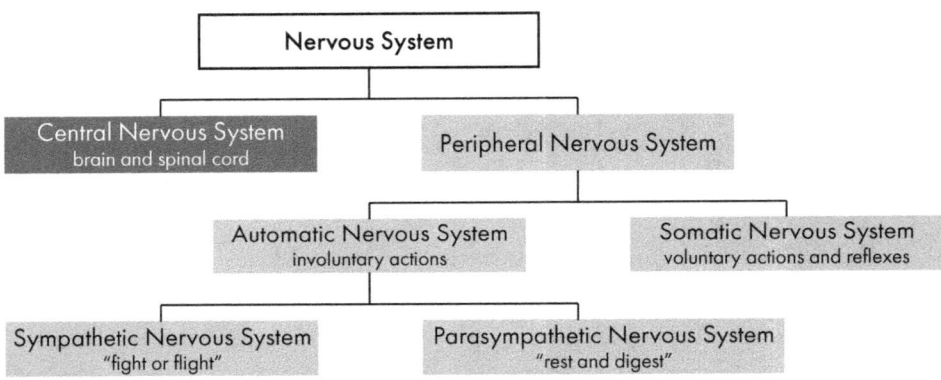

**Figure 7.8. Divisions of the Nervous System**

The second part of the peripheral nervous system, called the **somatic nervous system**, controls sensory information and motor control. Generally, nerve cells can be divided into two types. **Afferent** (sensory) cells relay messages to the central nervous system, and **efferent** (motor) cells carry messages to the muscles. In the motor nervous system, signals from the brain travel down the spinal cord before exiting and communicating with motor nerve cells, which synapse on muscle fibers at **neuromuscular junctions**. Because individuals can control the movement of skeletal muscle, this part of the nervous system is considered voluntary.

Some **reflexes**, or automatic response to stimuli, are able to occur rapidly by bypassing the brain altogether. In a **reflex arc**, a signal is sent from the peripheral nervous system to the spinal cord, which then sends a signal directly to a motor cells, causing movement.

## PATHOLOGIES OF THE NERVOUS SYSTEM

The nervous system can be affected by a number of degenerative diseases that result from the gradual breakdown of nervous tissue. These include:

- **Parkinson's disease**: caused by cell death in the basal ganglia; characterized by gradual loss of motor function
- **multiple sclerosis (MS)**: caused by damage to the myelin sheath; characterized by muscle spasms and weakness, numbness, loss of coordination, and blindness
- **amyotrophic lateral sclerosis (ALS)**: caused by the death of neurons that control voluntary muscle movement; characterized by muscle stiffness, twitches, and weakness
- **Alzheimer's disease**: caused by damaged neurons in the cerebral cortex; characterized by memory loss, confusion, mood swings, and problems with language

The nervous system is also susceptible to infections, some of which can be life threatening. **Meningitis** is inflammation of the meninges, the protective membrane that surrounds the brain and spinal cord, and **encephalitis** is inflammation of the brain. Both conditions can be caused by viral or bacterial pathogens.

**Epileptic seizures** are brief episodes caused by disturbed or overactive nerve cell activity in the brain. Seizures range widely in severity and may include confusion, convulsions, and loss of consciousness. They have many causes, including tumors, infections, head injuries, and medications.

### PRACTICE QUESTIONS

**8.** Which part of the nervous system controls only voluntary action?
- **A)** the peripheral nervous system
- **B)** the somatic nervous system
- **C)** the sympathetic nervous system
- **D)** the parasympathetic nervous system

**9.** Which of the following is the part of a nerve cell that receives information?
- **A)** axon
- **B)** dendrite
- **C)** Schwann cell
- **D)** myelin

# The Gastrointestinal System

## STRUCTURE AND FUNCTION OF THE GASTROINTESTINAL SYSTEM

Fueling the biological systems mentioned previously is the digestive system. The digestive system is essentially a continuous tube in which food is processed. During digestion, the body extracts necessary nutrients and biological fuels and isolates waste to be discarded.

**HELPFUL HINT**

The burning sensation called heartburn occurs when gastric acid from the stomach travels up the esophagus, often as a result of relaxation of the lower esophageal sphincter. This acid can damage the lining of the esophagus.

The breakdown of food into its constituent parts begins as soon as it is put into the mouth. Enzymes in **saliva** such as salivary amylase begin breaking down food, particularly starch, as mastication helps prepare food for swallowing and subsequent digestion. Food from this point is formed into a **bolus** that travels down the esophagus, aided by a process called **peristalsis**, rhythmic contractions that move the partially digested food towards the stomach. Upon reaching the **stomach**, food encounters a powerful acid (composed mainly of hydrochloric acid), which aids the breakdown of food into its absorbable components.

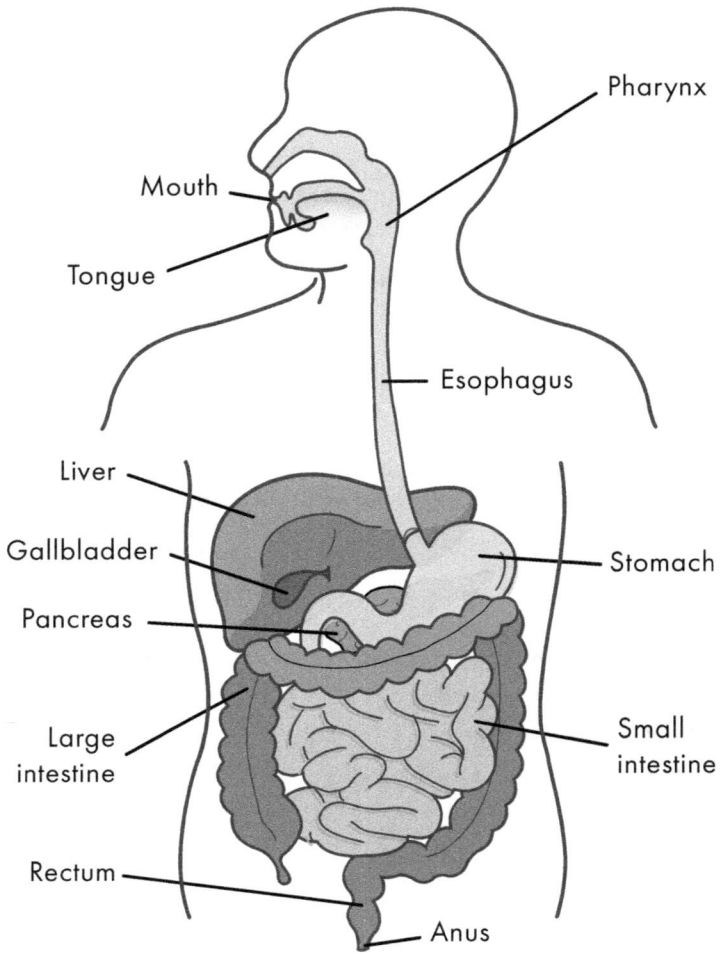

**Figure 7.9. The Digestive System**

The human body derives fuel primarily from three sources: proteins, sugars, and fats (lipids). Enzymes break proteins down into their constituent amino acids to produce new proteins for the body. Carbohydrates are broken down enzymatically if necessary and used for metabolism. Fats are broken down into constituent fatty acids and glycerol for a number of uses, including dense nutritional energy storage. Digestion of fat requires **bile** acids produced by the **liver**; bile is stored in the **gall bladder.**

The stomach produces a semifluid mass of partially digested food called **chyme** that passes into the **small intestine**, where nutrients are absorbed into the bloodstream. This absorption occurs through millions of finger-like projections known as **villi** that increase the surface area available for the absorption of nutrients.

The small intestine itself has three major segments. Proximal to the stomach is the **duodenum**, which combines digestive substances from the liver and pancreas; next is the **jejunum**, the primary site of nutrient absorption; finally, the **ileum** absorbs remaining nutrients and moves the remaining matter into the large intestine. The **large intestine** (also called the colon) absorbs water from the waste, which then passes into the **rectum** and out of the body through the **anus**.

## PATHOLOGIES OF THE DIGESTIVE SYSTEM

The digestive system is prone to several illnesses of varying severity. Commonly, gastrointestinal distress is caused by an acute infection (bacterial or viral) affecting the lining of the digestive system. A resulting immune response triggers the body, as an adaptive measure, to void the contents of the digestive system in order to purge the infection. Chronic gastrointestinal disorders include **irritable bowel syndrome** (the causes of which are largely unknown) and **Crohn's disease**, an inflammatory bowel disorder with an immune-related etiology.

### PRACTICE QUESTIONS

10. Where in the digestive tract are most of the nutrients absorbed?
    - **A)** the small intestine
    - **B)** the rectum
    - **C)** the stomach
    - **D)** the large intestine

11. Which of the following initiates the breakdown of carbohydrates?
    - **A)** salivary amylase
    - **B)** stomach acid
    - **C)** bile salts
    - **D)** peristalsis

# The Skeletal System
## STRUCTURE AND FUNCTION OF THE SKELETAL SYSTEM

The skeletal system is composed of tissue called **bone** that helps with movement, provides support for organs, and synthesizes blood cells. The outer layer of bone is composed of a matrix made of collagen and minerals that gives bones their strength and rigidity. The matrix is formed from functional units called **osteons** that include layers of compact bone called **lamellae**. The lamellae surround a cavity called the **Haversian canal**, which houses the bone's blood supply. These canals are in turn connected to the **periosteum**, the bone's outermost membrane, by another series of channels called **Volkmann's canals**.

Within osteons are blood cells called **osteoblasts**, mononucleate cells that produce bone tissue. When the bone tissue hardens around these cells, the cells are known as **osteocytes**, and the space they occupy within the bone tissue is known as **lacunae**. The lacunae are connected by a series of channels called **canaliculi**. **Osteoclasts**, a third type of bone cell, are responsible for breaking down bone tissue. They are located on the surface of bones and help balance the body's calcium levels by degrading bone to release stored calcium. The fourth type of bone cell, **lining cells**, are flatted osteoblasts that protect the bone and also help balance calcium levels.

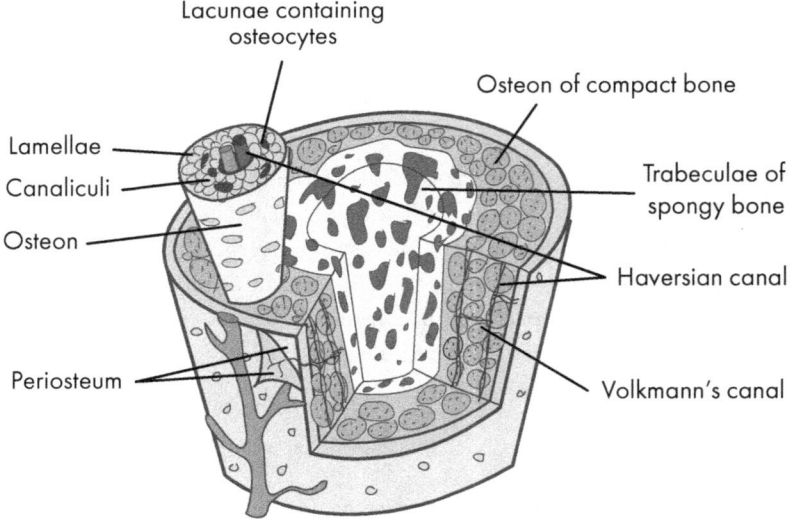

**Figure 7.10. Bone Structure**

**QUICK REVIEW**

How might diet affect the body's ability to rebuild bone after a fracture?

Within the hard outer layer of bone is the spongy layer called **cancellous bone**, which is made up of support structures called **trabeculae**. Within this layer is the bone marrow, which houses cells that produce red blood cells in a process called **hematopoiesis**. Bone marrow also produces many of the lymphocytes that play an important role in the immune system.

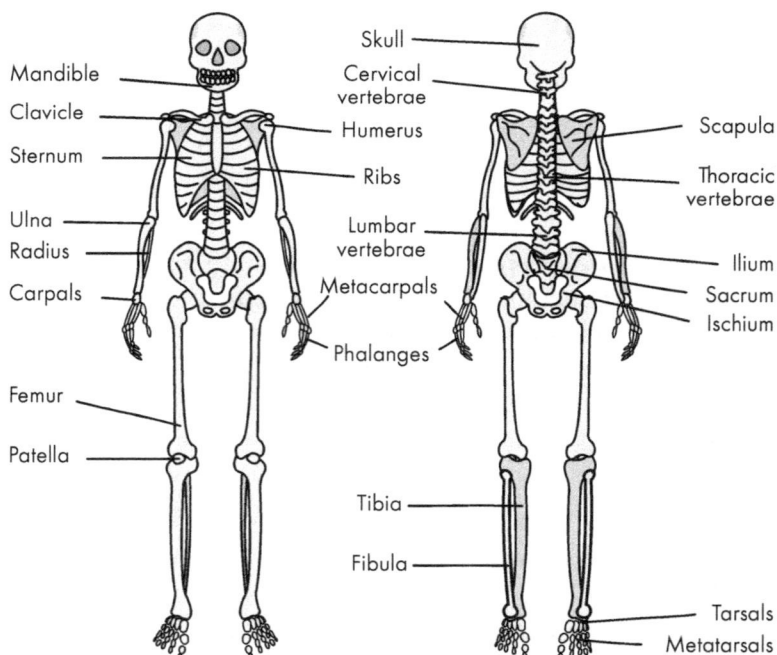

**Figure 7.11. The Skeletal System**

Bones are divided into four main categories. **Long bones**, such as the femur and humerus, are longer than they are wide. **Short bones**, in contrast, are wider than they are long. These include the clavicle and carpals. **Flat bones** are wide and flat, and usually provide protection. Examples of flat bones include the bones of the skull, pelvis, and rib cage. **Irregular bones**, as the name suggests, have an irregular shape that doesn't fit into the other categories. These bones include the vertebrae and bones of the jaw.

Bones are held together (articulated) at **joints** by connective tissue called **ligaments**. Joints can be classified based on the tissue that connects the bone. **Fibrous joints** are connected by dense, collagen-rich fibers, while **cartilaginous joints** are joined by special tissue called **hyaline cartilage**. Cartilage is more flexible than bone but denser than muscles. In addition to joining together bone, it also helps hold open passageways and provides support in structures like the nose and ears. The third type of joint, **synovial joints**, are joined by synovial fluid, which lubricates the joint and allows for movement. Bones are also joined to muscles by connective tissue called **tendons**.

Table 7.2. Types of Synovial Joints

| Name | Movement | Found In |
| --- | --- | --- |
| Hinge joint | movement through one plane of motion as flexion/extension | elbows, knees, fingers |
| Ball-and-socket joint | range of motion through multiple planes and rotation about an axis | hips, shoulders |
| Saddle joint | movement through multiple planes, but cannot rotate about an axis | thumbs |
| Gliding joint | sliding movement in the plane of the bones' surfaces | vertebrae, small bones in the wrists and ankles |
| Condyloid joint | movement through two planes as flexion/extension and abduction/adduction, but cannot rotate about an axis | wrists |
| Pivot joint | only movement is rotation about an axis | elbows, neck |

## PATHOLOGIES OF THE SKELETAL SYSTEM

Important pathologies of the skeletal system include **osteoporosis**, which occurs when minerals are leached from the bone, making bones more likely to break. Broken bones can also be caused by **brittle bone disease**, which results from a genetic defect that affects collagen production. Joint pain can be caused by **osteoarthritis**, which is the breakdown of cartilage in joints, and **rheumatoid arthritis**, which is an autoimmune disease that affects synovial membranes.

### PRACTICE QUESTIONS

**12.** Which type of cell is responsible for the degradation of bone tissue?
- **A)** osteoclasts
- **B)** osteoblasts
- **C)** osteocytes
- **D)** lining cells

**13.** Which joint allows for the most freedom of movement?
- **A)** fibrous joints
- **B)** hinge joints
- **C)** saddle joints
- **D)** ball-and-socket joints

# The Muscular System

## TYPES OF MUSCLE

The muscular system is composed of **muscles** that move the body, support bodily functions, and circulate blood. The human body contains three types of muscles. **Skeletal muscles** are voluntarily controlled and attach to the skeleton to allow movement in the body. **Smooth muscles** are involuntary, meaning they cannot be consciously controlled. Smooth muscles are found in many organs and structures, including the esophagus, stomach, intestines, blood vessels, bladder, and bronchi. Finally, **cardiac muscles**, found only in the heart, are the involuntary muscles that contract the heart in order to pump blood through the body.

**HELPFUL HINT**
Some skeletal muscles, such as the diaphragm and those that control blinking, can be voluntarily controlled but usually operate involuntarily.

## MUSCLE CELL STRUCTURE

The main structural unit of a muscle is the **sarcomere**. Sarcomeres are composed of a series of **muscle fibers**, which are elongated individual cells that stretch from one end of the muscle to the other. Within each fiber are hundreds of **myofibrils**, long strands within the cells that contain alternating layers of thin filaments made of the protein **actin** and thick filaments made of the protein **myosin**. Each of these proteins plays a role in muscle contraction and relaxation.

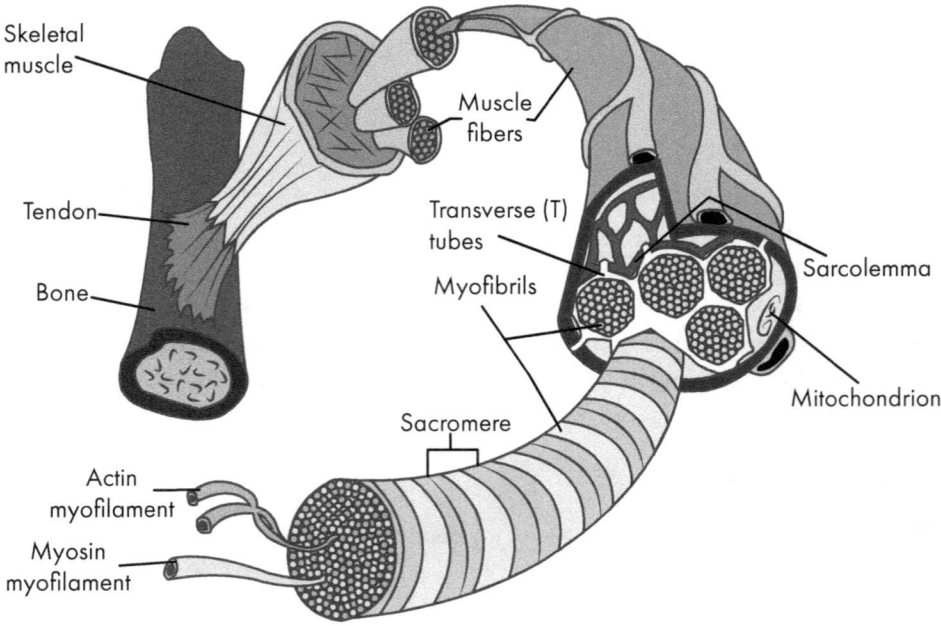

**Figure 7.12. Structure of Skeletal Muscle**

Muscle contraction is explained by the **sliding filament theory**. When the sarcomere is at rest, the thin filaments containing actin are found at both ends of the muscle, while the thick filaments containing myosin are found at the center. Myosin filaments contain "heads," which can attach and detach from actin filaments. The myosin attaches to actin and pulls the thin filaments to the center of the sarcomere, forcing the thin filaments to slide inward and causing the entire sarcomere to shorten, or contract, creating movement. The sarcomere can be broken down into zones that contain certain filaments.

- The **Z-line** separates the sarcomeres: a single sarcomere is the distance between two Z-lines.
- The **A-band** is the area of the sarcomere in which thick myosin filaments are found and does not shorten during muscular contraction.
- The **I-band** is the area in the sarcomere between the thick myosin filaments in which only thin actin filament is found.
- The **H-zone** is found between the actin filaments and contains only thick myosin filament.

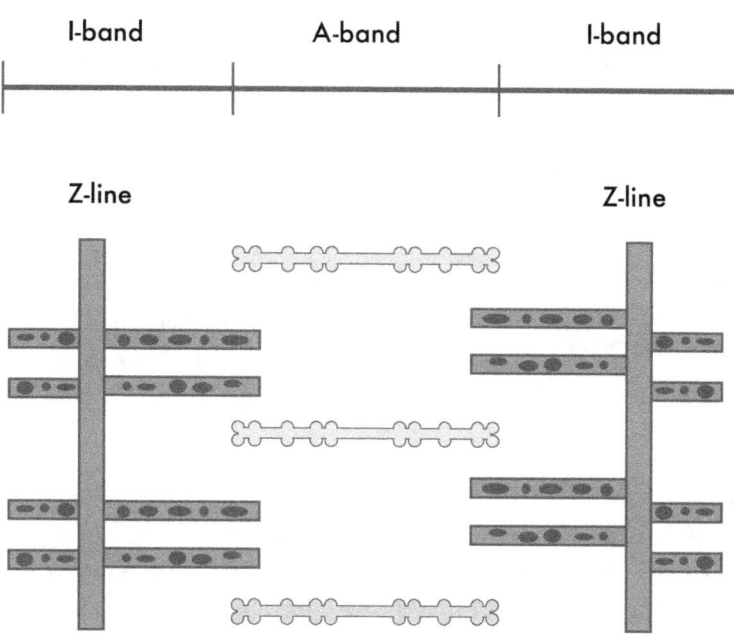

**Figure 7.13. Sliding Filament Theory**

## PATHOLOGIES OF THE MUSCULAR SYSTEM

Injuries to muscle can impede movement and cause pain. When muscle fibers are overstretched, the resulting **muscle strain** can cause pain, stiffness, and bruising. Muscle fibers can also be weakened by diseases, as with **muscular dystrophy** (MD). MD is a genetically inherited condition that results in progressive muscle wasting, which limits movement and can cause respiratory and cardiovascular difficulties.

**HELPFUL HINT**
Overstretching a ligament is called a **sprain**.

## PRACTICE QUESTIONS

**14.** Which type of muscle is responsible for voluntary movement in the body?
- **A)** cardiac
- **B)** visceral
- **C)** smooth
- **D)** skeletal

**15.** Which of the following causes a muscle strain?
- **A)** a lack of available energy
- **B)** the inability of muscle fibers to contract
- **C)** detachment of the ligament from the bone
- **D)** overstretching of muscle fibers

## The Immune System

The human immune system protects the body against bacteria and viruses that cause disease. The system is composed of two parts. The **innate** system includes nonspecific defenses that work against a wide range of infectious agents. This system includes both physical barriers that keep out foreign particles and organisms along with specific cells that attack invaders that move past barriers. The second part of the immune system is the **adaptive** immune system, which "learns" to respond only to specific invaders.

Table 7.3. Lines of Defense in the Immune System

| | |
|---|---|
| **1. External barriers** | skin, enzymes, mucus, earwax, native bacteria |
| **2. The innate response** | inflammation, neutrophils (a white blood cell), antimicrobial peptides, natural killer lymphocytes, interferon |
| **3. The adaptive response** | helper T-cells, cytotoxic T-cells, B-cells, memory B-cells |

### THE INNATE IMMUNE SYSTEM

The first line of defense in the immune system are barriers to entry. The most prominent is the **skin**, which leaves few openings for an infection-causing agent to enter. Bodily orifices exhibit other methods for preventing infection. The mouth is saturated with native bacteria that dominate the resources in the microenvironment, making it inhospitable to invading bacteria. In addition, enzymes in the mouth create a hostile environment for foreign organisms. The urethra flushes away potentially invasive microorganisms mechanically through the outflow of urine, while the vagina maintains a consistently low pH, deterring potential infections. The eyes and nose constantly produce and flush away tears and **mucus**, which trap pathogens before they can replicate and infect. Similarly, **earwax** serves as an additional barrier to entry.

Pathogens do occasionally breach these barriers and arrive within the body, where they attempt to replicate and cause an infection. When this occurs, the body mounts a number of nonspecific responses. The body's initial response is **inflammation**: infected cells release signaling molecules indicating that an infection has occurred, which causes increased blood flow to the area. This increase in blood flow includes the increased

**HELPFUL HINT**

Phagocytosis occurs when a cell completely surrounds a particle to form an enclosed vesicle. The particle can then be broken down either for nutrients or to neutralize a threat. Cells in the immune system that use phagocytosis are called macrophages.

presence of **white blood cells**, also called **leukocytes**. The most common type of leukocyte found at sites of inflammation are **neutrophils**, which engulf and destroy invaders.

Other innate responses include **antimicrobial peptides**, which destroy bacteria by interfering with the functions of their membranes or DNA, and **natural killer lymphocytes**, which respond to virus-infected cells. Because they can recognize damaged cells with the presence of antibodies, they are important in early defense against bacterial infection. In addition, infected cells may release **interferon**, which causes nearby cells to increase their defenses.

Table 7.4. Types of White Blood Cells

| Type of Cell | Name of Cell | Role | Innate or Adaptive | Prevalence |
|---|---|---|---|---|
| **Granulocytes** | Neutrophil | First responders that quickly migrate to the site of infections to destroy bacterial invaders | Innate | Very common |
| | Eosinophil | Attack multicellular parasites | Innate | Rare |
| | Basophil | Large cell responsible for inflammatory reactions, including allergies | Innate | Very rare |
| **Lymphocyte** | B-cells | Respond to antigens by releasing antibodies | Adaptive | Common |
| | T-cells | Respond to antigens by destroying invaders and infected cells | Adaptive | |
| | Natural killer cells | Destroy virus-infected cells and tumor cells | Innate and adaptive | |
| **Monocyte** | Macrophage | Engulf and destroy microbes, foreign substances, and cancer cells | Innate and adaptive | Rare |

## THE ADAPTIVE IMMUNE SYSTEM

The adaptive immune system is able to recognize molecules called **antigens** on the surface of pathogens to which the system has previously been exposed. Antigens are displayed on the surface of cells by the **major histocompatibility complex** (MHC), which can display either "self" proteins from their own cells or proteins from pathogens. In an **antigen-presenting cell**, the MHC on the cell's surface displays a particular antigen, which is recognized by **helper T-cells**. These cells produce a signal (cytokines) that activates **cytotoxic T-cells**, which then destroy any cell that displays the antigen.

The presence of antigens also activates **B-cells**, which rapidly multiply to create **plasma cells**, which in turn release **antibodies**. Antibodies will bind only to specific antigens, and in turn result in the destruction of the infected cell. Some interfere directly with the function of the cell, while others draw the attention of macrophages. **Memory B-cells** are created during infection. These cells "remember" the antigen that their parent cells responded to, allowing them to respond more quickly if the infection appears again.

Together, T- and B-cells are known as **lymphocytes**. T-cells are produced in the thymus, while B-cells mature in bone marrow. These cells circulate through the lymphatic system.

**HELPFUL HINT**

Memory B-cells are the underlying mechanisms behind vaccines, which introduce a harmless version of a pathogen into the body to activate the body's adaptive immune response.

## PATHOLOGIES OF THE IMMUNE SYSTEM

The immune system itself can be pathological. The immune system of individuals with an **autoimmune disease** will attack healthy tissues, as is the case in lupus, psoriasis, and multiple sclerosis. The immune system may also overreact to harmless particles, a condition known as an **allergy**. Some infections will attack the immune system itself. **Human immunodeficiency virus (HIV)** attacks helper T-cells, eventually causing **acquired immunodeficiency syndrome (AIDS)**, which allows opportunistic infections to overrun the body.

### PRACTICE QUESTIONS

16. Which of the following is NOT part of the innate immune system?
    A) interferon
    B) neutrophils
    C) antibodies
    D) natural killer lymphocytes

17. Which of the following is NOT considered a nonspecific defense of the innate immune system?
    A) the skin
    B) inflammation
    C) antimicrobial peptides
    D) antibody production

# The Reproductive System

## THE MALE REPRODUCTIVE SYSTEM

The male reproductive system produces **sperm**, or male gametes, and passes them to the female reproductive system. Sperm are produced in the **testes** (also called testicles), which are housed externally in a sac-like structure called the **scrotum**. The scrotum contracts and relaxes to move the testes closer or farther from the body. This process keeps the testes at the appropriate temperature for sperm production, which is slightly lower than regular body temperature.

Mature sperm are stored in the **epididymis**. During sexual stimulation, sperm travel from the epididymis through a long, thin tube called the **vas deferens**. Along the way, the sperm is joined by fluids from three glands to form **semen**. The **seminal vesicles** secrete the bulk of the fluid which makes up semen, which is composed of various proteins, sugars, and enzymes. The **prostate** contributes an alkaline fluid that counteracts the acidity of the vaginal tract. Finally, the **Cowper gland** secretes a protein-rich fluid that acts as a lubricant. Semen travels through the **urethra** and exits the body through the **penis**, which becomes rigid during sexual arousal.

The main hormone associated with the male reproductive system is **testosterone**, which is released by the testes (and in the adrenal glands in much smaller amounts). Testosterone is responsible for the development of the male reproductive system and male secondary sexual characteristics, including muscle development and facial hair growth.

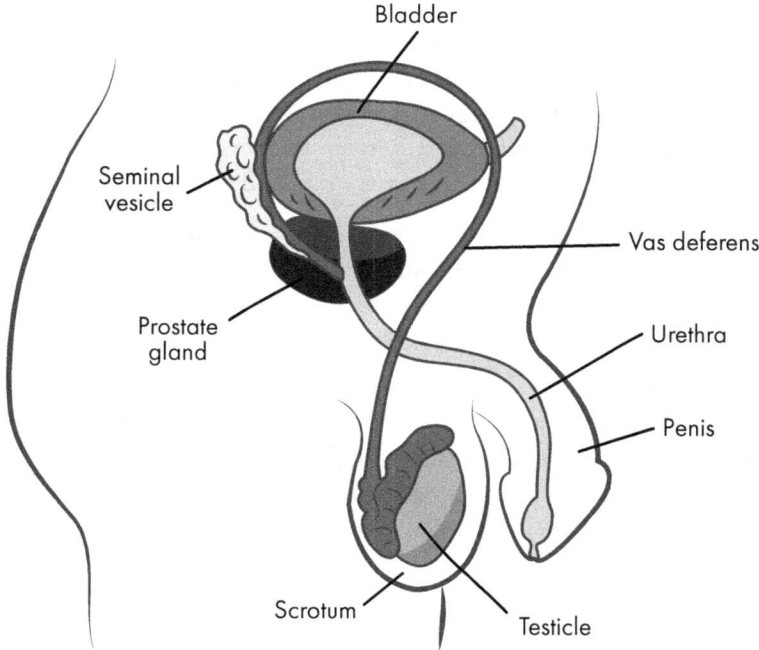

**Figure 7.14. The Male Reproductive System**

## THE FEMALE REPRODUCTIVE SYSTEM

The female reproductive system produces **eggs**, or female gametes, and gestates the fetus during pregnancy. Eggs are produced in the **ovaries** and travel through the **fallopian tubes** to the **uterus**, which is a muscular organ that houses the fetus during pregnancy. The uterine cavity is lined with a layer of blood-rich tissue called the **endometrium**. If no pregnancy occurs, the endometrium is shed monthly during **menstruation**.

**QUICK REVIEW**

What type of muscle is most likely found in the myometrium of the uterus?

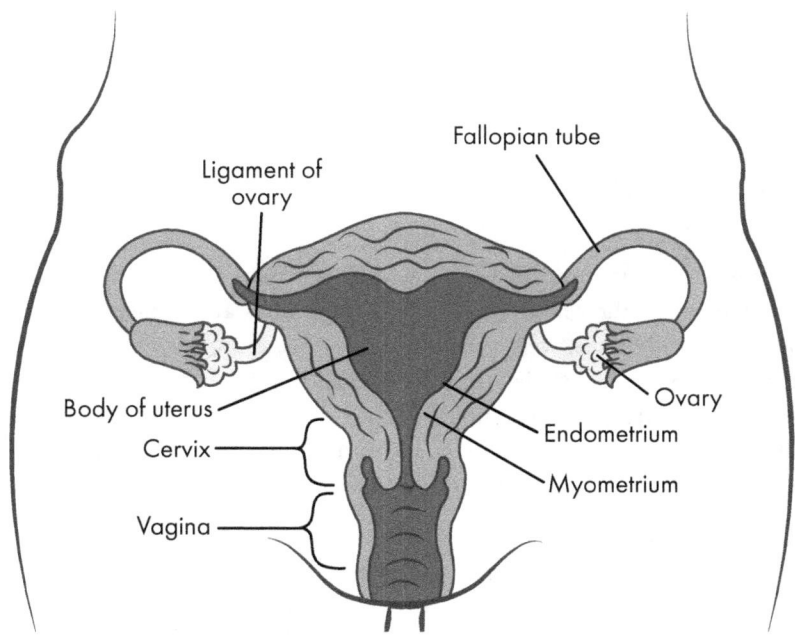

**Figure 7.15. The Female Reproductive System**

**ANATOMY AND PHYSIOLOGY**

Fertilization occurs when the egg absorbs the sperm; it usually takes place in the fallopian tubes but may happen in the uterus itself. After fertilization the new zygote implants itself in the endometrium, where it will grow and develop over thirty-eight weeks (roughly nine months). During gestation, the developing fetus acquires nutrients and passes waste through the **placenta**. This temporary organ is attached to the wall of the uterus and is connected to the baby by the **umbilical cord**.

When the fetus is mature, powerful muscle contractions occur in the myometrium, the muscular layer next to the endometrium. These contractions push the fetus through an opening called the **cervix** into the vagina, from which it exits the body. The placenta and umbilical cords are also expelled through the vagina shortly after birth.

The female reproductive cycle is controlled by a number of different hormones. Estrogen, produced by the ovaries, stimulates Graafian follicles, which contain immature eggs cells. The pituitary gland then releases luteinizing hormone, which causes the egg to be released into the fallopian tubes during **ovulation**. During pregnancy, estrogen and progesterone are released in high levels to help with fetal growth and to prevent further ovulation.

### PRACTICE QUESTIONS

**18.** Which of the following organs transports semen through the penis?
- **A)** urethra
- **B)** vas deferens
- **C)** prostate
- **D)** seminal vesicles

**19.** Which of the following organs provides nutrients to a fetus during gestation?
- **A)** ovary
- **B)** placenta
- **C)** uterus
- **D)** cervix

## The Endocrine System
### STRUCTURE AND FUNCTION OF THE ENDOCRINE SYSTEM

The endocrine system is composed of a network of organs called **glands** that produce signaling chemicals called **hormones**. These hormones are released by glands into the bloodstream and then travel to the other tissues and organs whose functions they regulate. When they reach their target, hormones bond to a specific receptor on cell membranes, which affects the machinery of the cell. Hormones play an important role in regulating almost all bodily functions, including digestion, respiration, sleep, stress, growth, development, reproduction, and immune response.

Much of the action of the endocrine system runs through the **hypothalamus**, which is highly integrated into the nervous system. The hypothalamus receives signals from the brain and in turn will release hormones that regulate both other endocrine organs and important metabolic processes. Other endocrine glands include the pineal, pituitary, thyroid, parathyroid, thymus, and adrenal glands.

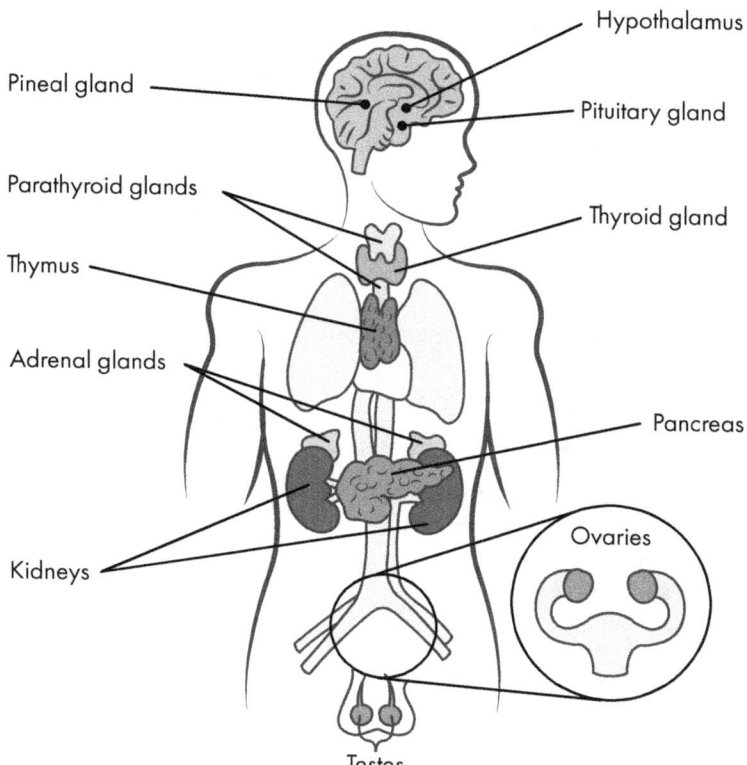

**Figure 7.16. The Endocrine System**

Organs from other systems, including the reproductive and digestive systems, can also secrete hormones, and thus are considered part of the endocrine system. The reproductive organs in both males (testes) and females (ovaries and placenta) release important hormones, as do the pancreas, liver, and stomach.

Table 7.5. Endocrine Glands

| Gland | Regulates | Hormones Produced |
|---|---|---|
| pineal gland | circadian rhythms (the sleep/wake cycle) | melatonin |
| pituitary gland | growth, blood pressure, reabsorption of water by the kidneys, temperature, pain relief, and some reproductive functions related to pregnancy and childbirth | human growth hormone (HGH), thyroid-stimulating hormone (TSH), prolactin (PRL), luteinizing hormone (LH), follicle-stimulating hormone (FSH), oxytocin, antidiuretic hormone (ADH) |
| hypothalamus | pituitary function and metabolic processes including body temperature, hunger, thirst, and circadian rhythms | thyrotropin-releasing hormone (TRH), dopamine, growth-hormone-releasing hormone (GHRH), gonadotropin-releasing hormone (GnRH), oxytocin, vasopressin |

**ANATOMY AND PHYSIOLOGY**

Table 7.5. Endocrine Glands (continued)

| Gland | Regulates | Hormones Produced |
|---|---|---|
| thyroid gland | energy use and protein synthesis | thyroxine (T4), triiodothyronine (T3), calcitonin |
| parathyroid | calcium and phosphate levels | parathyroid hormone (PTH) |
| adrenal glands | "fight or flight" response, regulation of salt and blood volume | epinephrine, norepinephrine, cortisol, androgens |
| pancreas | blood sugar levels and metabolism | insulin, glucagon, somatostatin |
| testes | maturation of sex organs, secondary sex characteristics | androgens (e.g., testosterone) |
| ovaries | maturation of sex organs, secondary sex characteristics, pregnancy, childbirth, and lactation | progesterone, estrogens |
| placenta | gestation and childbirth | progesterone, estrogens, human chorionic gonadotropin, human placental lactogen |

## PATHOLOGIES OF THE ENDOCRINE SYSTEM

Disruption of hormone production in specific endocrine glands can lead to disease. An inability to produce insulin results in uncontrolled blood glucose levels, a condition called **diabetes**. Over- or underactive glands can lead to conditions like **hypothyroidism**, which is characterized by slow metabolism, and hyperparathyroidism, which can lead to osteoporosis. Tumors on endocrine glands can also damage the functioning of a wide variety of bodily systems.

### PRACTICE QUESTIONS

20. Which gland in the endocrine system is responsible for regulating blood glucose levels?
    A) adrenal
    B) testes
    C) pineal
    D) pancreas

21. Damage to the parathyroid would most likely affect which of the following?
    A) stress levels
    B) bone density
    C) secondary sex characteristics
    D) circadian rhythms

# The Integumentary System

The **integumentary system** refers to the skin (the largest organ in the body) and related structures, including the hair and nails. Skin is composed of three layers. The **epidermis** is the outermost layer of the skin. This waterproof layer contains no blood vessels and acts mainly to protect the body. Under the epidermis lies the **dermis**, which consists of dense connective tissue that allows skin to stretch and flex. The dermis is home to blood vessels, glands, and **hair follicles**. The **hypodermis** is a layer of fat below the dermis that stores energy (in the form of fat) and acts as a cushion for the body. The hypodermis is sometimes called the **subcutaneous layer**.

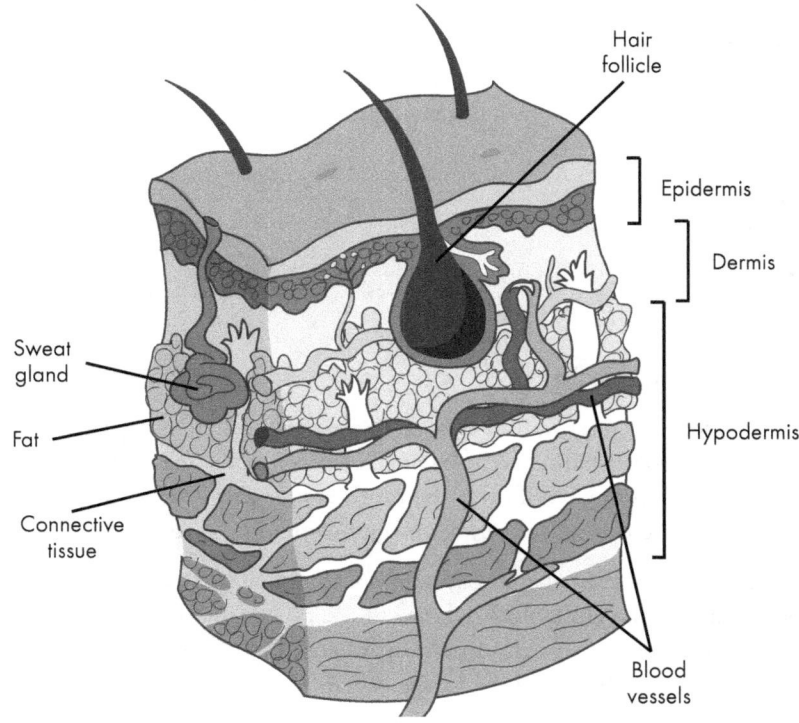

**Figure 7.17. The Skin**

The skin has several important roles. It acts as a barrier to protect the body from injury, the intrusion of foreign particles, and the loss of water and nutrients. It is also important for **thermoregulation**. Blood vessels near the surface of the skin can dilate, allowing for higher blood flow and the release of heat. They can also constrict to reduce the amount of blood that travels near the surface of the skin, which helps conserve heat. The skin also produces vitamin D when exposed to sunlight.

Because the skin covers the whole body, it plays a vital role in allowing organisms to interact with the environment. It is home to nerve endings that sense temperature, pressure, and pain, and it also houses glands that help maintain homeostasis. **Eccrine** glands, which are located primarily in the palms of the hands and soles of the feet (and to a lesser degree in other areas of the body), release the water and salt (NaCl) mixture called **sweat**. These glands help the body maintain the appropriate salt/water balance. Sweat can also contain small amounts of other substances the body needs to expel, including alcohol, lactic acid, and urea.

**QUICK REVIEW**

Why would flushing—the reddening of the skin caused by dilating blood vessels—be associated with fevers?

**Apocrine** glands, which are located primarily in the armpit and groin, release an oily substance that contains pheromones. They are also sensitive to adrenaline, and are responsible for most of the sweating that occurs due to stress, fear, anxiety, or pain. Apocrine glands are largely inactive until puberty.

### PRACTICE QUESTION

22. Which of the following is NOT a function of the skin?
    A) regulating body temperature
    B) protecting against injury
    C) producing adrenaline
    D) maintaining water/salt balance

23. Which of the following is the outermost layer of the skin?
    A) hypodermis
    B) dermis
    C) epidermis
    D) apocrine

## The Genitourinary System

The **urinary system** excretes water and waste from the body and is crucial for maintaining the body's electrolyte balance (the balance of water and salt in the blood). Because many organs function as part of both the reproductive and urinary systems, the two are sometimes referred to collectively as the **genitourinary system**.

The main organs of the urinary system are the **kidneys**, which filter waste from the blood; maintain the electrolyte balance in the blood; and regulate blood volume, pressure, and pH. The kidneys also function as an endocrine organ and release several important hormones. These include **renin**, which regulates blood pressure, and **calcitriol**, the active form of vitamin D. The kidney is divided into two regions: the **renal cortex**, which is the outermost layer, and the **renal medulla**, which is the inner layer.

> **HELPFUL HINT**
> A normal human kidney contains around one million nephrons.

The functional unit of the kidney is the **nephron**, which is a series of looping tubes that filter electrolytes, metabolic waste, and other water-soluble waste molecules from the blood. These wastes include **urea**, which is a nitrogenous byproduct of protein catabolism, and **uric acid**, a byproduct of nucleic acid metabolism. Together, these waste products are excreted from the body in **urine**.

Filtration begins in a network of capillaries called a **glomerulus** which is located in the renal cortex of each kidney. This waste is then funneled into **collecting ducts** in the renal medulla. From the collecting ducts, urine passes through the **renal pelvis** and then through two long tubes called **ureters**.

The two ureters drain into the urinary bladder, which holds up to 1000 milliliters of liquid. The bladder exit is controlled by two sphincters, both of which must open for urine to pass. The internal sphincter is made of smooth involuntary muscle, while the external sphincter can be voluntarily controlled. In males, the external sphincter also closes to prevent movement of seminal fluid into the bladder during sexual activity. (A sphincter is a circular muscle that controls movement of substances through passageways. Sphincters are found throughout the human body, including the bladder, esophagus, and capillaries.)

Urine exits the bladder through the **urethra**. In males, the urethra goes through the penis and also carries semen. In females, the much-shorter urethra ends just above the vaginal opening.

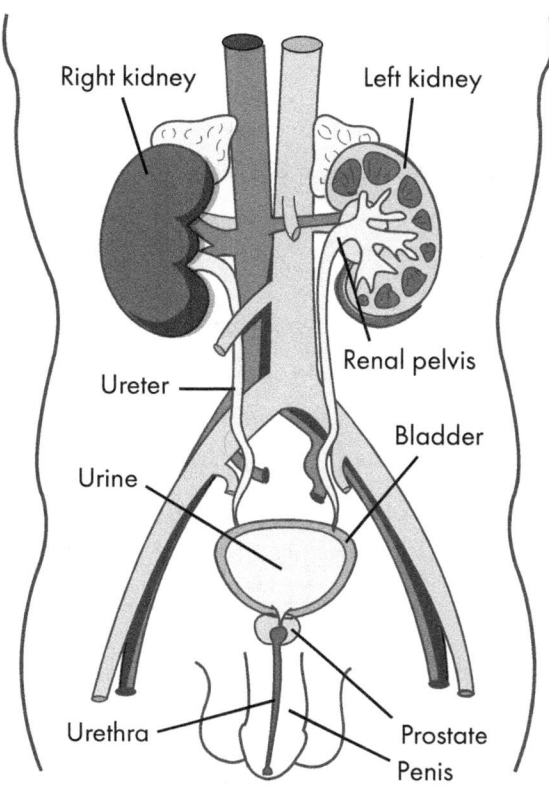

**Figure 7.18. Male Genitourinary System**

## PRACTICE QUESTIONS

**24.** Which of the following is the outermost layer of the kidney?
- **A)** renal cortex
- **B)** renal medulla
- **C)** renal pelvis
- **D)** nephron

**25.** Which of the following organs holds urine before it passes into the urethra?
- **A)** prostate
- **B)** kidney
- **C)** ureter
- **D)** urinary bladder

# ANSWER KEY

1. **C) is correct.** Superior means that something is above a reference point.
2. **A) is correct.** The wrist is distal, or further from the trunk, than the elbow.
3. **C) is correct.** The alveoli are sacs found at the terminal end of each bronchiole in the lungs and are the site of gas exchange with the blood.
4. **C) is correct.** Asthma is a negative reaction of the body to otherwise harmless particles.
5. **D) is correct.** These two structures form a junction at the mitral valve.
6. **C) is correct.** The iliac artery receives blood from the aorta to supply blood to the lower body.
7. **A) is correct.** The sinoatrial and atrioventricular nodes electrically stimulate the heart to pump.
8. **B) is correct.** The somatic nervous system controls voluntary actions.
9. **B) is correct.** Dendrites receive information in nerve cells.
10. **A) is correct.** Most nutrients are absorbed by the small intestine.
11. **A) is correct.** Salivary amylase in the mouth begins the breakdown of carbohydrates.
12. **A) is correct.** Osteoclasts break down and absorb bone tissue.
13. **D) is correct.** Ball-and-socket joints allow for the most freedom of movement.
14. **D) is correct.** Skeletal muscles are attached to the skeletal system and are controlled voluntarily.
15. **D) is correct.** A muscle strain is caused by the overstretching of muscle fibers, resulting in tearing of the muscle.
16. **C) is correct.** Antibodies are part of the body's adaptive immune system and only respond to specific pathogens.
17. **D) is correct.** Antibodies are produced by B-cells as part of an adaptive immune response.
18. **A) is correct.** The urethra carries semen through the penis.
19. **B) is correct.** The placenta provides nutrients to the growing fetus and also removes waste products.
20. **D) is correct.** The pancreas releases insulin and glucagon, which regulate glucose levels in the blood.
21. **B) is correct.** The parathyroid controls calcium and phosphate levels, which are maintained by producing and reabsorbing bone tissue.
22. **C) is correct.** The skin does not produce adrenaline. (Adrenaline is produced and released by the adrenal glands.)
23. **C) is correct.** The epidermis is the outermost layer of the skin. It is waterproof and does not contain any blood vessels.
24. **A) is correct.** The outermost layer of the kidney is the renal cortex.
25. **D) is correct.** The urinary bladder holds urine before it passes to the urethra to be excreted.

# EIGHT: PHYSICS

## Motion

To study motion, it is necessary to understand the concept of scalars and vectors. **Scalars** are measurements that have a quantity but no direction. **Vectors**, in contrast, have both a quantity and a direction. **Distance** is a scalar: it describes how far an object has traveled along a path. Distance can have values such as 54 m or 16 miles. **Displacement** is a vector: it describes how far an object has traveled from its starting position. A displacement value will indicate direction, such as 54 m east or −16 miles.

**EQUATIONS**

$d = \frac{1}{2}at^2 + v_i t$

($d = vt$ when $a = 0$)

$v_f = v_i + at$

$v_f^2 = v_i^2 + 2ad$

**HELPFUL HINT**

$m$ = mass (kg)
$d$ = displacement (m)
$v$ = velocity (m/s)
$a$ = acceleration (m/s²)
$t$ = time (s)

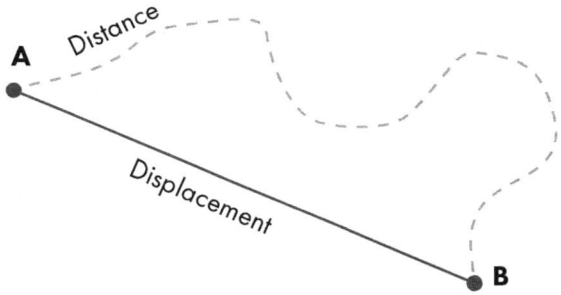

**Figure 8.1. Distance versus Displacement**

**Speed** describes how quickly something is moving. It is found by dividing distance by time, and so is a scalar value. **Velocity** is the rate at which an object changes position. Velocity is found by dividing displacement by time, meaning it is a vector value. An object that travels a certain distance and then returns to its starting point has a velocity of zero because its final position did not change. Its speed, however, can be found by dividing the total distance it traveled by the time it took to make the trip.

**Acceleration** describes how quickly an object changes velocity. It is also a vector: when acceleration is in the same direction as velocity, the object will move faster. When the acceleration is in the opposite direction of velocity, the object will slow down.

## PRACTICE QUESTION

1. A person starts from rest and increases his velocity to 5 m/s over a time period of 1 second. What is his acceleration?
   - **A)** −5 m/s²
   - **B)** 0 m/s²
   - **C)** 5 m/s²
   - **D)** 10 m/s²

# Forces

**EQUATIONS**

$G = 6.67408 \times 10^{-11} \text{ m}^3 \text{ kg}^{-1} \text{ s}^{-2}$ (gravitational constant)

$g = 9.8 \text{ m/s}^2$

$F_g = mg$ (for falling objects)

$F_g = \frac{Gm_1 m_2}{r_2}$ (for the gravitational force between two masses)

$F = ma$

$F_f = \mu_k F_N$

where $F$ = force (N)

A push or pull that causes an object to move or change direction is called a **force**. Forces can arise from a number of different sources.

- **Gravity** is the attraction of one mass to another mass. For example, the earth's gravitational field pulls objects toward it, and the sun's gravitational field keeps planets in motion around it.
- **Electrical force** is the creation of a field by charged particles that will cause other charged objects in that field to move.
- **Tension** is found in ropes pulling or holding up an object.
- **Friction** is created by two objects moving against each other.
- **Normal force** occurs when an object is resting on another object.
- **Buoyant force** is the upward force experienced by floating objects.

In 1687, Isaac Newton published **three laws of motion** that describe the behavior of force and mass. Newton's first law is also called the **law of inertia**. It states that an object will maintain its current state of motion unless acted on by an outside force.

Newton's **second law** is an equation, $F = ma$. The equation states that increasing the force on an object will increase its acceleration. In addition, the mass of the object will determine its acceleration: under the same force, a small object will accelerate more quickly than a larger object.

An object in equilibrium is either at rest or is moving at constant velocity; in other words, the object has no acceleration, or $a = 0$. Using Newton's second law, an object is in equilibrium if the net force on the object is 0, or $F = 0$ (this is called the equilibrium condition).

Newton's **third law** states that for every action (force), there will be an equal and opposite reaction (force). For instance, if a person is standing on the floor, there is a force of gravity pulling him toward the earth. However, he is not accelerating toward the earth; he is simply standing at rest on the floor (in equilibrium). So, the floor must provide a force that is equal in magnitude and in the opposite direction to the force of gravity.

## PRACTICE QUESTIONS

2. When a car moving forward stops abruptly, which of the following describes what happens to the driver if she is wearing a seat belt?

- **A)** The driver's body will continue to move forward due to inertia, and the seat belt will apply the required force to keep her in her seat.
- **B)** The driver is inside the car, so she will stop with the car whether or not she is wearing a seat belt.
- **C)** Due to inertia, the driver's body wants to be at rest, so she will stop automatically once the car stops moving.
- **D)** The driver's body will slow down because inertia is passed from the seat belt in the car to the driver.

**3.** Which example describes an object in equilibrium?
- **A)** a parachutist after he jumps from an airplane
- **B)** an airplane taking off
- **C)** a person sitting still in a chair
- **D)** a soccer ball when it is kicked

# Work

**Work** is a scalar value that is defined as the application of a force over a distance. It is measured in Joules (J).

A person lifting a book off the ground is an example of someone doing work. The book has a weight because it is being pulled toward the earth. As the person lifts the book, her hand and arm are producing a force that is larger than that weight, causing the book to rise. The higher the person lifts the book, the more work is done.

The sign of the work done is important. In the example of lifting a book, the person's hand is doing positive (+) work on the book. However, gravity is always pulling the book down, which means that during a lift, gravity is doing negative (−) work on the book. If the force and the displacement are in the same direction, then the work is positive (+). If the force and the displacement are in opposite directions, then the work is negative (−). In the case of lifting a book, the net work done on the book is positive.

**EQUATIONS**

$W = Fd$

$P = \frac{W}{t}$

where $P$ = power (W)

### PRACTICE QUESTION

**4.** Which situation requires the most work done on a car?
- **A)** pushing on the car, but it does not move
- **B)** towing the car up a steep hill for 100 meters
- **C)** pushing the car 5 meters across a parking lot
- **D)** painting the car

# Energy

**Energy** is an abstract concept, but everything in nature has an energy associated with it. Energy is measured in Joules (J). There are many types of energy:
- mechanical: the energy of motion
- chemical: the energy in chemical bonds
- thermal: the energy of an object due to its temperature

**EQUATIONS**

$KE = \frac{1}{2} mv^2$

$PE_g = mgh$

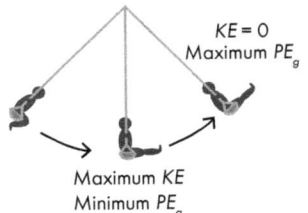

**Figure 8.2. Conservation of Energy in a Swing**

- nuclear: the energy in the nucleus of an atom
- electric: the energy arising from charged particles
- magnetic: the energy arising from a magnetic field

There is an energy related to movement called the **kinetic energy** (**KE**). Any object that has mass and is moving will have a kinetic energy.

**Potential energy** (**PE**) is the energy stored in a system; it can be understood as the potential for an object to gain kinetic energy. There are several types of potential energy.

- **Electric potential energy** is derived from the interaction between positive and negative charges.
- Compressing a spring stores **elastic potential energy**.
- Energy is also stored in chemical bonds as **chemical potential energy**.
- The energy stored by objects due to their height is **gravitational potential energy**.

Energy can be converted into other forms of energy, but it cannot be created or destroyed. This principle is called the **conservation of energy**. A swing provides a simple example of this principle. Throughout the swing's path, the total energy of the system remains the same. At the highest point of a swing's path, it has potential energy but no kinetic energy (because it has stopped moving momentarily as it changes direction). As the swing drops, that potential energy is converted to kinetic energy, and the swing's velocity increases. At the bottom of its path, all its potential energy has been converted into kinetic energy (meaning its potential energy is zero). This process repeats as the swing moves up and down. At any point in the swing's path, the kinetic and potential energies will sum to the same value.

### PRACTICE QUESTIONS

5. Imagine a roller coaster that does not have its own power and starts on a hill at a height of 100 meters. There is no air resistance or friction. It falls down to a height of 50 meters in the first dip and begins to move up the next hill, which is 200 meters high. What will happen to the coaster on this hill?

   **A)** It will slow down but will make it over the 200 meter hill.
   **B)** It will make it 150 meters up the hill and move back down to the first dip.
   **C)** It will make it 100 meters up the hill and move back down to the first dip.
   **D)** It will make it 75 meters up the hill and move back down to the first dip.

6. A pendulum with mass *m* is swinging back and forth. Which of the following statements about the pendulum's speed is true?

   **A)** The maximum speed of the mass will occur when it's closest to the ground.
   **B)** The maximum speed of the mass will occur when it's farthest from the ground.
   **C)** The mass will always travel at the same speed.
   **D)** The maximum speed of the mass will occur when it is halfway between its lowest and highest point.

# Waves

Energy can also be transferred through **waves**, which are repeating pulses of energy. Waves that travel through a medium, like ripples on a pond or compressions in a Slinky, are called **mechanical waves**. Waves that vibrate up and down (like the ripples on a pond) are **transverse waves**, and those that travel through compression (like the Slinky) are **longitudinal waves**. Mechanical waves will travel faster through denser mediums; for example, sound waves will move faster through water than through air.

**EQUATIONS**

$v = \lambda f = \frac{\lambda}{T}$

$T = \frac{1}{f}$

$I_0 = 1 \times 10^{-12}$ W/m² (smallest intensity that can be heard by the human ear)

$DB = 10 \log\left(\frac{I}{I_0}\right)$ where $I$ = intensity

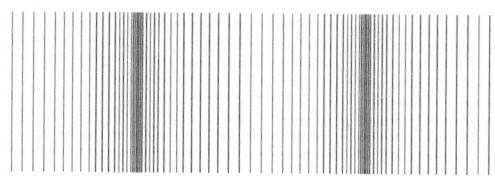

Longitudinal Wave

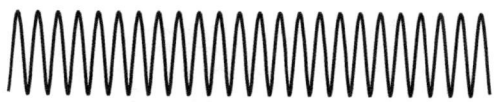

Transverse Wave

**Figure 8.3. Types of Waves**

Waves can be described using a number of different properties. A wave's highest point is called its **crest**, and its lowest point is the **trough**. A wave's **midline** is halfway between the crest and trough; the **amplitude** describes the distance between the midline and the crest (or trough). The distance between crests (or troughs) is the **wavelength**. A wave's **period** is the time it takes for a wave to go through one complete cycle, and the number of cycles a wave goes through in a specific period of time is its **frequency**.

**Sound** is a special type of longitudinal wave created by vibrations. Our ears are able to interpret these waves as particular sounds. The frequency, or rate, of the vibration determines the sound's **pitch**. **Loudness** depends on the amplitude, or height, of a sound wave.

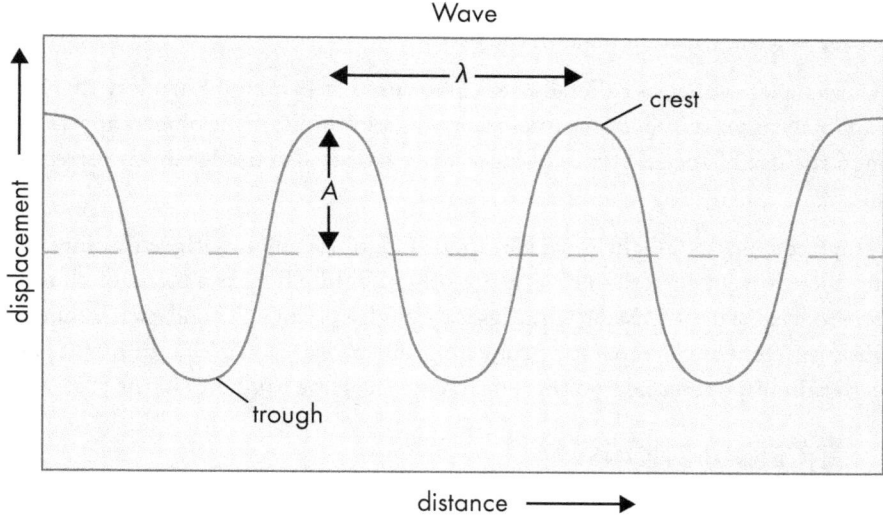

$\lambda$ = wavelength
A = amplitude

**Figure 8.4. Parts of a Wave**

**PHYSICS**

The **Doppler effect** is the difference in perceived pitch caused by the motion of the object creating the wave. For example, as an ambulance approaches an observer, the siren's pitch will appear to increase, and then as the ambulance moves away, the siren's pitch will appear to decrease. This occurs because sound waves are compressed as the ambulance approaches the observer and are spread out as the ambulance moves away from the observer.

**Electromagnetic waves** are composed of oscillating electric and magnetic fields and thus do not require a medium through which to travel. The electromagnetic spectrum classifies the types of electromagnetic waves based on their frequency. These include radio waves, microwaves, X-rays, and visible light.

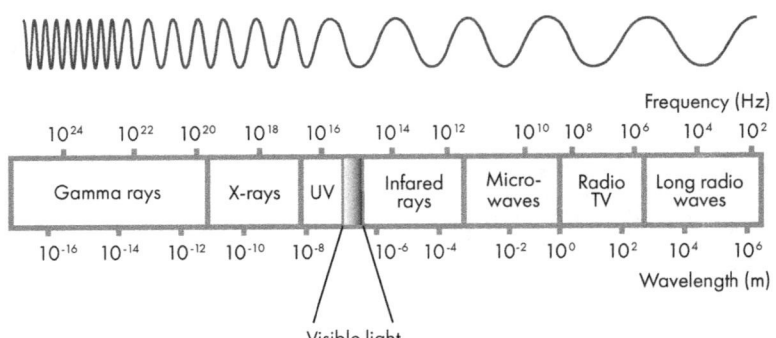

**Figure 8.5. The Electromagnetic Spectrum**

The study of light is called **optics**. Because visible light is a wave, it will display properties that are similar to other waves. It will **reflect**, or bounce off, surfaces, which can be observed by shining a flashlight on a mirror. Light will also **refract**, or bend, when it travels between substances. This effect can be seen by placing a pencil in water and observing the apparent bend in the pencil.

Curved pieces of glass called **lenses** can be used to bend light in a way that affects how an image is perceived. Some microscopes, for example, make objects appear larger through the use of specific types of lenses. Eyeglasses also use lenses to correct poor vision.

The frequency of a light wave is responsible for its color, with red/orange colors having a lower frequency than blue/violet colors. White light is a blend of all the frequencies of visible light. Passing white light through a prism will bend each frequency at a slightly different angle, separating the colors and creating a rainbow. Sunlight passing through raindrops can undergo this effect, creating large rainbows in the sky.

## PRACTICE QUESTIONS

**7.** Which type of wave is a longitudinal wave?
- **A)** ocean wave
- **B)** light wave
- **C)** sound wave
- **D)** X-ray wave

**8.** Which of the following events is caused by refraction?
- **A)** a rainbow during a rainstorm
- **B)** an echo in a cave
- **C)** a candle appearing in a mirror
- **D)** the Doppler effect

## Electricity and Magnetism

**Electric charge** is created by a difference in the balance of protons and electrons, which creates a positively or negatively charged object. Charged objects create an **electric field** that spreads outward from the object. Other charged objects in that field will experience a force: objects that have opposite charges will be attracted to each other, and objects with the same charge will be repelled, or pushed away, from each other.

**EQUATIONS**

$k = 9 \times 10^9$ N·m²/C²

$F = k\dfrac{q_1 q_2}{r^2}$

$\Delta V = Ed$

$V = IR$

$P = IV = \dfrac{V^2}{I}$

where $q$ = charge (C), $E$ = electric field (N/C), $V$ = voltage (V), $I$ = current (A), $R$ = resistance (Ω), and $P$ = power

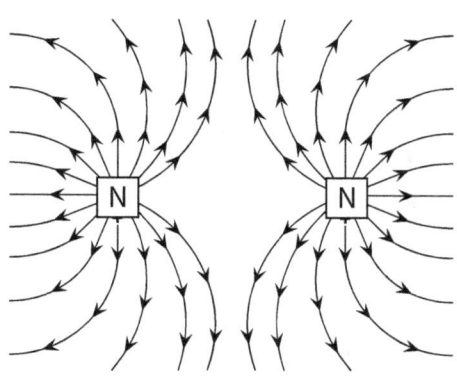

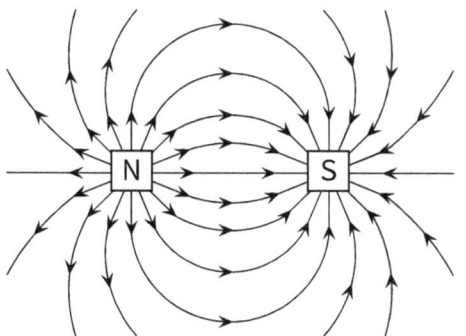

**Figure 8.6. Magnetic Field Lines**

Because protons cannot leave the nucleus, charge is created by the movement of electrons. **Static electricity**, or electrostatic charge, occurs when a surface has a buildup of charges. For example, if a student rubs a balloon on her head, the friction will cause electrons to move from her hair to the balloon. This creates a negative charge on the balloon and a positive charge on her hair; the resulting attraction will cause her hair to move toward the balloon.

**Electricity** is the movement of electrons through a conductor, and an electric circuit is a closed loop through which electricity moves. Circuits include a **voltage** source, which powers the movement of electrons known as **current**. Sources of voltage include batteries, generators, and wall outlets (which are in turn powered by electric power stations). Other elements, such as lights, computers, and microwaves, can then be connected to the circuit and then powered by its electricity.

A **resistor** is an electrical component that provides resistance to the flow of current through an electric circuit. A resistor is usually composed of a series of materials that are not conducive to electron flow. The units of resistance are Ω. According to Ohm's law, current and resistance are inversely related, and both are proportional to voltage.

Resistors in a circuit can be wired in series or in parallel. In a **series** circuit, the current can only follow one path, while in a **parallel** circuit the current can follow multiple pathways.

Table 8.1. Series and Parallel Circuits

|  | Series | Parallel |
| --- | --- | --- |
| Current | $I_1 = I_2 = I_3 = ... = I_n$ | $I_t = I_1 + I_2 + ... + I_n$ |
| Voltage | $V_t = V_1 + V_2 + ... + V_n$ | $V_1 = V_2 = V_3 = ... = V_n$ |
| Resistance | $R_t = R_1 + R_2 + ... + R_n$ | $\frac{1}{R_t} = \frac{1}{R_1} + \frac{1}{R_2} + ... + \frac{1}{R_n}$ |

**Magnets** are created by the alignment of spinning electrons within a substance. This alignment will occur naturally in some substances, including iron, nickel, and cobalt, all of which can be used to produce permanent magnets. The alignment of electrons creates a magnetic field, which, like an electric or gravitational field, can act on other objects. Magnetic fields have a north and a south pole that act similarly to electric charges: opposite poles will attract, and same poles will repel each other. However, unlike electric charge, which can be either positive or negative, a magnetic field ALWAYS has two poles. If a magnet is cut in half, the result is two magnets, each with a north and a south pole.

Electricity and magnetism are closely related. A moving magnet creates an electric field, and a moving charged particle creates a magnetic field. A specific kind of temporary magnet known as an **electromagnet** can be made by coiling a wire around a metal object and running electricity through it. A magnetic field will be created when the wire contains a current but will disappear when the flow of electricity is stopped.

## PRACTICE QUESTIONS

**9.** What part of the atom flows through a circuit to power a light bulb?
- **A)** protons
- **B)** neutrons
- **C)** electrons
- **D)** nucleus

**10.** Which metal attracts magnets?
- **A)** iron
- **B)** copper
- **C)** silver
- **D)** gold

# ANSWER KEY

1. **C) is correct.** Acceleration is the change in velocity over the change in time:
   $a = \frac{v}{t} = \frac{(5 \text{ m/s} - 0 \text{ m/s})}{1 \text{ s}} = $ **5 m/s²**

2. **A) is correct.** The driver's body will continue moving forward due to inertia. A force is required to slow the driver down (Newton's first law).

3. **C) is correct.** A person sitting in a chair is not accelerating. All the other choices describe objects that are accelerating, or changing velocity.

4. **B) is correct.** A steep hill requires a large force to counter the gravitational force. The large distance will also lead to a large amount of work done. Less work is done in choice C), and no work is done in choice A). Choice D) is incorrect because painting the car is "work," but not the technical definition of work. The car is not moving while being painted, so no work is done on the car.

5. **C) is correct.** Its maximum energy is from its starting point, the potential energy at 100 meters, so it can never move higher than 100 meters.

6. **A) is correct.** The mass always has the same total energy. When the height is the lowest, the potential energy is at its minimum, and so the kinetic energy is at its maximum. When kinetic energy is high, the mass's velocity will be at its height.

7. **C) is correct.** Sound waves are longitudinal waves because the vibrations travel in the same direction as the energy.

8. **A) is correct.** The light of the sun hits rain droplets and bends into a band of colors. The bending of waves is refraction.

9. **C) is correct.** Electrons are negatively charged subatomic particles that exist outside the nucleus of an atom. A power source forces moving electrons through a circuit.

10. **A) is correct.** Magnets readily attract iron. The other metals are not attracted to magnets.

# NINE: PRACTICE TEST

## Mathematics

Directions: Work the problem carefully, and choose the best answer.

1. Solve: $8x + 2 = 3x + 17$
   A) −3
   B) 3
   C) 5
   D) −6

2. A pharmacy technician fills 13 prescriptions in 30 minutes. At that rate, how many prescriptions can he fill in a 7-hour shift?
   A) 91
   B) 45
   C) 182
   D) 208

3. The diameter of a round table is 60 inches. What is the diameter of the table in meters?
   A) 1.667 m
   B) 2.5 m
   C) 1.524 m
   D) 0.75 m

4. Alice ran $3\frac{1}{2}$ miles on Monday, and she increased her distance by $\frac{1}{4}$ mile each day. What was her total distance from Monday to Friday?
   A) $17\frac{1}{2}$ mi
   B) 20 mi
   C) $18\frac{1}{2}$ mi
   D) 19 mi

5. $75.00 − $39.73 =
   A) $36.73
   B) $46.27
   C) $44.73
   D) $35.27

6. Simplify the following expression:
   $5 − 7(3^2 − 4)$
   A) −5
   B) 1
   C) −9
   D) −30

**7.** Fried's rule for computing an infant's dose of medication is:

$$\frac{\text{child's age in months} \times \text{adult dosage}}{150}$$

If the adult dose is 25 milligrams, how much should be given to a one-and-a-half-year-old child?

- **A)** 3 mg
- **B)** 6 mg
- **C)** 4 mg
- **D)** 5 mg

**8.** Cotton swabs can be ordered in boxes of 125. If the doctor's office needs to order 4,250 cotton swabs, how many boxes should be ordered?

- **A)** 34 boxes
- **B)** 17 boxes
- **C)** 42 boxes
- **D)** 40 boxes

**9.** Simplify the following expression:

$16 + 10 \div 2$

- **A)** 13
- **B)** 21
- **C)** 19
- **D)** 11

**10.** Find the total weight of three cartons weighing 6.5 kilograms, 3.59 kilograms, and 2 kilograms.

- **A)** 4.26 kg
- **B)** 0.91 kg
- **C)** 10.11 kg
- **D)** 12.09 kg

**11.** Solve: $-9b - 4 = 2b + 7$

- **A)** 11
- **B)** 3
- **C)** −1
- **D)** 1

**12.** Evaluate the following expression for $a = -10$: $\frac{a^2}{4 - 3a + 4}$

- **A)** 54
- **B)** 9
- **C)** −1
- **D)** 59

**13.** A carpenter is planning to add wood trim along three sides of a doorway. The sides of the doorway measure $7\frac{1}{2}$ feet, $2\frac{5}{8}$ feet, and $7\frac{1}{2}$ feet. How much wood trim is needed?

- **A)** $16\frac{5}{8}$ ft
- **B)** $17\frac{5}{8}$ ft
- **C)** $16\frac{1}{2}$ ft
- **D)** $17\frac{1}{2}$ ft

**14.** Which of the following rational numbers is the least?

- **A)** $-3\frac{1}{3}$
- **B)** 2.73
- **C)** 0
- **D)** $-\frac{24}{5}$

**15.** What fraction is equivalent to 0.7?

- **A)** $\frac{7}{5}$
- **B.** $\frac{3}{10}$
- **C)** $\frac{7}{10}$
- **D)** $\frac{7}{100}$

**16.** The average high temperature in Paris, France, in July is 25°C. Convert the temperature to Fahrenheit.

- **A)** 13°F
- **B)** 43°F
- **C)** 77°F
- **D)** 57°F

17. Evaluate the following expression for $x = -7$, $y = -9$, and $z = -4$: $x + y - z$
    A) −2
    B) 6
    C) −12
    D) 8

18. In a class of 25 students, four students were absent. What percent of the students were absent?
    A) 4%
    B) 16%
    C) 21%
    D) 84%

19. A patient's chart indicates that she was administered pain medication at 1400 hours. The patient can have another dose in 4 hours. At what time can the patient have another dose?
    A) 8:00 p.m.
    B) 12:00 a.m.
    C) 6:00 p.m.
    D) 2:00 p.m.

20. The ratio of fiction to nonfiction books in a small public library is 2 to 5. If there are 735 total books in the library, how many are fiction?
    A) 294 books
    B) 210 books
    C) 184 books
    D) 257 books

21. A food label says that the box holds 2.5 servings. How many boxes would be needed to provide 10 servings?
    A) 4 boxes
    B) 25 boxes
    C) 10 boxes
    D) 6 boxes

22. In 2016, LeBron James averaged 26.4 points per game over 74 games. How many points did James score that year? (Round to the nearest whole number.)
    A) 1954 points
    B) 2803 points
    C) 100 points
    D) 2640 points

23. A patient weighs 110 pounds. What is her weight in kilograms?
    A) 55 kg
    B) 50 kg
    C) 11 kg
    D) 20 kg

24. If $285.48 will be shared equally by six people, how much will each person receive?
    A) $1712.88
    B) $47.58
    C) $885.46
    D) $225.48

25. A hardcover best-selling book is on sale for $18. If the book is discounted 25%, what was its original price?
    A) $20.50
    B) $24.00
    C) $4.50
    D) $30.00

26. One day during flu season, 23% of a company's staff was absent. If the company employs 127 people, how many staff members were present on that day? (Round your answer to the nearest whole number.)
    A) 98 people
    B) 29 people
    C) 104 people
    D) 46 people

27. What is $\frac{2}{3}$ of $\frac{3}{10}$?
    A) $\frac{9}{20}$
    B) $\frac{5}{13}$
    C) $\frac{2}{5}$
    D) $\frac{1}{5}$

28. A nurse records a patient's vital signs during a 3:00 p.m. to 11:00 p.m. shift. The clock in the patient's room reads 6:45. What time should be written in the patient's chart?
    A) 0645
    B) 1845
    C) 1645
    D) 1045

29. $\frac{1}{2} \div \frac{2}{3} =$
    A) $\frac{1}{3}$
    B) $\frac{3}{4}$
    C) $\frac{3}{5}$
    D) $\frac{5}{6}$

30. On a history test, Robert answered fifteen questions correctly. If he answered approximately 94% of the questions correctly, how many questions were on the test?
    A) 20 questions
    B) 25 questions
    C) 16 questions
    D) 32 questions

31. Solve: $12x + 5 = 77$
    A) −6
    B) 6
    C) 10
    D) 8

32. Simplify the following expression:
    $\frac{4x^2}{2x} + 7x$
    A) $11x^2$
    B) $2x^3 + 7$
    C) $2x + 7$
    D) $9x$

33. Convert 0.64 to a fraction in lowest terms.
    A) $\frac{8}{125}$
    B) $\frac{16}{25}$
    C) $\frac{2}{3}$
    D) $\frac{4}{5}$

34. Solve: $5(x + 3) - 12 = 43$
    A) 8
    B) 12
    C) 9
    D) 10

35. $7\frac{1}{3} \div \frac{4}{5} =$
    A) $9\frac{1}{6}$
    B) $5\frac{13}{15}$
    C) $\frac{6}{55}$
    D) $\frac{15}{88}$

36. Marcus works maintenance for a large apartment complex. He averages $\frac{2}{3}$ hour per maintenance call. How many calls can he take in an 8-hour work day?
    A) 6 calls
    B) 12 calls
    C) 24 calls
    D) 36 calls

**37.** How many fluid ounces are in a 300-milliliter bottle of shampoo?

  **A)** 10.15 fl oz
  **B)** 101.5 fl oz
  **C)** 8.87 fl oz
  **D)** 20.7 fl oz

**38.** Solve: $\frac{x}{4} + \frac{2}{3} = \frac{29}{12}$

  **A)** 5
  **B)** 12
  **C)** 7
  **D)** 10

**39.** Carlos spent $1.68 on bananas. If bananas cost 48 cents per pound, how many pounds of bananas did he buy?

  **A)** 2.06 lb
  **B)** 1.2 lb
  **C)** 8.1 lb
  **D)** 3.5 lb

**40.** Angelica bought a roast weighing 3.2 pounds. If the roast cost $25.44, how much did it cost per pound?

  **A)** $5.95
  **B)** $7.95
  **C)** $7.44
  **D)** $8.14

**41.** The instructions for an over-the-counter liquid medication say to take 15 milliliters every four hours. If Janice has only standard measuring spoons, how many teaspoons of the medication should she take? (Note: 1 m = 0.2 tsp)

  **A)** 7.5 tsp
  **B)** 2 tsp
  **C)** 3 tsp
  **D)** 1.5 tsp

**42.** Simplify the following expression:
$3xy(x^2 - 11xy + 10y^2)$

  **A)** $3x^4y^4$
  **B)** $3x^3y - 33x^2y^2 + 30xy^3$
  **C)** $3x^3y - 11xy + 10y^2$
  **D)** $3x^3y + 33x^2y^2 - 30xy^3$

**43.** Simplify the following expression:
$\frac{10x^9y^6}{5x^3y^2}$

  **A)** $2x^6y^4$
  **B)** $2x^3y^3$
  **C)** $5x^3y^3$
  **D)** $5xy$

**44.** Find 9% of 81.

  **A)** 9
  **B)** 7.29
  **C)** 90
  **D)** 72

**45.** An old TV ad states, "Four out of five dentists surveyed recommend sugarless gum for their patients who chew gum." If 450 dentists were surveyed, how many recommended sugarless gum?

  **A)** 360 dentists
  **B)** 400 dentists
  **C)** 50 dentists
  **D)** 90 dentists

**46.** $17 - 4\frac{3}{5} =$

  **A)** $6\frac{1}{5}$
  **B)** $13\frac{2}{5}$
  **C)** $12\frac{2}{5}$
  **D)** $13\frac{3}{5}$

47. Terrence has 63 hours of sick leave. If he donates 15.75 hours to a coworker with a long-term illness, how much sick leave does he have left?
    A) 78.75 hr
    B) 48.75 hr
    C) 15.12 hr
    D) 47.25 hr

48. $(-9)(-4) =$
    A) $-13$
    B) $13$
    C) $-36$
    D) $36$

49. $-2(11) =$
    A) $22$
    B) $-22$
    C) $18$
    D) $-18$

50. $8.653 + 2 + 1.06 =$
    A) $8.761$
    B) $11.713$
    C) $9.715$
    D) $9.913$

51. $\frac{1}{2} + \frac{5}{6} - \frac{3}{4} =$
    A) $\frac{7}{12}$
    B) $\frac{3}{4}$
    C) $\frac{7}{36}$
    D) $\frac{25}{36}$

52. The electric company uses the formula $C = 0.057k + 23.50$, where $k$ represents the number of kilowatt-hours used by the customer, to determine the amount of a customer's bill. Find the bill amount for a customer who uses 1210 kilowatt-hours.
    A) $68.97
    B) $713.20
    C) $30.40
    D) $92.47

53. Jim is taking care of 8 patients during his shift. So far it has taken him 25 minutes to see two patients. At this rate, how long will it take Jim to check in on all 8 patients?
    A) 2 hr
    B) 50 min
    C) 100 min
    D) 1 hr

54. Jack missed 5% of 260 work days last year, some for illness and some for vacation. How many days did Jack work?
    A) 13 days
    B) 208 days
    C) 247 days
    D) 255 days

55. A patient enters the emergency room at 11:15 a.m. The patient is discharged 4 hours later. Express the time the patient left the ER in military time.
    A) 1515
    B) 0315
    C) 0515
    D) 0715

# Reading

Directions: Read the passage carefully, and then read the questions that follow and choose the most correct answer.

The endocrine system is made up of glands—such as the parathyroid, thyroid, pituitary, and adrenals—that produce hormones. Men and women have different reproductive glands: men have testes and women have ovaries. The pituitary gland serves as the "master gland" of the endocrine system.

The endocrine system's function is to produce and distribute hormones. Endocrine glands release hormones into the bloodstream, where they are carried to other tissues or organs. When the hormones reach other tissues, they catalyze certain chemical reactions, stimulating various processes or activities. For instance, hormones are responsible for important bodily processes such as puberty and menstruation. Hormones are also released in humans in moments of fear or anxiety and can trigger the fight-or-flight response. The endocrine system is the primary source of a wide range of physiological activities and is sometimes referred to as the "hardworking chemical control center" of the human body.

1. What is the best summary of the passage?
   A) The endocrine system controls hormones that stimulate processes in the body.
   B) Endocrine glands differ in men and women.
   C) The pituitary gland is the "master gland" of the endocrine system.
   D) Hormones are responsible for puberty and menstruation.

2. What is the author's primary purpose in writing this essay?
   A) to warn people about the dangers of hormonal imbalance
   B) to persuade people to take care of their endocrine glands
   C) to advise people about different hormones and what they do
   D) to inform people about the endocrine system's parts and functions

3. What is the meaning of the word *stimulating* in the second paragraph?
   A) to make something happen
   B) to reproduce something
   C) to create fear or anxiety
   D) to destroy or diminish a tissue

4. Which of the following statements can be considered a statement of FACT according to the content offered in the paragraphs above?
   A) The endocrine system is the most important system in the human body.
   B) The endocrine system is the only "chemical control center in the body."
   C) The endocrine system only has one organ: the pancreas.
   D) The endocrine system stimulates reactions in the body by releasing hormones.

5. According to the passage, what is true about hormones?
   A) They are only secreted by the pancreas.
   B) They can help trigger fight-or-flight responses.
   C) They almost always cause negative reactions.
   D) Their sole purpose is to stimulate reproductive activities.

6. According to the passage, what serves as the major organ associated with the endocrine system?
   A) the pituitary gland
   B) the testicles
   C) the ovaries
   D) the spinal cord

Every medical professional should understand the root causes and potential effects of hypoglycemia because it can actually be a matter of life or death for a patient with diabetes. Hypoglycemia—which literally means low (*hypo*) blood sugar (*glycemia*)—is one of the most common medical emergencies for patients who have diabetes. Hypoglycemia can occur when a patient either takes too much insulin or has not consumed enough sugar. At other times, hypoglycemia stems from overexertion. A person can even become hypoglycemic if they vomit an important meal, depriving the body of the sugar and nutrients it needs to stay balanced.

Any medical professional interacting with diabetic patients should know the telltale signs of hypoglycemia. When a diabetic patient's blood sugar plummets, their mental state becomes altered. This can lead to unconsciousness or, in more severe cases, a diabetic coma and/or brain damage. If you notice the rapid onset of nervousness or anxiety, shakiness, and/or profuse sweating in someone with diabetes, you will likely need to help administer glucose to them as soon as possible (as long as they are conscious enough to swallow). Most diabetic patients manage their condition by using glucometers.

Glucometers measure the level of glucose in the bloodstream. During a potential hypoglycemic episode, if at all possible, ask the person if they have used their glucometer lately or encourage them to use it immediately. If the person is still cognizant but looks "out of it," you may have to assist in the process. A blood glucose value of less than 80 milligrams per deciliter can be considered a hypoglycemic episode. This kind of reading would prompt a swift glucose administration and, in worst-case scenarios, a trip to the emergency room.

**7.** What is the main idea of the passage?

**A)** Medical professionals should know what causes hypoglycemia and how to manage it.

**B)** Glucometers help patients with diabetes monitor their glucose levels.

**C)** Patients with diabetes can slip into a diabetic coma if they do not monitor their glucose levels.

**D)** Profuse sweating is one of the most telltale signs of a hypoglycemic episode.

**8.** Which of the following is NOT listed as a detail in the passage?

**A)** Glucometers help patients and medical professionals measure the level of glucose in the bloodstream.

**B)** Any blood glucose value that reads less than 80 milligrams per deciliter can be considered a hypoglycemic episode.

**C)** Only people with diabetes can become hypoglycemic.

**D)** Hypoglycemia literally means low (*hypo*) blood sugar (*glycemia*).

**9.** What is the author's primary purpose in writing this essay?

**A)** to inform health care workers and the public about the symptoms of hypoglycemia and how to respond to it

**B)** to persuade people to purchase more glucometers so that they can properly handle all hypoglycemic episodes

**C)** to dramatize a hypoglycemic episode so readers will know what to expect if they encounter a patient with diabetes who is undergoing one

**D)** to recount a time when a medical professional failed to properly respond to a hypoglycemic episode

**10.** What is the meaning of the word *administer* in the second paragraph?

**A)** adorn

**B)** give

**C)** revive

**D)** withdraw

**11.** Which of the following statements can the reader infer from the passage?

- **A)** Diabetic comas, which can be triggered by untreated episodes of hypoglycemia, can cause permanent brain damage.
- **B)** Glucometers are too expensive for most diabetic patients to purchase, making cases of hypoglycemia frequent.
- **C)** Medical professionals should ignore the personal perspectives of people experiencing hypoglycemic episodes.
- **D)** Diabetes is a dangerous disease that cannot be managed properly.

**12.** Which of the following statements is a fact stated in the passage?

- **A)** Profuse sweating is the number one sign that tells a medical professional a hypoglycemic episode has concluded.
- **B)** Any blood glucose value that reads less than 80 milligrams per deciliter can be considered a hypoglycemic episode.
- **C)** Most diabetic patients do not know how to monitor their own condition, so health care workers must help them.
- **D)** Most personal glucometers are outdated, and medical professionals should purchase their own.

Communicating with any human being in crisis—whether that crisis is physical or emotional—is going to be more difficult than normal, everyday communication. Thus, emergency responders and medical practitioners, like many other social service providers, need to learn how to be sensitive in interpersonal communication. Here are some tips about how to hone your craft as a communicator while working with people in crisis. These tips can also be used for everyday communication.

First, it is essential that you are aware of cultural differences. In some cultures, direct eye contact can be unsettling or disrespectful. People from different cultures may have different comfort levels with personal space: some might find physical closeness comforting; others might find it threatening. Your body language speaks volumes. Be sure you are aware of the symbolic nature of your posture, hand motions, and gestures.

It is also important to enunciate your verbal statements and directions in a clear, relevant way. Use terminology and directions that a patient will understand, and avoid lofty medical jargon. Believe it or not, you also want to be honest with the person in crisis, even if the conditions are dire. Also explain, if possible, what you might do to help alleviate even the most drastic conditions so that the person feels supported. Lastly, and most importantly, be prepared to listen. Even if there is a language barrier, condition, or disability limiting your communication with the person in crisis, try to position yourself as an active listener. These tips will help you support people who need clarity and sensitivity.

**13.** What is the meaning of the phrase *speaks volumes* in the second paragraph?

- **A)** talks too much
- **B)** reads instructions
- **C)** communicates many things
- **D)** reads novels in several volumes

**14.** According to the passage, what do most people in crisis need?

- **A)** medical care
- **B)** psychological counseling
- **C)** cultural understanding
- **D)** sensitivity and clarity

15. Which of the following statements can be considered a statement of FACT according to the content offered in the paragraphs above?

    A) Most people cannot handle it if you look them in the eye and tell "dire" truths.

    B) Communicating with someone in crisis is more difficult than normal communication.

    C) The most important part of sensitive communication is establishing physical contact.

    D) Communicating with patients is not as important as dealing quickly with their injuries.

16. According to the passage, what is true about cultural differences?

    A) People from most cultures can recognize a thumbs-up gesture.

    B) In some cultures, people are uncomfortable with direct eye contact.

    C) When a crisis occurs, cultural differences usually disappear.

    D) No matter what someone's culture is, everyone needs a hug in a crisis.

17. What is the best summary of the passage?

    A) In some cultures, direct eye contact can be unsettling or disrespectful.

    B) Posture, hand motions, and gestures can symbolize respect or disrespect.

    C) Medical practitioners must learn to be sensitive with people who are in crisis.

    D) Medical practitioners should give clear directions and avoid using lofty medical jargon.

18. What is the author's primary purpose in writing this essay?

    A) to warn people about the dangers of disrespectful communication

    B) to persuade medical personnel to speak only when it is necessary

    C) to tell an interesting story about a paramedic who offended a patient

    D) to advise medical practitioners about communicating with patients in crisis

---

A variety of environmental factors can inhibit the body's ability to naturally keep itself cool. Humid conditions, for instance, mean that sweat evaporates slowly, reducing the body's ability to radiate heat. On the other hand, extremely dry heat may encourage people to push beyond their normal boundaries of exertion because they do not "feel" the heat as much as in humid environments. Overexertion in either moist or dry heat forces the body to alter its heat-coping mechanisms, placing people at risk of experiencing heat cramps, heat exhaustion, or heat stroke. These physiological responses to heat exposure can impair important bodily functions and can even result in death.

Heat cramps occur when an excessive amount of water and salts are released from the body—in the form of sweat—in hot conditions. Prolonged loss of water and salts will lead to muscle cramps, usually in the legs or abdomen. Excessive loss of fluids and salts can also lead to heat exhaustion, a state in which a person experiences shallow breathing, an altered mental state, unresponsiveness, dizziness or faintness, and/or moist and cool skin. These symptoms occur as a result of circulatory dysfunction; the overexposure to heat combined with the loss of fluids disrupts normal blood flow.

If not addressed promptly, heat exhaustion can lead to heatstroke, which is a life-threatening heat-exposure emergency. Heatstroke occurs when the body gets so overheated that it becomes hyperthermic; the patient stops sweating and the skin becomes hot and can appear flushed. Heatstroke can lead to loss of consciousness, muscle twitching, seizures, or even cardiac arrest. For these reasons, it is essential to immediately remove a person experiencing heat exposure from the hot environment so they can cool off and replenish fluids. The best prevention for heat-exposure illnesses is to limit time spent in the heat (for example, by taking frequent breaks), limit exertion, and hydrate regularly.

**19.** What is the main idea of the passage?

**A)** Heat exhaustion can lead to heatstroke, a life-threatening emergency.

**B)** A range of environmental conditions can prevent the body from cooling itself.

**C)** The best prevention for heat exposure is to limit time spent in the heat.

**D)** Overexposure to heat can lead to circulatory dysfunction.

**20.** Which of the following is NOT listed as a detail in the passage?

**A)** Humidity can cause sweat to evaporate too slowly, and this can impede natural cooling.

**B)** Dry heat may allow people to overexert themselves because they do not "feel" the heat.

**C)** Heat cramps occur when people drink too much water before exercising.

**D)** A hyperthermic patient stops sweating and has hot skin that looks flushed.

**21.** What is the author's primary purpose in writing this essay?

**A)** to inform readers about symptoms of heat exposure and how to respond to it

**B)** to persuade older readers to move to regions with cooler climates

**C)** to dramatize a hyperthermic episode so readers will know what to expect if they treat a patient who is undergoing one

**D)** to recount a time when a medical professional failed to properly respond to a hyperthermic episode

**22.** What is the meaning of the word *inhibit* in the first sentence?

**A)** embarrass

**B)** cause

**C)** enhance

**D)** hinder

**23.** Which of the following statements is a FACT stated in the passage?

**A)** While heat exposure can impair important bodily functions, it rarely results in death.

**B)** A patient who is experiencing heat exposure should not be moved; instead, the hot environment should be cooled immediately.

**C)** The best treatment for heat-exposure illnesses is to acclimate to high temperatures.

**D)** A patient who has heat exhaustion may have shallow breathing, an altered mental state, and dizziness.

**24.** Which of the following statements can the reader infer from the passage?

**A)** Some people die because they do not know how dangerous overexposure to heat can be.

**B)** Most of the patients who die as a result of overexposure to heat are over sixty years old.

**C)** Athletes who train in hot climates can tolerate heat better than those who train in cooler places.

**D)** Excessive sweating is a sign that a patient is hyperthermic and needs immediate treatment.

---

Medical professionals not only have to handle physical medical emergencies; they also have to be prepared to manage behavioral emergencies. Behavioral emergencies occur when a person's behavior—an observable response to the environment—is unreasonable to the point that it disrupts normal, everyday activities. Extreme cases of a behavioral emergency may result when someone's behavior is creating a danger to themselves or others. Chronic cases of extreme behavioral emergencies may eventually be classified as a mental disorder. Psychological and behavioral effects can result from any number of illnesses; they can also be the result of a chemical imbalance, genetic disorder, or psychological disturbance. People suffering from mental disorders are at risk for increased incidents of behavioral emergencies because their behavioral patterns are typically impaired or disrupted. Consequently, medical professionals must be trained in crisis management to deal with behavioral emergencies that may increase the possibility of self-harm or interpersonal conflict. While medical practitioners must be trained for emergency situations that demand physical restraint, extreme cases of behavioral emergency may be directed to police for appropriate support.

**25.** What is the author's primary purpose in writing this paragraph?

- **A)** to warn readers about dangerous behavioral emergencies
- **B)** to persuade family members to call 911 to prevent suicides
- **C)** to advise readers about ways to treat someone who is mentally ill
- **D)** to inform readers about managing patients in behavioral emergencies

**26.** Which of the following statements can be considered a statement of FACT according to the content offered in the paragraph above?

- **A)** It is unlawful for a medical professional to attempt to treat a violent, mentally ill patient without calling for police assistance.
- **B)** When a person's actions pose a threat to him- or herself—or to others—professionals consider this an extreme form of behavioral emergency.
- **C)** People suffering from mental illness almost always cause behavioral emergencies because they cannot stop themselves from picking fights with others.
- **D)** Medical professionals with crisis-management training are better equipped to deal with behavioral emergencies than police officers are.

**27.** According to the passage, what is true of genetic disorders?

- **A)** They are one cause of mental illness.
- **B)** They do not cause mental illness.
- **C)** They almost always cause mental illness.
- **D)** They are the main cause of mental illness.

**28.** Which of the following statements can the reader infer from the passage?

- **A)** People who are mentally ill are harder to deal with than physically ill patients.
- **B)** Most people who are psychologically disturbed try to harm themselves or others.
- **C)** In a behavioral emergency, police officers may have to put handcuffs on a mentally ill person.
- **D)** Most medical professionals are unwilling or unable to cope with violent or suicidal patients.

**29.** According to the passage, when should a medical professional call for police support in dealing with a behavioral emergency?

- **A)** in every case
- **B)** very rarely
- **C)** when the medical professional needs help with physically restraining someone
- **D)** when the patient is irrational to the extent that it interferes with everyday activities

1) The thyroid is an important endocrine gland located in the neck. 2) Normally, when thyroid hormones drop below a certain level, the pituitary gland releases thyroid-stimulating hormone. 3) Once stimulated, the thyroid gland floods the body with another hormone, thyroxine. 4) Thyroxine is one of the drivers of weight loss and weight gain; it affects the increase or decrease of the metabolic rate in the body tissues. 5) However, when something goes wrong, the thyroid can either produce too much thyroxine or not enough. 6) An excess of thyroxine in the circulatory system

may result in a condition known as hyperthyroidism, which produces a rapid metabolic rate. 7) Hyperthyroidism may result in extended periods of irritability and anxiety. 8) A deficit of thyroxine in the circulatory system may result in a condition known as hypothyroidism. 9) People with hypothyroidism typically suffer from obesity and fatigue. 10) Fortunately, medications are available to help patients regulate their thyroid function when they have been diagnosed with hyperthyroidism or hypothyroidism.

**30.** Which sentence best summarizes the paragraph's main idea?

- **A)** Sentence 1: "The thyroid is an important endocrine gland located in the neck."
- **B)** Sentence 2: "Normally, when thyroid hormones drop below a certain level, the pituitary gland releases thyroid-stimulating hormone."
- **C)** Sentence 4: "Thyroxine is one of the drivers of weight loss and weight gain; it affects the increase or decrease of the metabolic rate in the body tissues."
- **D)** Sentence 10: "Fortunately, medications are available to help patients regulate their thyroid function when they have been diagnosed with hyperthyroidism or hypothyroidism."

**31.** Which of the following is NOT listed as a detail in the passage?

- **A)** When thyroid hormones drop below normal, the pituitary gland releases a hormone that stimulates the thyroid to produce more thyroxine.
- **B)** Too much thyroxine in the circulatory system is a condition called hyperthyroidism.
- **C)** Too little thyroxine in the circulatory system is a condition called hypothyroidism.
- **D)** Patients with hyperthyroidism are usually very overweight and easily tired.

**32.** What is the meaning of the word *deficit* in sentence 8?

- **A)** surplus
- **B)** trade
- **C)** insufficiency
- **D)** budget

**33.** What is the author's primary purpose in writing this paragraph?

- **A)** to inform readers about the thyroid's normal function and disorders of the gland
- **B)** to persuade readers with hypothyroidism to take medication and lose weight
- **C)** to encourage readers with thyroid disorders by telling them that medication is available
- **D)** to recount a time when a patient was successfully treated for a serious thyroid disorder

**34.** Which of the following statements is a FACT stated in the passage?

- **A)** Most older patients have either hyperthyroidism or hypothyroidism.
- **B)** Hypothyroidism is common among children who do not get enough exercise.
- **C)** Hyperthyroidism is common among young parents with busy, stressful lives.
- **D)** Medications are available to help patients regulate their thyroid function.

**35.** Which of the following statements can the reader infer from the passage?

- **A)** The pituitary gland's main function is regulating the thyroid gland.
- **B)** Thyroxine is one of the medications patients can take to regulate thyroid function.
- **C)** The prefix *hyper* means "too much" and the prefix *hypo* means "not enough."
- **D)** Hyperthyroidism is one cause of eating disorders such as anorexia and bulimia.

The spinal cord is the central messaging stem of the nervous system. Almost all sensory information the human body experiences must pass through the spinal cord in order to reach the brain. The spinal cord also coordinates reflexes, or motor responses.

When the spinal cord is cross-sectioned, it becomes apparent that it possesses an outer layer of myelinated motor and sensory axons (also referred to as white matter) and an inner layer of nerve cell bodies (gray matter). Sensory information the body takes in enters the spinal cord through neurons located on its dorsal plane (the back side). The cell bodies of these dorsally located neurons form a cluster called a dorsal root ganglion. Motor information, on the other hand, exits the spinal cord ventrally, meaning from the front side. Every nerve branch that enters and exits the spinal cord is called a nerve root.

The entire spinal cord has five regions. From top to bottom, these regions are cervical, thoracic, lumbar, sacral, and coccygeal. Each region innervates a corresponding area of the body. Spinal nerves "direct" the incoming and outgoing messages of the central nervous system, making the spinal cord the main neurological conduit of the human body.

**36.** Which of the following statements can the reader infer from the passage?

- **A)** When the human body is in pain, the spinal cord conveys that information to the brain.
- **B)** Orthopedic surgeons cross-section patients' spinal cords to treat spinal injuries.
- **C)** The coccygeal region is located near the top of the spinal cord, below the cervical region.
- **D)** Dorsally located neurons can be found on the front side of the spinal cord, near the top.

**37.** According to the passage, what is true of the spinal cord's cervical region?

- **A)** It is in the middle of the spinal cord.
- **B)** It is the lowest region of the spinal cord.
- **C)** It is at the top of the spinal cord.
- **D)** It is on the back side of the spinal cord.

**38.** What is the meaning of the word *conduit* in the last sentence?

- **A)** current
- **B)** channel
- **C)** artery
- **D)** area

**39.** Which sentence best summarizes the passage's main idea?

- **A)** "The spinal cord also coordinates reflexes, or motor responses."
- **B)** "The spinal cord is the central messaging stem of the nervous system."
- **C)** "Sensory information the body takes in enters the spinal cord through neurons located on its dorsal plane (the back side)."
- **D)** "The cell bodies of these dorsally located neurons form a cluster called a dorsal root ganglion."

**40.** What is the author's primary purpose in writing this essay?

- **A)** to show that the spinal cord is more important than other body parts
- **B)** to persuade readers to take better care of their spines and spinal cords
- **C)** to advise readers about ways to treat spinal cord disorders
- **D)** to inform readers about the spinal cord's functions and parts

**41.** According to the passage, which part of the spinal cord coordinates reflexes, or motor responses?

- **A)** the cervical region
- **B)** the lumbar region
- **C)** the back side
- **D)** the front side

Scientists only partially understand carcinogenesis—the process by which normal cells become cancer cells. Yet most scientists agree that this malignant transformation results from damaged genetic material within a cell. In a normal cell, DNA helps control processes such as mitosis, or cell division, and protein synthesis. DNA provides the "master codes" for these two biological processes.

However, cells that are becoming cancerous demonstrate disturbances in these processes. The damage to the genetic material can cause unchecked growth and reproduction, continuing to pass the abnormalities on to further generations of cells. Altered cellular programs and altered DNA can lead cancerous cells to proliferate, invade, move, or spread. Anaplasia, a process by which cells become undifferentiated, is characteristic of some cancerous tumors. Some cells even mutate in a way in which they lose elements of programmed cell death, or apoptosis. In fact, apoptosis is what causes cancer to grow at such high rates and, in some extreme cases, live indefinitely.

**42.** According to the passage, what is something scientists do NOT know?

- **A)** what happens to cells during carcinogenesis
- **B)** all aspects of the process of carcinogenesis
- **C)** the fact that damaged DNA helps to cause carcinogenesis
- **D)** the fact that normal DNA helps to control mitosis and protein synthesis

**43.** What is the meaning of the word *malignant* in the first paragraph?

- **A)** damaged
- **B)** undifferentiated
- **C)** cancerous
- **D)** fast-growing

**44.** Which sentence best summarizes the passage's main idea?

- **A)** "Scientists only partially understand carcinogenesis—the process by which normal cells become cancer cells."
- **B)** "Yet most scientists agree that this malignant transformation results from damaged genetic material within a cell."
- **C)** "In a normal cell, DNA helps control processes such as mitosis, or cell division, and protein synthesis."
- **D)** "In fact, apoptosis is what causes cancer to grow at such high rates and, in some extreme cases, live indefinitely."

**45.** Which of the following is NOT listed as a detail in the passage?

- **A)** DNA helps control mitosis, or cell division, and protein synthesis.
- **B)** Cells going through carcinogenesis show disturbances in mitosis and protein synthesis.
- **C)** Normal DNA, too, can cause abnormal unchecked growth and reproduction of cells.
- **D)** Apoptosis (losing aspects of programmed cell death) causes cancer to grow at high rates.

**46.** What is the author's primary purpose in writing this essay?

- **A)** to speculate on environmental—rather than genetic—causes for cancer
- **B)** to recount times when genetic testing saved the lives of cancer patients
- **C)** to inform readers about cause-effect relationships between genetic material and cancer
- **D)** to persuade readers to undergo genetic testing to predict whether they will develop cancer

**47.** Which of the following statements can the reader infer from the passage?

- **A)** Scientists disagree about the cause-effect relationship between damaged genetic material and carcinogenesis.
- **B)** All human diseases and disorders can be traced back to damaged DNA.
- **C)** Scientists do not yet know exactly how genetic material becomes damaged.
- **D)** Most cancerous tumors are the result of anaplasia, a process by which cells become undifferentiated.

Most people think of respiration as the mechanical exchange of air between human lungs and the environment. They think about oxygen filling up the tiny air sacs in the lungs. They think about how this process feeds the capillaries surrounding the air sacs, which then infuse the bloodstream with the oxygen it needs. They may even think about how carbon dioxide is exhaled from the lungs back into the environment. But this process—known as external respiration—is just one form of respiration that occurs in the human body. Did you know there are actually two types of respiration in humans? The second form of respiration is equally important; it is known as internal, or cellular, respiration.

Whereas external respiration centers on an exchange between the lungs and the environment, internal respiration centers on a molecular exchange between cells and capillaries. All organs inside the human body rely on cellular respiration to function properly. Cells within the organs are surrounded by thousands of tiny capillaries that act as channels for the exchange of gases. Oxygen is carried through these microscopic blood vessels, moving from red blood cells to the surrounding tissue. Additionally, built-up carbon dioxide in the tissues flows through the capillaries back to the lungs. This second form of respiration may be invisible to the human eye, but it is crucial for the maintenance of human life.

**48.** Which of the following statements can the reader infer from the passage?

- **A)** The author believes that most people know what capillaries are.
- **B)** The idea that the human lungs contain tiny air sacs is a myth.
- **C)** The term "external respiration" does not accurately describe breathing.
- **D)** The author believes that most people have never heard of internal respiration.

**49.** What is the author's primary purpose in writing this essay?

- **A)** to inform readers about external and internal respiration
- **B)** to advise readers about ways to treat patients with lung disease
- **C)** to prove that most people are ignorant about internal respiration
- **D)** to persuade readers to take better care of their lungs and other organs

**50.** How does the author define the word *capillaries* in the passage?

- **A)** "tiny air sacs" (paragraph 1)
- **B)** "two types of respiration" (paragraph 1)
- **C)** "[a]ll organs inside the human body" (paragraph 2)
- **D)** "these microscopic blood vessels" (paragraph 2)

**51.** According to the passage, external respiration is an exchange between what and what?

- **A)** the lungs and the environment
- **B)** oxygen and carbon dioxide
- **C)** capillaries and cells
- **D)** blood vessels and blood cells

**52.** Which sentence best summarizes the passage's main idea?

- **A)** "Most people think of respiration as the mechanical exchange of air between human lungs and the environment."
- **B)** "They may even think about how carbon dioxide is exhaled from the lungs back into the environment."
- **C)** "The second form of respiration is equally important; it is known as internal, or cellular, respiration."
- **D)** "Cells within the organs are surrounded by thousands of tiny capillaries that act as channels for the exchange of gases."

**53.** According to the passage, how does carbon dioxide escape during internal respiration?

- **A)** The lungs draw it into tiny air sacs.
- **B)** The lungs release it into the bloodstream.
- **C)** It travels from the tissues through the capillaries back to the lungs.
- **D)** It travels from the capillaries into the red blood cells to the tissues.

---

Scientists separate hormones into two major categories: peptide hormones and steroid hormones. Peptide hormones are made of amino acids, while steroid hormones are made of cholesterol. Two examples of peptide hormones are insulin and glucagon. Insulin decreases glucose levels in the blood, while glucagon increases glucose levels. They work together as part of a feedback system to regulate blood sugar. An increase in insulin may cause a decrease in glucagon and vice versa.

Hormone feedback systems can also involve steroid hormones. For example, testosterone is a steroid hormone that influences male secondary sexual characteristics that develop during puberty. Its level is influenced by the production of follicle-stimulating hormone (FSH) and luteinizing hormone (LH) in a negative feedback loop. The release of FSH and LH stimulates the production of testosterone. When testosterone reaches a certain level, it inhibits the production of FSH and LH. As testosterone levels fall, FSH and LH begin to be released again, starting the cycle over. A similar but more complex feedback loop occurs in women with FSH and LH stimulating the production of estrogen, resulting in the cycle of ovulation and menstruation.

---

**54.** According to the second paragraph, what happens immediately after "testosterone reaches a certain level [by rising]"?

- **A)** "[T]estosterone levels fall."
- **B)** "FSH and LH begin to be released again."
- **C)** "[I]t inhibits the production of FSH and LH."
- **D)** "[It stimulates] the production of estrogen."

**55.** What does the word *feedback* mean in the passage?

- **A)** criticism
- **B)** reaction
- **C)** advice
- **D)** opinion

# Vocabulary

Directions: Read the question and then choose the most correct answer.

1. Which word is not spelled correctly in the context of this sentence?

   The six-toed Hemingway cats are an exseption among domestic cat species, which usually have five toes.

   A) exseption
   B) domestic
   C) species
   D) usually

2. Select the meaning of the underlined word in the sentence.

   The administration of the HPV vaccination before the onset of adolescence is recommended as a precaution against the sexually transmitted human papillomavirus.

   A) warning
   B) detriment
   C) prevention
   D) diagnosis

3. Select the meaning of the underlined word in the sentence.

   The triage system gives priority to patients based on the severity of their condition.

   A) medical care
   B) transportation
   C) precedence
   D) insurance

4. A patient with co-morbidities

   A) has chronic pain.
   B) is near death.
   C) presents with two disorders.
   D) has no symptoms of a disorder.

5. Select the word that means "dependent on something else."

   The contract specified that the nurse's hiring was conditional on her passing a drug test.

   A) contract
   B) specified
   C) conditional
   D) passing

6. Select the word that best completes the sentence.

   The scaly rash on the child's forearm was a _____ of eczema.

   A) laceration
   B) manifestation
   C) treatment
   D) transmission

7. Which word means "reduce in strength"?

   A) restore
   B) dilute
   C) combine
   D) suppress

8. Select the meaning of the underlined word in the sentence.

   A constant prone state, coupled with respiratory co-morbidities, may lead to pneumonia.

   A) excited
   B) flat
   C) unconscious
   D) uncomfortable

9. Select the meaning of the underlined word in the sentence.

   Excess consumption of salt can cause patients to <u>retain</u> water.

   A) excrete
   B) shed
   C) filter
   D) hold

10. Select the meaning of the underlined word in the sentence.

    <u>Excessive</u> supplements can be harmful and may interfere with the effectiveness of medications.

    A) too many
    B) a variety of
    C) prescribed by a doctor
    D) taken orally

11. Select the word that best completes the sentence.

    She was told that the procedure would be endoscopic and therefore minimally _____ .

    A) effective
    B) invasive
    C) inflamed
    D) expensive

12. Which word is not spelled correctly in the context of this sentence?

    Tests of mental ability in the elderly often include recalling the placment of objects.

    A) ability
    B) recalling
    C) placment
    D) objects

13. What best describes the term *predispose*?

    A) to get rid of
    B) to wash thoroughly
    C) to make susceptible
    D) to have a poor attitude

14. Select the meaning of the underlined word in the sentence.

    <u>Asymmetric</u> moles are often indications of an underlying pathology.

    A) patterned
    B) unbalanced
    C) circular
    D) aligned

15. Select the meaning of the underlined word in the sentence.

    The patient asked the nightshift nurse for a <u>soporific</u>.

    A) stimulant
    B) muscle relaxer
    C) sleeping pill
    D) anti-diarrheal

16. A collateral blood vessel is a vessel that

    A) carries blood from the limbs to the heart.
    B) moves blood around vessels that are impaired.
    C) is easily obstructed by blood clots.
    D) has been damaged by trauma.

17. What best describes the term *syndrome*?

    A) a disease that is getting worse
    B) a set of symptoms characteristic of a disease
    C) a series of tests used to diagnose an illness
    D) a condition inherited from a parent

18. Select the meaning of the underlined word in the sentence.

    Many pharmacists recommend taking vitamin B-12 sublingually to promote absorption.

    A) by mouth
    B) with meals
    C) under the tongue
    D) after eating

19. Select the word that best completes the sentence.

    The Ebola virus is a(n) _____ disease requiring strict protocols to prevent its spread.

    A) asymptomatic
    B) neurologic
    C) innocuous
    D) pathogenic

20. When a physician orders a hematologic study on a patient,

    A) a study will be conducted on the patient's neurovascular system.
    B) the nurse will take the patient's blood pressure.
    C) the lab will do a blood workup on the patient.
    D) the lab will examine the patient's urine for blood.

21. Select the meaning of the underlined word in the sentence.

    Health care workers must remain poised, professional, and pragmatic under pressure.

    A) practical
    B) logical
    C) emotional
    D) aloof

22. Select the meaning of the underlined word in the sentence.

    After extensive physical therapy, the patient was once again ambulatory.

    A) healthy
    B) recovered
    C) symptomatic
    D) walking

23. A room equipped with special acoustic equipment may be used for

    A) cardiovascular procedures.
    B) procedures related to sound or hearing.
    C) oral surgery.
    D) ocular surgery.

24. Select the meaning of the underlined word in the sentence.

    Progress is being made in developing effective treatments for triple-negative breast cancer.

    A) an agreement
    B) an improvement
    C) a decision
    D) a description

25. Select the word that means "severe and destructive."

    The virulent infection worsened rapidly, and the patient was admitted to the Intensive Care Unit.

    A) virulent
    B) worsened
    C) admitted
    D) Intensive

**26.** Which word means "the tearing of soft body tissue resulting in a wound"?
- **A)** paroxysmal
- **B)** precipitous
- **C)** laceration
- **D)** surgical

**27.** Select the meaning of the underlined word in the sentence.

Some medicines are best administered via a transdermal patch.
- **A)** in the muscle
- **B)** under the tongue
- **C)** through the skin
- **D)** in the mouth

**28.** Select the meaning of the underlined word in the sentence.

Dysfunctional bureaucracies in a hospital can endanger patients.
- **A)** vast
- **B)** expensive
- **C)** intricate
- **D)** flawed

**29.** What is the best description of the term *external*?
- **A)** totally open
- **B)** hidden action
- **C)** occurring once
- **D)** located outside

**30.** Select the meaning of the underlined word in the sentence.

Following strokes that cause vascular damage, patients can suffer shock or heart failure.
- **A)** circulatory
- **B)** digestive
- **C)** respiratory
- **D)** endocrine

**31.** Select the meaning of the underlined word in the sentence.

The interview process was an amalgam of performance tasks, psychological tests, and one-to-one meetings.
- **A)** blend
- **B)** process
- **C)** schedule
- **D)** conference

**32.** Select the word that means "to widen."

Vasodilators are drugs that dilate blood vessels, increasing blood flow and lowering blood pressure.
- **A)** vasodilators
- **B)** dilate
- **C)** increasing
- **D)** pressure

**33.** Select the meaning of the underlined word in the sentence.

Studies show that the normal respiration rate in relaxed adults varies with cardiovascular health.
- **A)** breathing
- **B)** sleeping
- **C)** digestion
- **D)** heart beat

**34.** Select the word that means "unobstructed."

In an emergency, maintaining a patent airway is often the priority nursing intervention.
- **A)** emergency
- **B)** patent
- **C)** priority
- **D)** intervention

**35.** What best describes the term *paroxysmal*?
- **A)** occurring on the left side
- **B)** experiencing a seizure
- **C)** undergoing a procedure
- **D)** experiencing confusion

**36.** Select the meaning of the underlined word in the sentence.

Rather than showing improvement, the patient's ability to walk <u>regressed</u> after his knee replacement.
- **A)** got better
- **B)** strengthened
- **C)** worsened
- **D)** failed

**37.** When using a cannula, a nurse would be
- **A)** measuring the patient's blood pressure.
- **B)** applying compression where necessary.
- **C)** cleaning a wound of debris and dead tissue.
- **D)** inserting a thin tube into the body to drain fluid.

**38.** Which word means "unstable"?
- **A)** obverse
- **B)** enteral
- **C)** labile
- **D)** occult

**39.** Which word means "the opposite"?
- **A)** primary
- **B)** obverse
- **C)** intact
- **D)** distended

**40.** Select the word that best completes the sentence.

The patient requested a _____ drug in the hopes of getting some sleep.
- **A)** soporific
- **B)** localized
- **C)** systemic
- **D)** stimulating

**41.** Select the meaning of the underlined word in the sentence.

Many high school teachers who want to show a movie must <u>justify</u> their decision and receive approval.
- **A)** understand
- **B)** explain
- **C)** organize
- **D)** introduce

**42.** Select the meaning of the underlined word in the sentence.

Daily exercise is <u>sensible</u> for those striving for health and well-being.
- **A)** confusing
- **B)** prohibited
- **C)** necessary
- **D)** wise

**43.** A manipulation of a patient with abduction requires
- **A)** the movement of a limb away from the body's midline.
- **B)** assisting the patient with ambulation.
- **C)** palpation of the patient's peripheral arteries.
- **D)** attenuation of the heart muscle.

**44.** Select the meaning of the underlined word in the sentence.

The wound proved to be underline{superficial} and did not require sutures.

- **A)** shallow
- **B)** impressive
- **C)** gruesome
- **D)** jagged

**45.** Select the meaning of the underlined word in the sentence.

The boss succumbed to pressure from his employees and let them leave early for the holiday.

- **A)** ignored
- **B)** fought
- **C)** surrendered
- **D)** enjoyed

**46.** Select the meaning of the underlined word in the sentence.

The surgeon had to resect a portion of the intestine due to a diagnosis of volvulus.

- **A)** remove
- **B)** repair
- **C)** replace
- **D)** relocate

**47.** Select the meaning of the underlined word in the sentence.

A nutritional deficiency will slow down the bone healing process in adults and children.

- **A)** foundation
- **B)** solution
- **C)** injury
- **D)** shortage

**48.** Which word means "affecting only the surface"?

- **A)** superficial
- **B)** persistent
- **C)** transdermal
- **D)** occult

**49.** What is the best description of the term *ossify*?

- **A)** loss of bone density
- **B)** a bone fracture
- **C)** to remedy
- **D)** to harden

**50.** Select the meaning of the underlined word in the sentence.

Long-distance swimming requires attention to hydration, as excessive sweating can go unnoticed.

- **A)** measuring temperature
- **B)** maintaining cleanliness
- **C)** consuming fluids
- **D)** taking vitamins

**51.** Select the meaning of the underlined word in the sentence.

The medicine affected the patient adversely, exacerbating the pain rather than relieving it.

- **A)** consequently
- **B)** harmfully
- **C)** helpfully
- **D)** expectedly

**52.** What best describes the term *superficial*?

- **A)** concerning the face
- **B)** serious in demeanor
- **C)** thorough and complete
- **D)** on the surface

**53.** Select the meaning of the underlined word in the sentence.

Delayed recognition of subtle changes in a patient's appetite can lead to patient deterioration.

- **A)** obvious
- **B)** rapid
- **C)** slight
- **D)** large

**54.** Select the meaning of the underlined word in the sentence.

Many cardiac conditions are emergent and require immediate medical care.

- **A)** pertaining to the lungs
- **B)** pertaining to the heart
- **C)** pertaining to respiration
- **D)** pertaining to the chest

**55.** Select the word that best completes the sentence.

The patient's _____ was affected by his stroke, and he could not recall simple facts.

- **A)** hydration
- **B)** acuity
- **C)** balance
- **D)** temperament

# Grammar

Directions: Read the question and then choose the most correct answer.

1. Which of the following sentences is grammatically correct?
   A) Kiana went to class; but Lara stayed home.
   B) Kiana went to class, but Lara stayed home.
   C) Kiana went to class, Lara stayed home though.
   D) Kiana went to class but Lara stayed home.

2. Which word from the following sentence is an adverb?
   Our boss has recently hired two new employees.
   A) Our
   B) boss
   C) has
   D) recently

3. Which two words are used incorrectly in the following sentence?
   After the bus driver spoke to the passenger, she realized that she might have acted rudely.
   A) After/realized
   B) spoke/acted
   C) she/she
   D) realized/rudely

4. Which is a list of only homophones?
   A) accept, except, expect
   B) aloud, allowed, louder
   C) they're, there, their
   D) where, wear, weary

5. Which of the following sentences is grammatically correct?
   A) I'm sorry, but I can't drive any further today.
   B) I'm sorry, but I can't drive any father today.
   C) I'm sorry, but I can't drive any fatter today.
   D) I'm sorry, but I can't drive any farther today.

6. Select the best punctuation marks for the blanks in the following sentence.
   "Jean ____" I asked, "Can you come over for dinner ____"
   A) a colon and an exclamation point
   B) a comma and a question mark
   C) a semicolon and a period
   D) a period and a question mark

7. Which word is used incorrectly in the following sentence?
   Liz's love about praise was reflected in how happy she seemed during the birthday toasts in her honor.
   A) love
   B) about
   C) reflected
   D) toasts

8. Which of the following is a dependent clause?
   A) I want to get something hot to eat.
   B) Sometimes we hike in the mountains.
   C) She drives straight home every day.
   D) If you are ready to leave the party.

9. Select the best words for the blanks in the following sentence.

   Mateo was ____ busy studying for an exam ____ attend the party with his roommate.

   A) too, too
   B) two, too
   C) to, two
   D) too, to

10. Select the best words for the blanks in the following sentence.

    It is not a good idea to throw a ____ indoors; when Sam did it, he knocked over a ____ full of cereal and milk.

    A) bull, bawl
    B) bowl, ball
    C) ball, bowl
    D) bawl, bull

11. Which word from the following sentence is an adverb?

    Don't wolf down your food so hastily—you will get a stomachache.

    A) wolf
    B) food
    C) hastily
    D) stomachache

12. Select the best words for the blanks in the following sentence.

    ____ I love tomato sauces, I dislike the texture of raw tomatoes, ____ I avoid salads that contain them.

    A) Because, yet
    B) Although, so
    C) If, but
    D) So, nor

13. Which word is used incorrectly in the following sentence?

    I wish I could except your invitation, but I am going out of town that weekend.

    A) wish
    B) could
    C) except
    D) town

14. Which punctuation mark is used incorrectly in the following sentence?

    I continued, "Lets' wait until 8:00 p.m. to eat dinner."

    A) , (comma)
    B) " (opening quotation mark)
    C) ' (apostrophe)
    D) " (closing quotation mark)

15. Which of the following sentences is grammatically correct?

    A) The cat eat their food while the dog sleep in their bed.
    B) The cats eats its food while the dog sleep in their bed.
    C) The cat eat their food while the dogs sleep in their bed.
    D) The cat eats its food while the dogs sleep in their beds.

16. Select the best words for the blanks in the following sentence.

    ____ is nobody over ____. Did you think you saw someone?

    A) They're, their
    B) Their, they're
    C) They're, there
    D) There, there

**17.** Which word from the following sentence is a preposition?

Whenever they get scared, our cats hide under the bed.

- A) whenever
- B) our
- C) hide
- D) under

**18.** Which is the best way to rewrite the following incorrectly written sentence?

Walking to school, Javi's basketball was stolen by a gang of mean older boys.

- A) As Javi was walking to school, a gang of mean older boys stole his basketball.
- B) Walking to school, a gang of mean older boys stole Javi's basketball.
- C) When Javi and a gang of mean older boys were walking to school, the gang of mean older boys noticed Javi's basketball, so they stole it.
- D) Javi took his basketball to school one day, and it got stolen.

**19.** Select the best words for the blanks in the following sentence.

Finding a ____ in your sock is not enough to ruin your ____ day, I hope!

- A) whole, hole
- B) hole, whole
- C) howl, whale
- D) whale, howl

**20.** Select the best words for the blanks in the following sentence.

The ____ teammates were practicing ____ the big game on the following Friday.

- A) fore, four
- B) four, for
- C) fewer, for
- D) four, fore

**21.** Which of the following sentences is grammatically correct?

- A) My teacher and the school principal has worked together for many years.
- B) My teacher and the school principal have worked together for many years.
- C) My teacher and the school principal have been worked together for many years.
- D) My teacher and the school principal had working together for many years.

**22.** Which of the following sentences uses capitalization correctly?

- A) We're going to Austin, Texas, next weekend so that we can attend my brother's graduation.
- B) We're going to Austin, Texas, next Weekend so that we can attend my brother's Graduation.
- C) We're going to austin, Texas, next weekend so that we can attend my Brother's graduation.
- D) We're going to Austin, texas, next Weekend so that we can attend my brother's graduation.

**23.** Which word is used incorrectly in the following sentence?

How are you feeling on this sunny Saturday mourning?

- A) How
- B) feeling
- C) Saturday
- D) mourning

**24.** Which of the following sentences is grammatically correct?

- A) Is that purple jacket Shelby's or yours?
- B) Is that purple jacket Shelbys or yours?
- C) Is that purple jacket Shelby's or your?
- D) Is that purple jacket Shelby's or you?

**25.** Select the best words for the blanks in the following sentence.

My mechanic says that if a driver ____ incorrectly, he or she might eventually ____ the car's brakes by wearing them out.

- **A)** brains, bray
- **B)** brays, brain
- **C)** breaks, brake
- **D)** brakes, break

**26.** Which word is used incorrectly in the following sentence?

There was a heat wave in October, even though Summer was long over.

- **A)** wave
- **B)** October
- **C)** Summer
- **D)** long

**27.** Which word from the following sentence is a <u>subordinating</u> conjunction?

Because we love animals, our family has adopted a rescue dog and four rescue cats.

- **A)** Because
- **B)** love
- **C)** family
- **D)** and

**28.** Which of the following is a compound sentence?

- **A)** The ferryboat ride from Oakland to San Francisco does not take long at all.
- **B)** Last weekend we took the ferry to San Francisco, and we stayed in the city for two nights.
- **C)** Although the BART train is convenient, too, the ferryboat ride is more enjoyable.
- **D)** If you decide to drive over the Bay Bridge, it will probably take you far longer, and you will not enjoy being stuck in traffic.

**29.** Which word is used incorrectly in the following sentence?

You're rite: the best time to write a thank-you note is right after you receive a gift or a big favor.

- **A)** You're
- **B)** rite
- **C)** write
- **D)** right

**30.** Which of the following choices uses punctuation correctly?

- **A)** My cat Katrina isn't the only female in our home, there's Hollie the dog, and I am female, too.
- **B)** My cat Katrina isnt the only female in our home: theres Hollie the dog, and I am female, too.
- **C)** My cat Katrina isn't the only female in our home: there's Hollie the dog, and I am female, too.
- **D)** My cat Katrina isnt' the only female in our home? There's Hollie the dog, and I am female, too.

**31.** Which two words from the following sentence are homophones?

It rained hard during the afternoon, so I reined in my horse, turned her toward home, and we galloped for shelter.

- **A)** rained, reined
- **B)** It, I
- **C)** turned, toward
- **D)** horse, home

**32.** Which of the following sentences is grammatically correct?

- **A)** It is so hot today that I can scarcely bare it.
- **B)** It is so hot today that I can scarcely bore it.
- **C)** It is so hot today that I can scarcely bear it.
- **D)** It is so hot today that I can scarcely burn it.

**33.** Which of the following sentences is grammatically correct?

- A) One of my teammates hope to be the star player tonight.
- B) Two of my teammates hopes to be star players tonight.
- C) All my teammates hopes to play their best tonight.
- D) Of course, no one on our team wants to play poorly.

**34.** Which of the following sentences contains a possessive pronoun?

- A) I love thin-crust pizza topped with roasted red peppers and caramelized onions.
- B) Ana's favorite pizza is the deep-dish kind they sell at the Chicago airport.
- C) Mom makes pizza dough from scratch; it contains flour, yeast, and other ingredients.
- D) Go ahead and take the last slice—it's yours!

**35.** Select the best words for the blanks in the following sentence.

One medication _____ me poorly, but the other medication had no _____ at all.

- A) effected; affect
- B) affected; effect
- C) effected; effect
- D) affected; affect

**36.** Which of the following sentences is grammatically correct?

- A) I have about six sweaters, and the most soft one is cashmere.
- B) My softest sweater is made of cashmere.
- C) I have about six sweaters, and the softer one is cashmere.
- D) My most softest sweater is made of cashmere.

**37.** Which word is incorrectly capitalized or lowercased in the following sentence?

The Summer season is made up of June, July, and August.

- A) Summer
- B) season
- C) June
- D) August

**38.** Which word or phrase is used incorrectly in the following sentence?

We could have went out last night, but it was raining.

- A) could have
- B) went
- C) but
- D) was raining

**39.** Select the best words for the blanks in the following sentence.

After the king received a ____ wound in battle and died, his whole country was in ____ for a year.

- A) mortal, mourning
- B) mourning, mortal
- C) morning, mooring
- D) mooring, mourning

**40.** Which word is used incorrectly in the following sentence?

There are two bedrooms, a bathroom, and a sitting room in our hotel sweet.

- A) There
- B) bathroom
- C) hotel
- D) sweet

**41.** Which words from the following sentence are pronouns?

I offered to help her study for the test, but she was too busy.

- **A)** I, her, she
- **B)** offered, help, study
- **C)** to, for, but, was
- **D)** test, too, busy

**42.** Select the best word or phrase for the blank in the following sentence.

By the time Emma arrived at my house, we _____ already late for the party, so I was irritated with her.

- **A)** were
- **B)** was
- **C)** had been
- **D)** were being

**43.** Which word is used incorrectly in the following sentence?

Please bring that unsafe toy away from your little brother.

- **A)** Please
- **B)** bring
- **C)** unsafe
- **D)** brother

**44.** Which of the following sentences is grammatically correct?

- **A)** I don't think the outcome will effect me much, so I won't worry about it.
- **B)** I don't think the outcome will infect me much, so I won't worry about it.
- **C)** I don't think the outcome will inspect me much, so I won't worry about it.
- **D)** I don't think the outcome will affect me much, so I won't worry about it.

**45.** Which of the choices is a homophone for a word in the sentence below?

The new member of the royal family has a sweet smile and a poised manner.

- **A)** knew
- **B)** rayon
- **C)** sweat
- **D)** manure

**46.** Select the best words for the blanks in the following sentence.

I _____ busy studying for my exam, and my brothers _____ busy studying for theirs.

- **A)** are, are
- **B)** are, am
- **C)** am, am
- **D)** am, are

**47.** Which word is used incorrectly in the following sentence?

My elementary school principle's name was Mrs. Woodnancy.

- **A)** elementary
- **B)** school
- **C)** principle's
- **D)** Mrs.

**48.** Which word from the following sentence is an interjection?

I was considering majoring in English, but then I thought, hey, why not major in biology?

- **A)** considering
- **B)** English
- **C)** hey
- **D)** biology

**49.** Which of the following sentences is grammatically correct?

- **A)** DeQuan loves eating pizza, but meat toppings make him feel queasy.
- **B)** Though he avoids meat toppings, pizza is one of DeQuan's favorite foods.
- **C)** Meat toppings on pizza makes DeQuan feel queasy.
- **D)** Pizza is one of DeQuan's favorite foods but he can't put meat on it.

**50.** Select the best words for the blanks in the following sentence.

Our ____ says she lives by this ____: "Honesty is the best policy."

- **A)** principle, principal
- **B)** prince, principle
- **C)** principal, invincible
- **D)** principal, principle

**51.** Which of the following sentences is correctly punctuated?

- **A)** "Im so relieved that the storm is over!" Robyn exclaimed.
- **B)** "I'm so relieved that the storm is over! Robyn exclaimed.
- **C)** "I'm so relieved that the storm is over?" Robyn exclaimed.
- **D)** "I'm so relieved that the storm is over!" Robyn exclaimed.

**52.** Which word is used incorrectly in the following sentence?

Hundreds of years ago (in days of yore), if you were female, you're destiny was not yours to decide: your father, brother, or husband made all your decisions for you.

- **A)** Hundreds
- **B)** yore
- **C)** you're
- **D)** yours

**53.** Which of the following sentences is grammatically correct?

- **A)** I used flour to bake a cake, and I decorated it with flowers.
- **B)** I used flower to bake a cake, and I decorated it with flour.
- **C)** I used fleer to bake a cake, and I decorated it with flowing.
- **D)** I used flair to bake a cake, and I decorated it with flours.

**54.** Select the best word for the blank in the following sentence.

Gold is a valuable precious _____ used in jewelry, medicine, and technology.

- **A)** meddle
- **B)** medal
- **C)** mettle
- **D)** metal

**55.** Which of the following is a compound-complex sentence?

- **A)** This mug, the large, pale-blue ceramic one, is my favorite cup from which to drink coffee.
- **B)** First I pour in about two inches of coffee, and then I fill the rest of the cup with hot milk.
- **C)** Although it is not a good idea to consume sweets in the morning, I always add two teaspoons of raw sugar.
- **D)** Because caffeine keeps me awake, I can't have it in the evening, but I need one cup of coffee in the morning.

# Biology

Directions: Read the question carefully, and then choose the most correct answer.

1. Water molecules are considered polar because they:
   A) form hydrogen bonds.
   B) are held together by a covalent bond.
   C) have a high specific heat.
   D) have partial positive and negative charges.

2. Why do the tails of phospholipids not interact with water?
   A) The phospholipids' tails are too large to interact with water.
   B) Nonpolar molecules do not interact with water.
   C) Inorganic molecules interact with each other.
   D) Water molecules have a high specific heat.

3. Which of the following is found in plant cells but not in animal cells?
   A) cell wall
   B) Golgi apparatus
   C) plasma membrane
   D) proteins

4. Tay-Sachs disease is caused by a four-codon insertion that causes errors in the production of the enzyme beta-hexosaminidase. What kind of mutation causes Tay-Sachs disease?
   A) point mutation
   B) base substitution
   C) frameshift mutation
   D) deletion

5. The purpose of oxygen in the electron transport chain is to:
   A) form water.
   B) drive the proton gradient.
   C) act as the final electron acceptor.
   D) carry protons.

6. To form nucleosomes, DNA is wrapped around:
   A) histones.
   B) chromatin.
   C) centromeres.
   D) ATP.

7. In which phase of the cell cycle do chromosomes become visible?
   A) S
   B) G2
   C) interphase
   D) prophase

8. Which of the following is produced during transcription?
   A) DNA
   B) mRNA
   C) lipids
   D) proteins

9. If an egg cell has 14 chromosomes, how many chromosomes would a skin cell from the same organism contain?
   A) 7
   B) 14
   C) 28
   D) 56

10. Which type of bond holds the oxygen and hydrogen atoms in water molecules together?
    A) ionic bond
    B) covalent bond
    C) hydrogen bond
    D) metallic bond

11. Red-green color blindness is an X-linked recessive trait. If the mother is a carrier and the father is color blind, what is the percent chance that they will have a child who has red-green color blindness?
    A) 0 percent
    B) 25 percent
    C) 50 percent
    D) 75 percent

12. Organic molecules must contain which element?
    A) carbon
    B) phosphorous
    C) nitrogen
    D) oxygen

13. Where do the light reactions of photosynthesis occur in plants?
    A) mitochondria
    B) chloroplast
    C) cytoplasm
    D) vacuole

14. Which molecule is produced during the Calvin cycle?
    A) carbon dioxide
    B) glucose
    C) water
    D) ATP

15. Why is one strand of DNA synthesized in Okazaki fragments?
    A) DNA is synthesized in the 5' to 3' direction.
    B) Replication of DNA occurs one strand at a time.
    C) Synthesis of one of the strands is incomplete.
    D) Large strands of DNA cannot be ligated.

16. The primary purpose of meiosis is to:
    A) replicate DNA.
    B) grow specialized tissues.
    C) prevent mutations in DNA.
    D) produce gametes.

17. During protein synthesis, the purpose of tRNA is to:
    A) carry the mRNA to the ribosome.
    B) align the next amino acid with the growing protein.
    C) detach the finished protein from the ribosome.
    D) package the protein for transport out of the cell.

18. Cystic fibrosis is a recessive trait. If the mother does not carry the recessive gene, but the father carries a single copy, what are the chances that their child will have cystic fibrosis?
    A) 0 percent
    B) 25 percent
    C) 50 percent
    D) 75 percent

19. Which of the following is a carbohydrate?
    A) DNA polymerase
    B) vegetable oil
    C) fructose
    D) mRNA

20. Which organelle produces energy in the form of ATP?
    A) mitochondria
    B) nucleus
    C) vacuole
    D) Golgi apparatus

21. Which of the following is removed from ATP to release energy?
    A) adenosine
    B) a phosphate group
    C) oxygen
    D) an electron

22. Which of the following is found at the end of a chromosome?
    A) telomere
    B) centromere
    C) centrosome
    D) promoter

23. During meiosis, the number of chromosomes is reduced from 2n to 1n during:
    A) metaphase I.
    B) anaphase II.
    C) prophase II.
    D) telophase I.

24. Protein synthesis takes place at which organelle?
    A) nucleus
    B) vacuole
    C) ribosome
    D) chloroplast

25. How many nucleotides are in a codon?
    A) 3
    B) 4
    C) 5
    D) 6

26. During cellular respiration, electrons are carried by:
    A) NADH.
    B) ADP.
    C) cyclic AMP.
    D) glucose.

27. The codon for the amino acid methionine is AUG. Which anticodon would be found on the tRNA that carries methionine?
    A) AUG
    B) TAC
    C) UAC
    D) TUG

28. An organism has 8 pairs of chromosomes. How many chromosomes does each egg or sperm cell contain?
    A) 4
    B) 8
    C) 16
    D) 32

29. In which phase of the cell cycle is DNA replicated?
    A) G1
    B) S
    C) G2
    D) mitosis

30. When a scientist crosses a red flower with a white flower, the F1 generation has pink flowers. In this flower, the allele for red is:
    A) dominant over white.
    B) codominant with white.
    C) incompletely dominant over white.
    D) recessive to white.

# Chemistry

Directions: Read the question carefully, and then choose the most correct answer.

1. Which element has the greatest number of protons? Refer to the periodic table.
   A) $Mg^{2+}$
   B) $Br^-$
   C) $Na^+$
   D) $N^{3-}$

2. Which of the following elements will form an ion with a charge of −2? Refer to the periodic table.
   A) F and Be
   B) Cl and Br
   C) Se and Br
   D) Se and O

3. What type of bond is formed between one positively charged atom and one negatively charged atom?
   A) ionic bond
   B) hydrogen bond
   C) covalent bond
   D) metallic bond

4. A solution that contains less than the maximum amount of solute that can be dissolved in it is:
   A) heterogeneous.
   B) homogeneous.
   C) unsaturated.
   D) saturated.

5. Which of the following elements is the most electronegative?
   A) radon (Rn)
   B) tin (Sn)
   C) sulfur (S)
   D) fluorine (F)

6. Which of the following is a chemical property?
   A) viscosity
   B) density
   C) toxicity
   D) color

7. What are the coefficients needed to balance the equation below?
   $\_Pb(NO_3)_2 + \_K_2CrO_4 \rightarrow \_PbCrO_4 + \_KNO_3$
   A) 1, 1, 1, 2
   B) 2, 2, 2, 3
   C) 1, 1, 1, 1
   D) 3, 3, 3, 1

8. Which of the following is a base?
   A) $Ba(OH)_2$
   B) HCl
   C) $HClO_4$
   D) HI

9. If 10 moles of $Pb(NO_3)_2$ react completely with $K_2CrO_4$, how many moles of $KNO_3$ are produced?
   $Pb(NO_3)_2 + K_2CrO_4 \rightarrow PbCrO_4 + 2KNO_3$
   A) 2 moles of $KNO_3$
   B) 5 moles of $KNO_3$
   C) 10 moles of $KNO_3$
   D) 20 moles of $KNO_3$

10. A particular substance has a half-life of twenty days. If the initial sample was 100 g, how many grams will remain after forty days?
    A) 75 g
    B) 50 g
    C) 33 g
    D) 25 g

11. The half-life of an unknown radioactive element X is four days. How much of a 100 g sample of element X will remain after four days?
    A) 25 g
    B) 50 g
    C) 75 g
    D) 100 g

12. The identity of an element is determined by its number of:
    A) neutrons.
    B) nuclei.
    C) protons.
    D) electrons.

13. Which of the following elements will form an ion with a charge of +2? Refer to the periodic table.
    A) Ca and Mn
    B) Li and Be
    C) Na and Mg
    D) Mg and Ca

14. Which type of bond occurs when electrons are shared between two atoms?
    A) hydrogen bond
    B) covalent bond
    C) metallic bond
    D) ionic bond

15. The number of neutrons in an atom is equal to:
    A) the atomic mass minus the number of electrons.
    B) the number of protons plus the number of electrons.
    C) the number of protons minus the number of electrons.
    D) the atomic mass minus the atomic number.

16. What state of matter has a definite shape and definite volume?
    A) solid
    B) liquid
    C) gas
    D) plasma

17. Solutions that have a sour taste and react strongly with metals are:
    A) acidic.
    B) basic.
    C) neutral.
    D) salts.

18. What type of reaction is shown below?
    $2Li + Cl_2 \rightarrow 2LiCl$
    A) synthesis reaction
    B) decomposition reaction
    C) single displacement reaction
    D) double displacement reaction

19. Which of the following is a negatively charged subatomic particle?
    A) neutron
    B) proton
    C) cation
    D) electron

20. How many electrons are needed to complete the valence shell of the halogens?
    A) 1
    B) 2
    C) 6
    D) 7

21. The weak attraction between temporary dipoles creates:
    A) the London dispersion force.
    B) a hydrogen bond.
    C) dipole-dipole interactions.
    D) a covalent bond.

22. How many moles of $O_2$ are needed to produce 20 moles of $KClO_3$?
    $2KCl + 3O_2 \rightarrow 2KClO_3$
    A) 1.5 moles of $O_2$
    B) 15 moles of $O_2$
    C) 20 moles of $O_2$
    D) 30 moles of $O_2$

23. Which process occurs when a substance goes from gas to liquid, such as when dew forms on grass in the morning?
    A) condensation
    B) sublimation
    C) evaporation
    D) deposition

24. Which of the following is a heterogeneous mixture?
    A) sugar water
    B) air
    C) vegetable oil
    D) cereal in milk

25. What type of reaction is shown below?
    $2H_2O_2 \rightarrow 2H_2O + O_2$
    A) synthesis reaction
    B) decomposition reaction
    C) single displacement reaction
    D) double displacement reaction

26. Which elements have the same number of electrons in their valence shell? Refer to the periodic table.
    A) Na, K, Ca
    B) Mg, Be, Cr
    C) F, Cl, Br
    D) P, N, C

27. What type of reaction is shown below?
    $2K(s) + Cl_2(g) \rightarrow 2KCl(s)$
    A) decomposition
    B) synthesis
    C) single displacement
    D) double displacement

28. How many electrons are needed to complete the valence shell of the noble gases?
    A) 0
    B) 1
    C) 2
    D) 3

29. Which process occurs when water vapor becomes a solid?
    A) condensation
    B) sublimation
    C) evaporation
    D) deposition

30. What type of reaction is shown below?
    $Zn + CuCl_2 \rightarrow ZnCl_2 + Cu$
    A) synthesis reaction
    B) decomposition reaction
    C) single displacement reaction
    D) double displacement reaction

PRACTICE TEST

# Anatomy and Physiology

Directions: Read the question carefully, and then choose the most correct answer.

1. Which of the following heart valves prevents blood from going back into the right ventricle?
   A) aortic
   B) mitral
   C) pulmonary
   D) tricuspid

2. Which of the following is the layer of bone that houses blood vessels and nerve endings?
   A) periosteum
   B) compact bone
   C) spongy bone
   D) trabecula

3. Which part of the digestive system is the appendix attached to?
   A) stomach
   B) cecum
   C) jejunum
   D) ileum

4. Which of the following statements is anatomically correct?
   A) The knees are superior to the shoulder.
   B) The stomach is lateral to the kidneys.
   C) The fingers are proximal to the shoulders.
   D) The urethral meatus is anterior to the anus.

5. Which artery branches off directly from the aortic arch?
   A) right common carotid
   B) right subclavian
   C) pulmonary
   D) left subclavian

6. Which type of nerve allows a person to determine the temperature of an object?
   A) interneurons
   B) cranial nerves
   C) spinal nerves
   D) afferent neurons

7. Which of the following is a response by the innate immune system when tissue is damaged?
   A) The skin dries out.
   B) The temperature increases.
   C) The blood flow to the area decreases.
   D) The heart rate slows.

8. Which layer of the skin contains large numbers of blood vessels?
   A) epidermis
   B) dermis
   C) hypodermis
   D) subcutaneous

9. Which of the following is released when bone is broken down?
   A) phosphorous
   B) iron
   C) calcium
   D) zinc

10. Which part of a nerve cell holds the cellular organelles?
    A) soma
    B) dendrite
    C) axon
    D) synapse

11. Which hormone produced by the pineal gland causes drowsiness?
    A) oxytocin
    B) dopamine
    C) thyroxine
    D) melatonin

12. Where are apocrine glands of the integumentary system located?
    A) armpit
    B) hands
    C) feet
    D) abdomen

13. Which zone of the sarcomere has myosin filaments that are thick and do not shorten during muscle contraction?
    A) Z-line
    B) A-band
    C) I-band
    D) H-zone

14. Which of the following secretes progesterone and estradiol after the egg is fertilized?
    A) oocyte
    B) corpus luteum
    C) fallopian tube
    D) fimbriae

15. Which of the following describes a function of the large intestine?
    A) It absorbs approximately 25 percent of the available nutrients from food.
    B) It secretes enzymes that break down nucleic acids.
    C) It produces enzymes that regulate blood sugar level.
    D) It absorbs water and electrolytes before waste is expelled.

16. Which of the following is the largest and outermost part of the brain?
    A) pons
    B) cerebellum
    C) cerebrum
    D) thalamus

17. Which of the following connects the ribs to the sternum?
    A) costal cartilage
    B) synovial joint
    C) cardiac muscle
    D) collagen fiber

18. Which of the following is true about air in the lungs?
    A) During expiration, air completely leaves the lungs.
    B) There is always about a liter of air in the lungs.
    C) Shallow breathing does not circulate any air through the lungs.
    D) Deep breathing moves a maximum of two liters of air through the lungs.

19. Which of the following bones are directly connected to the ulna and radius?
    A) carpal
    B) metacarpal
    C) tarsal
    D) metatarsal

20. Which of the following stores oxygen to help muscles perform work under stress?
    A) myofibril
    B) transverse tube
    C) myoglobin
    D) filament

21. Which of the following provides the energy muscles need to contract?
    A) sarcolemma
    B) mitochondria
    C) myofibril
    D) sarcomere

22. Which of the following joins the left and right hemispheres of the cerebrum?
    A) corpus callosum
    B) corpus luteum
    C) corpus sulci
    D) corpus gyri

23. A patient has recently been diagnosed with a bone marrow disorder that leads to slow blood clotting. The patient is likely low in which of the following?
    A) red blood cells
    B) plasma
    C) platelets
    D) hemoglobin

24. A patient came to the emergency department complaining of severe lower back pain after a fall. Which vertebrae has the patient most likely injured?
    A) cervical
    B) thoracic
    C) cranial
    D) lumbar

25. Which of the following describes the triceps when the elbow is extended?
    A) agonist
    B) antagonist
    C) fixator
    D) synergist

26. Which of the following is the outer and most durable layer of the meninges?
    A) pia mater
    B) dura mater
    C) arachnoid mater
    D) subarachnoid space

27. What type of muscle is found in the external sphincter of the bladder?
    A) involuntary
    B) voluntary
    C) undifferentiated
    D) multinucleated

28. What is the role of the liver in digestion?
    A) It produces the bile needed to digest fats.
    B) It stores bile produced by the gallbladder.
    C) It regulates feelings of hunger.
    D) It collects the waste that is the end product of digestion.

29. Which granular leukocyte digests bacteria?
    A) neutrophil
    B) eosinophil
    C) basophil
    D) lymphocyte

30. What is the role of the thyroid gland?
    A) It controls the release of hormones from the pituitary gland.
    B) It regulates the sleep cycle.
    C) It controls the body's metabolic rate.
    D) It regulates blood sugar level.

# Physics

Directions: Read the question carefully, and then choose the most correct answer.

1. A race car accelerates from 0 miles per hour to 60 miles per hour in 4 seconds. What is the race car's acceleration?
   A) 6.7 m/s$^2$
   B) 15.0 m/s$^2$
   C) 15.7 m/s$^2$
   D) 240.0 m/s$^2$

2. A mover exerts a constant 400 newton force to push a sofa up a 10 meter-long truck ramp. How much work does the mover do?
   A) 40 J
   B) 400 J
   C) 4000 J
   D) 40,000 J

3. On Mars, the acceleration due to gravity is 3.8 meters per second squared. What is the weight of an 80 kilogram person on Mars?
   A) 0.05 N
   B) 21.1 N
   C) 304 N
   D) 3040 N

4. A radio transmitter emits what type of wave?
   A) mechanical
   B) electromagnetic
   C) longitudinal
   D) transverse

5. The International Space Station orbits Earth at 17,500 miles per hour. What is its speed in meters per second?
   A) 5000 m/s
   B) 7822 m/s
   C) 17,500 m/s
   D) 39,155 m/s

6. What is the gravitational potential energy stored in a 2.5 gram penny held over the edge of a building that is 400 meters tall?
   A) 9.8 J
   B) 98 J
   C) 980 J
   D) 9800 J

7. Electrons move through a conducting wire at a constant speed, producing a constant current. What type of field do they produce?
   A) electric field
   B) magnetic field
   C) gravitational field
   D) no field

8. What magnitude of force does a 1 kilogram object exert on the surface of the earth?
   A) 0.10 N
   B) 0.98 N
   C) 9.8 N
   D) 98 N

9. How much time does it take a 100 watt light bulb to do 100 joules of work?
   A) 0.01 s
   B) 1 s
   C) 100 s
   D) 1 hour

10. What is the intensity of a sound that delivers 0.5 watts of power to a square space with sides of 2 meters?
    A) 0.125 W/m$^2$
    B) 1 W/m$^2$
    C) 2 W/m$^2$
    D) 12.5 W/m$^2$

11. A water balloon is launched at 47 meters per second at an angle of 39 degrees above the horizontal. What is the vertical component of its velocity?
    A) 26.5 m/s
    B) 28.5 m/s
    C) 29.6 m/s
    D) 36.5 m/s

12. A child swings a tennis ball above her head on the end of a 1 meter rope. She lets go and it flies off at 2.5 meters per second. What was the centripetal acceleration of the tennis ball the moment before the girl let it go?
    A) 2.5 m/s$^2$
    B) 6.25 m/s$^2$
    C) 62.5 m/s$^2$
    D) 112.5 m/s$^2$

13. A force meter attached to a rope swinging an 88 gram baseball reads 0.5 newtons. If the rope is 80 centimeters long, what is the tangential velocity of the baseball?
    A) 2.1 m/s
    B) 4.5 m/s
    C) 21 m/s
    D) 45 m/s

14. Light entering a diamond from air at 30 degrees from the surface normal is refracted at 12 degrees. What is the index of refraction of the diamond?
    A) 2.02
    B) 2.40
    C) 3.00
    D) 2.42 × 10$^2$

15. What is the velocity of a wave with a frequency of 100 hertz and a wavelength of 400 meters?
    A) 4 m/s
    B) 4 × 10$^4$ m/s
    C) 4 × 10$^8$ m/s
    D) 3 × 10$^8$ m/s

16. A 17 nanocoulomb charge is placed 8 centimeters from a 22 nanocoulomb charge. What is the magnitude of the electric force between them? ($k = 9 \times 10^9$ N m$^2$/C$^2$)
    A) 4.21 × 10$^{-5}$ N
    B) 5.26 × 10$^{-4}$ N
    C) 4.21 × 10$^4$ N
    D) 5.26 × 10$^4$ N

17. How much resistance is required for a high-voltage power supply of 3 kilovolts to only supply 0.1 ampere?
    A) 30 Ω
    B) 30,000 Ω
    C) 300,000 Ω
    D) 30,000,000 Ω

18. Eight AA batteries of 1.5 volts are connected in series. What current flows if they are connected to a single 10 ohm resistor?
    A) 0.15 A
    B) 0.27 A
    C) 2.7 A
    D) 27 A

19. A mass triples its speed. By what factor is its kinetic energy increased?
    A) $\frac{1}{3}$
    B) $\frac{1}{9}$
    C) 3
    D) 9

20. Before being pushed across a floor, a crate is weighed on a scale as 47 kilograms. If the coefficient of friction between the crate and a rug is known to be 0.40, with what force will friction oppose the crate's motion?

   A) 74 N
   B) 84 N
   C) 174 N
   D) 184 N

21. A 0.5 kilogram ball moving at 5 meters per second bounces off a wall at 3 meters per second. What magnitude of impulse was delivered to the wall?

   A) 0.75 kg m/s
   B) 1 kg m/s
   C) 2.25 kg m/s
   D) 4 kg m/s

22. What is the magnitude of the electric field between two parallel plates separated by 2 millimeters and held at a potential difference of 30 volts?

   A) 0.06 V/m
   B) 6.0 V/m
   C) 15 V/m
   D) 15,000 V/m

23. A laser is directed at a reflective mirror 50 degrees from the normal to the mirror surface. At what angle from the normal is the beam reflected?

   A) 0°
   B) 40°
   C) 50°
   D) 90°

24. Seventeen 12 ohm resistors are connected in series. What is the total resistance of this circuit?

   A) 0.71 Ω
   B) 1.42 Ω
   C) 194 Ω
   D) 204 Ω

25. A proton in free space is being accelerated by a force of $3 \times 10^{-9}$ newtons. What electric field is present?

   A) $1.8 \times 10^{10}$ N/C
   B) $0.53 \times 10^{10}$ N/C
   C) $1.8 \times 10^{19}$ N/C
   D) $0.53 \times 10^{19}$ N/C

26. Far away from any massive objects, an asteroid moves with a constant velocity of 8 kilometers per second. What is the magnitude of the force acting on the asteroid?

   A) 0 N
   B) 9.8 N
   C) 78.4 N
   D) 78,400 N

27. A charged object with a mass of 5 kilograms is placed in a vertical electric field of $4 \times 10^4$ newtons per coulomb and released. If the object remains stationary, what is the magnitude of charge on the object?

   A) $1.23 \times 10^{-9}$ C
   B) $1.23 \times 10^{-6}$ C
   C) $1.23 \times 10^{-3}$ C
   D) 1.23 C

**28.** A friend is trying to spin a tennis ball on a string at 1 revolution per second, but does not want to exceed an angular acceleration of 1 radian per second squared. What is the shortest time it would take them to accomplish this?

- **A)** 1 s
- **B)** 3.14 s
- **C)** 6.28 s
- **D)** 10 s

**29.** Two identical waves each with an amplitude of 2 meters and a frequency of 7 hertz interfere in phase. What is the final amplitude and frequency of the resulting wave?

- **A)** 0 m, 0 Hz
- **B)** 2 m, 14 Hz
- **C)** 4 m, 7 Hz
- **D)** 4 m, 14 Hz

**30.** Light from air enters a material of $n = 1.5$ at an angle of 45 degrees from the normal. At what angle from the normal is the light inside the material?

- **A)** 0.008°
- **B)** 18.33°
- **C)** 28.13°
- **D)** 45°

# ANSWER KEY

## MATHEMATICS

1. **B)**
   $8x + 2 = 3x + 17$
   $8x = 3x + 15$
   $5x = 15$
   **$x = 3$**

2. **C)**
   30 minutes = 0.5 hour
   $\frac{13}{0.5} = \frac{x}{7}$
   $0.5x = 91$
   **$x = 182$**

3. **C)**
   $60 \text{ in} \times \frac{2.54 \text{ cm}}{\text{in}} \times \frac{1 \text{ m}}{100 \text{ cm}} = \mathbf{1.524 \text{ m}}$

4. **B)**
   $3\frac{2}{4} + 3\frac{3}{4} + 4 + 4\frac{1}{4} + 4\frac{2}{4} = 18\frac{8}{4} = 18 + 2 = \mathbf{20}$

5. **D)**
   $\$75.00 - \$39.73 = \mathbf{\$35.27}$

6. **D)**
   $5 - 7(3^2 - 4) = 5 - 7(9 - 4)$
   $= 5 - 7(5) = 5 - 35 = \mathbf{-30}$

7. **A)**
   $1\frac{1}{2}$ years = 18 months
   $\frac{18 \times 25}{150} = \mathbf{3}$

8. **A)**
   $4250 \div 125 = \mathbf{34}$

9. **B)**
   $16 + 10 \div 2 = 16 + 5 = \mathbf{21}$

10. **D)**
    $6.5 + 3.59 + 2 = \mathbf{12.09}$

11. **C)**
    $-9b - 4 = 2b + 7 \rightarrow -9b = 2b + 11$
    $-11b = 11 \rightarrow \mathbf{b = -1}$

12. **D)**
    $\frac{(-10)^2}{4} - 3(-10) + 4$
    $\frac{100}{4} + 30 + 4$
    $25 + 30 + 4 = \mathbf{59}$

13. **B)**
    $7\frac{4}{8} + 2\frac{5}{8} + 7\frac{4}{8} = 16\frac{13}{8} = 16 + 1\frac{5}{8} = \mathbf{17\frac{5}{8}}$

14. **D)**
    $-3\frac{1}{3} = -3.\overline{3}$
    $-\frac{24}{5} = -4.8$
    **$-4.8 < -3.3 < 0 < 2.73$**

15. **C)**
    $0.7 = \mathbf{\frac{7}{10}}$

16. **C)**
    $F = 1.8C + 32$
    $F = 1.8(25) + 32$
    **$F = 77°$**

17. **C)**
    $-7 + (-9) - (-4) = -16 + 4 = \mathbf{-12}$

18. **B)**
    percent = $\frac{\text{part}}{\text{whole}}$
    $\frac{4}{25} = 0.16 = \mathbf{16\%}$

19. **C)**
    1400 hours is 2:00 p.m. In 4 hours, it will be **6:00 p.m.**

20. **B)**
    If the ratio of fiction to nonfiction books is 2 to 5, the ratio of fiction to the total number of books is 2 to 7.
    $\frac{2}{7} = \frac{x}{735}$
    $7x = 1470$
    **$x = 210$**

21. **A)**
$\frac{1}{2.5} = \frac{x}{10}$
$2.5x = 10$
**x = 4**

22. **A)**
$26.4 \times 74 = 1953.6 \approx$ **1954**

23. **B)**
$110 \text{ lb} \times \frac{1 \text{ kg}}{2.2 \text{ lb}} =$ **50 kg**

24. **B)**
$\$285.48 \div 6 =$ **$47.58**

25. **B)**
$100\% - 25\% = 75\%$
$\text{whole} = \frac{\text{part}}{\text{percent}}$
$\frac{18}{0.75} =$ **24**

26. **A)**
part = whole × percent
$127 \times 0.23 = 29.21 \rightarrow 29$ people absent
$127 - 29 =$ **98**

27. **D)**
$\frac{2}{3} \times \frac{3}{10} = \frac{1}{5}$

28. **B)**
The nurse is working an afternoon/evening shift; therefore, it is 6:45 p.m., which is **1845 in military time**.

29. **B)**
$\frac{1}{2} \div \frac{2}{3} = \frac{1}{2} \times \frac{3}{2} = \frac{3}{4}$

30. **C)**
$\text{whole} = \frac{\text{part}}{\text{percent}}$
$\frac{15}{0.94} \approx$ **16**

31. **B)**
$12x + 5 = 77$
$12x = 72$
**x = 6**

32. **D)**
$\frac{4x^2}{2x} + 7x = 2x + 7x =$ **9x**

33. **B)**
$\frac{64 \div 4}{100 \div 4} = \frac{16}{25}$

34. **A)**
$5(x + 3) - 12 = 43$
$5x + 15 - 12 = 43$
$5x + 3 = 43$
$5x = 40$
**x = 8**

35. **A)**
$7\frac{1}{3} \div \frac{4}{5} = \frac{22}{3} \div \frac{4}{5} = \frac{22}{3} \times \frac{5}{4}$
$= \frac{11}{3} \times \frac{5}{2} = \frac{55}{6} = \mathbf{9\frac{1}{6}}$

36. **B)**
$8 \div \frac{2}{3} = \frac{8}{1} \times \frac{3}{2} = \frac{4}{1} \times \frac{3}{1} =$ **12**

37. **A)**
$300 \text{ ml} \times \frac{1 \text{ L}}{1000 \text{ ml}} \times \frac{1 \text{ gal}}{3.785 \text{ L}} \times \frac{128 \text{ fl oz}}{1 \text{ gal}}$
$\approx$ **10.15 fl oz**

38. **C)**
Multiply by the least common denominator to clear the fractions.
$(12)\frac{x}{4} + (12)\frac{2}{3} = (12)\frac{29}{12}$
$3x + 8 = 29$
$3x = 21$
**x = 7**

39. **D)**
48 cents = $0.48
$\$1.68 \div \$0.48 =$ **3.5**

40. **B)**
$\$25.44 \div 3.2 =$ **$7.95**

41. **C)**
$15 \text{ mL} \times \frac{0.2 \text{ tsp}}{1 \text{ mL}} =$ **3 tsp**

42. **B)**
Distribute by multiplying coefficients and adding exponents.
$3xy(x^2 - 11xy + 10y^2) =$ **$3x^3y - 33x^2y^2 + 30xy^3$**

43. **A)**
Reduce coefficients, subtract exponents.
$\dfrac{10x^9y^6}{5x^3y^2} =$ **$2x^6y^4$**

44. **B)**
part = whole × percent
$81 \times 0.09 =$ **7.29**

45. **A)**
$\dfrac{4}{5} = \dfrac{x}{450} \rightarrow 5x = 1800$
**$x = 360$**

46. **C)**
$17 - 4\dfrac{3}{5} = \dfrac{85}{5} - \dfrac{23}{5} = \dfrac{62}{5} =$ **$12\dfrac{2}{5}$**

47. **D)**
$63 - 15.75 =$ **47.25**

48. **D)**
negative × negative = positive
$(-9)(-4) =$ **36**

49. **B)**
negative × positive = negative
$-2(11) =$ **−22**

50. **B)**
$8.653 + 2 + 1.06 =$ **11.713**

51. **A)**
$\dfrac{1}{2} + \dfrac{5}{6} - \dfrac{3}{4} = \dfrac{6}{12} + \dfrac{10}{12} - \dfrac{9}{12} =$ **$\dfrac{7}{12}$**

52. **D)**
$0.057(1210) + 23.50 = 68.97 + 23.50 =$ **92.47**

53. **C)**
$\dfrac{25}{2} = \dfrac{x}{8} \rightarrow 2x = 200$
**$x = 100$**

54. **C)**
part = whole × percent
$260 \times 0.05 = 13$
$260 - 13 =$ **247**

55. **A)**
11:15 a.m. is 1115 hours.
$1115 + 400 =$ **1515**

# READING

1. **A)**
   The answer provides an adequate summary of the passage overall. The other choices only provide specific details from the passage.

2. **D)**
   The primary purpose of the essay is to inform; its focus is the endocrine system's parts and functions. It is not persuasive or cautionary.

3. **A)**
   In the second paragraph, the author writes, "When the hormones reach other tissues, they catalyze certain chemical reactions, stimulating various processes or activities." The writer then goes on to describe those activities in detail, making it clear that the hormones caused those events to occur.

4. **D)**
   In the second paragraph, the author writes, "The endocrine system's function is to produce and distribute hormones."

5. **B)**
   The author writes, "Hormones are also released in humans in moments of fear or anxiety and can trigger the fight-or-flight response." There are no sentences supporting the other claims.

6. **A)**
   In the first paragraph, the author writes, "The pituitary gland serves as the 'master gland' of the endocrine system."

7. **A)**
   The passage is about how important it is for medical professionals to understand hypoglycemia, especially when it comes to patients who have diabetes. The other answer choices are details from the passage.

8. **C)**
   This detail is not found in the passage. The passage strongly focuses on patients with diabetes, but it does not state that only those patients are affected by hypoglycemia.

9. **A)**
   The text is informative, not persuasive or dramatic. It does not recount a specific event, but simply informs the audience of potential general scenarios.

10. **B)**
    In the second paragraph, the author writes, "[Y]ou will likely need to help administer glucose to them as soon as possible." In this case, administer means to give glucose to a patient.

11. **A)**
    In the second paragraph, the author states, "When a diabetic patient's blood sugar plummets, their mental state becomes altered. This can lead to unconsciousness or, in more severe cases, a diabetic coma and/or brain damage." The reader can infer from this information that diabetic comas could cause permanent brain damage.

12. **B)**
    In the third paragraph, the author writes, "A blood glucose value of less than 80 milligrams per deciliter can be considered a hypoglycemic episode."

13. **C)**
    In the second paragraph, the author writes, "Your body language speaks volumes." The writer then goes on to detail ways that body language can convey messages (with "posture, hand motions, and gestures").

14. **D)**
    In the last sentence, the author writes, "These tips will help you support people who need clarity and sensitivity."

15. **B)**
    In the first paragraph, the author writes, "Communicating with any human being in crisis—whether that crisis is physical or emotional—is going to be more difficult than normal, everyday communication."

16. **B)**
    The author writes, "In some cultures, direct eye contact can be unsettling or disrespectful." There are no sentences supporting the other claims.

17. **C)**

    The answer provides an adequate summary of the passage overall. The other choices only provide specific details from the passage.

18. **D)**

    The primary purpose of the essay is to advise; its focus is communication with patients in crisis. It is not persuasive or cautionary, and it does not tell a story.

19. **B)**

    The passage is about heat exposure's causes and results. The other answer choices are details from the passage.

20. **C)**

    The passage does not contain this detail. The passage deals with overexposure to heat, not with results of drinking too much water.

21. **A)**

    The text is informative, not persuasive or dramatic. It does not recount a specific event, but simply informs readers about symptoms and treatment of patients experiencing overexposure to heat.

22. **D)**

    In the first sentence, the author writes, "A variety of environmental factors can inhibit the body's ability to naturally keep itself cool." In this case, inhibit means "hinder or prevent."

23. **D)**

    In the second paragraph, the author writes, "Excessive loss of fluids and salts can also lead to heat exhaustion, a state in which a person experiences shallow breathing, an altered mental state, unresponsiveness, dizziness or faintness, and/or moist and cool skin."

24. **A)**

    In the first paragraph, the author states, "[E]xtremely dry heat may encourage people to push beyond their normal boundaries of exertion because they do not 'feel' the heat as much as in humid environments. Overexertion in either moist or dry heat forces the body to alter its heat-coping mechanisms, placing people at risk of experiencing heat cramps, heat exhaustion, or heat stroke. These physiological responses to heat exposure can impair important bodily functions and can even result in death." The reader can infer from this information that ignorance about symptoms could lead people to exercise too hard in hot weather and die as a result.

25. **D)**

    The primary purpose of the essay is to inform; its focus is on managing behavioral emergencies. It is not persuasive or cautionary. It does not deal with treating mentally ill patients.

26. **B)**

    In the third sentence, the author writes, "Extreme cases of a behavioral emergency may result when someone's behavior is creating a danger to themselves or others."

27. **A)**

    The author writes, "Psychological and behavioral effects can result from any number of illnesses; they can also be the result of a chemical imbalance, genetic disorder, or psychological disturbance." There are no sentences supporting the other claims.

28. **C)**

    In the last sentence, the author states, "While medical practitioners must be trained for emergency situations that demand physical restraint, extreme cases of behavioral emergency may be directed to police for appropriate support." The reader can infer from this information that "physical restraint" means handcuffing or otherwise restraining a mentally ill patient who is violent.

29. **C)**

    In the last sentence, the author writes, "While medical practitioners must be trained for emergency situations that demand physical restraint, extreme cases of behavioral emergency may be directed to police for appropriate support."

30. **A)**

    The paragraph is about the thyroid gland. The other sentences give details about the main idea.

31. **D)**

    The passage does not contain this detail. According to sentence 9, hypothyroidism causes obesity and fatigue, not hyperthyroidism.

**32.** C)

In sentences 6 – 8, the author writes, "An excess of thyroxine in the circulatory system may result in a condition known as hyperthyroidism.... A deficit of thyroxine in the circulatory system may result in a condition known as hypothyroidism." The context shows that excess and deficit are antonyms. Insufficiency, too, is an antonym for excess.

**33.** A)

The text is informative, not persuasive. It does not recount a specific event, but informs readers about the thyroid gland's function, as well as symptoms of hyper- and hypothyroidism.

**34.** D)

In sentence 10, the author writes, "Fortunately, medications are available to help patients regulate their thyroid function when they've been diagnosed with hyperthyroidism or hypothyroidism." There is no support for any of the other claims.

**35.** C)

In sentences 6 – 8, the author writes, "An excess of thyroxine in the circulatory system may result in a condition known as hyperthyroidism.... A deficit of thyroxine in the circulatory system may result in a condition known as hypothyroidism." The words excess and deficit are antonyms. The reader can infer from this information that hyper (as in hyperactive) means "too much," and that hypo (as in hypoglycemic) means the opposite: "too little" or "under the normal requirement."

**36.** A)

In the first paragraph, the author states, "Almost all sensory information the human body experiences must pass through the spinal cord in order to reach the brain." The reader can infer from this information that the spinal cord conveys to the brain sensory information such as pain, heat, coldness, and other "human body experiences."

**37.** C)

The author writes, "From top to bottom, these regions are: cervical, thoracic, lumbar, sacral, and coccygeal."

**38.** B)

In the last sentence, the author writes, "Spinal nerves 'direct' the incoming and outgoing messages of the central nervous system, making the spinal cord the main neurological conduit of the human body." In the first sentence, the author calls the spinal cord a "central messaging stem." In other words, the spinal cord channels messages from other parts of the body to the brain.

**39.** B)

The essay is about the spinal cord's function and parts. The other sentences give details about the main idea.

**40.** D)

The primary purpose of the essay is to inform; its focus is on the spinal cord's functions and parts. It is not persuasive or advisory. It does not make value judgments about body parts' comparative importance.

**41.** D)

In the second paragraph, the author writes, "Motor information, on the other hand, exits the spinal cord ventrally, meaning from the front side."

**42.** B)

In the first sentence, the author writes, "Scientists only partially understand carcinogenesis—the process by which normal cells become cancer cells."

**43.** C)

In the first two sentences, the author writes, "Scientists only partially understand carcinogenesis—the process by which normal cells become cancer cells. Yet most scientists agree that this malignant transformation results from damaged genetic material within a cell." The context shows that by "malignant transformation" the author means changing from normal cells to cancer cells.

**44.** B)

The passage is about ways that damaged genetic material can cause carcinogenesis. The first sentence introduces but does not summarize the main idea. The other two answer choices give details from the passage.

**45.** C)

The passage does not contain this detail. According to the passage, damaged genetic material—not normal DNA—causes cells to become cancerous.

**46. C)**
The text is informative, not persuasive or speculative. It does not recount specific events, but simply informs readers about ways that damaged DNA can cause carcinogenesis.

**47. C)**
In the first paragraph, the author states, "Scientists only partially understand carcinogenesis—the process by which normal cells become cancer cells. Yet most scientists agree that this malignant transformation results from damaged genetic material within a cell." During the remainder of the passage, the author does not explain how genetic material becomes damaged. The reader can infer from this information that scientists do not know exactly how such damage occurs.

**48. D)**
The first paragraph begins with "Most people think ...." The author goes on to describe external respiration and then asks, "Did you know there are actually two types of respiration in humans?" Finally, the author describes the other type: internal respiration. The author is probably correct in assuming that most people—excluding biologists and medical professionals—have never heard of internal respiration.

**49. A)**
The primary purpose of the essay is to inform; its focus is on the two types of respiration. It is not persuasive or advisory. The author is not trying to prove a point.

**50. D)**
In paragraph 2, the author writes, "Cells within the organs are surrounded by thousands of tiny capillaries that act as channels for the exchange of gases. Oxygen is carried through these microscopic blood vessels, moving from red blood cells to the surrounding tissue." Readers can infer from context that the phrase "these microscopic blood vessels" refers to the "thousands of tiny capillaries" in the previous sentence.

**51. A)**
In paragraph 2, the author writes, "Whereas external respiration centers on an exchange between the lungs and the environment, internal respiration centers on a molecular exchange between cells and capillaries."

**52. C)**
As the title shows, the passage is about the two types of respiration: external and internal.

**53. C)**
In the second paragraph, the author writes, "Additionally, built-up carbon dioxide in the tissues flows through the capillaries back to the lungs."

**54. C)**
In the fifth sentence in the second paragraph, the author writes, "When testosterone reaches a certain level, it inhibits the production of FSH and LH."

**55. B)**
The last sentence reads, "A similar but more complex feedback loop occurs in women with FSH and LH stimulating the production of estrogen, resulting in the cycle of ovulation and menstruation." Readers can infer from context that by "feedback loop," the author means the hormones FSH and LH cause a reaction that stimulates "the production of estrogen, resulting in" other reactions: "the cycle of ovulation and menstruation."

## VOCABULARY

1. **A)**
   *Exseption* should be spelled "exception."

2. **C)**
   *Precaution* means "an act done in advance to ensure safety or benefit" or "protection against something or someone."

3. **C)**
   *Priority* means "right of precedence; order of importance."

4. **C)**
   *Co-morbidity* means "two disorders that occur at the same time."

5. **C)**
   *Conditional* means "dependent on something else."

6. **B)**
   *Manifestation* means "display."

7. **B)**
   *Dilute* means "weaken by a mixture of water or other liquid; reduce in strength."

8. **B)**
   *Prone* means "lying flat."

9. **D)**
   *Retain* means "to hold or keep in possession." Fluid retention can be a symptom of a medical condition.

10. **A)**
    *Excessive* means "exceeding what is normal or necessary."

11. **B)**
    Endoscopic procedures are considered minimally invasive procedures because they rely on fiberoptic tools and small incisions. *Invasive* means "intrusive."

12. **C)**
    *Placment* should be spelled "placement."

13. **C)**
    *Predispose* means "to make susceptible or to have a tendency to."

14. **B)**
    *Asymmetric* means "lacking symmetry or unbalanced."

15. **C)**
    A *soporific* is "a sleep-inducing drug."

16. **B)**
    *Collateral* means "parallel" or "secondary." Collateral blood vessels provide an alternate circulation route around injured or blocked vessels.

17. **B)**
    A *syndrome* is "a set of symptoms characteristic of a specific disease or condition."

18. **C)**
    *Sublingual* means "under the tongue."

19. **D)**
    *Pathogenic* means "causing disease." Pathogenic diseases, or infections, require protocols to prevent their spread.

20. **C)**
    A *hematologic* study examines the blood.

21. **A)**
    *Pragmatic* means "concerned with practical matters and results."

22. **D)**
    *Ambulatory* means "able to walk."

23. **B)**
    *Acoustic* means "of or related to sound or hearing."

24. **B)**
    *Progress* means "gradual betterment or improvement."

25. **A)**
Virulent means "severe and destructive."

26. **C)**
Laceration means "the tearing of soft body tissue resulting in a wound."

27. **C)**
Transdermal means "passing through the skin."

28. **D)**
Dysfunctional means "not functioning properly."

29. **D)**
External means "located outside of something."

30. **A)**
Vascular means "pertaining to bodily ducts (vessels) that convey fluids."

31. **A)**
Amalgam means "a mixture or blend."

32. **B)**
Dilate means "to widen."

33. **A)**
Respiration means "breathing."

34. **B)**
Patent means "unobstructed."

35. **B)**
Paroxysmal means "pertaining to a seizure, spasm, or violent outburst."

36. **C)**
Regress means "to move backward, often to a worse state."

37. **D)**
A cannula is "a thin tube inserted into the body to remove fluid."

38. **C)**
Labile means "unstable or easily changed." A patient's blood pressure may be labile.

39. **B)**
Something that is obverse is "the opposite" of something else.

40. **A)**
A soporific drug induces sleep.

41. **B)**
Justify means "to show to be just or right."

42. **D)**
Sensible means having "good sense or reason."

43. **A)**
Abduction means "the movement of a limb away from the body's midline."

44. **A)**
As used in this sentence, superficial means "shallow in character or attitude; on the surface." Therefore, a shallow or superficial wound does not require stitches.

45. **C)**
Succumb means "to yield or stop resisting."

46. **A)**
Resect means "to remove or cut out organs or tissue."

47. **D)**
Deficiency means "an amount that is lacking or inadequate."

48. **A)**
Superficial means "only concerned with things on the surface."

49. **D)**
Ossify means "to harden."

50. **C)**
Hydration refers to "the act of meeting body fluid demands."

51. **B)**
Adversely means "harmful to one's interest; unfortunate."

**52. D)**
*Superficial* means "located on the surface or not penetrating the surface."

**53. C)**
*Subtle* means "delicate or difficult to observe."

**54. B)**
*Cardiac* means "of or pertaining to the heart."

**55. B)**
*Acuity* means "mental sharpness or quickness."

## GRAMMAR

**1. B)**

Choice B correctly connects two independent clauses ("Kiana went to class" and "Lara stayed home") with a comma and the coordinating conjunction *but*. Choice A incorrectly uses a semicolon instead of a comma. Choice C is a comma splice, using a comma without a coordinating conjunction. Choice D is a run-on sentence, since it lacks a comma before the coordinating conjunction *but*.

**2. D)**

Choice D is correct. The adverb *recently* modifies the verb *has . . . hired*. Choice A, *Our*, is a possessive pronoun; choice B, *boss*, is a common noun; and choice C, *has*, is a helping verb.

**3. C)**

Choice C is correct. Since the bus driver and the passenger are not identified by name, using the feminine subject pronoun *she* is confusing to the reader. The reader cannot tell who spoke or who acted rudely. The whole sentence needs rewriting. For example: *After Joe, the bus driver, spoke too loudly to an elderly passenger, he realized that he might have acted rudely.*

**4. C)**

All three words in choice C are homophones; they sound alike, and they have different spellings and meanings. In choice A, *expect* rhymes with *accept* and *except*, but *expect/accept* and *expect/except* are not homophone pairs. In choice B, the first syllable in *louder* sounds like the second syllables in *aloud* and *allowed*, but *louder/aloud* and *louder/allowed* are not homophone pairs. In choice D, *where/wear* is a homophone pair and *wear* and *weary* begin with the same four letters. However, *weary* (which rhymes with *dreary* and *theory*) does not sound like *where* and *wear*, so the three are not homophones.

**5. D)**

Choice D correctly uses the adverb *farther*, which describes a measurable distance, such as twenty miles. In choice A, the adverb *further* describes an amount that cannot be measured in units. In choices B and C, the words *father* and *fatter* do not make logical sense—the first implies that the speaker cannot drive around any person who is a male parent, and the second implies that the speaker cannot drive if he or she gains any more weight today.

**6. B)**

Choice B is correct. The correct answers are a comma and a question mark. Correctly completed, the sentence looks like this: *"Jean," I asked, "Can you come over for dinner?"* Choice A is incorrect because a quotation cannot end in a colon. A colon denotes that the two sentence parts are closely related. In addition, the second half of the quotation is a question, which means an exclamation point is not the correct choice. Choice C is incorrect because a quotation cannot end in a semicolon and because a semicolon can only be used to join two complete independent clauses or items in a list. A question should not end in a period. Choice D is incorrect because a comma is used when attaching a speaker tag (*I asked*) to a quotation.

**7. B)**

Choice B is correct. The preposition *about* is unidiomatic in the phrase "love about praise" and should be replaced with the preposition *of* to create the idiomatic phrase "love of praise."

**8. D)**

Choice D is correct; the clause in this choice cannot stand on its own. While it contains a subject (*you*) and a verb (*are*), it begins with the subordinating conjunction *if*. It therefore cannot stand on its own and must be connected to another independent clause. Choice A has a subject (*I*) and a verb (*want*). Choice B has a subject (*we*) and a verb (*hike*). Choice C has a subject (*She*) and a verb (*drives*). Choices A, B, and C can all stand alone as full sentences and do not need to be connected to any other clauses.

**9. D)**

The correct answers are *too* and *to*. The adverb *too* correctly modifies the adjective *busy*. *To* combined with *attend* forms the infinitive verb *to attend*.

**10. C)**

The correct answers are *ball* and *bowl* in choice C. These two nouns make sense in the sentence. In choice A and D, *bull* is a noun that means "a male animal such as a steer or moose" and *bawl* is a verb that means "to cry." Choice B incorrectly reverses the two words *bowl* and *ball*.

11. **C)**
Choice C is correct. The adverb *hastily* modifies the verb "to wolf [down]," which means "to devour." *Food* is a noun, and *stomachache* is a noun.

12. **B)**
The correct answers are *Although* and *so* in choice B. The subordinating conjunction *although* correctly connects the opening dependent clause, "I love tomato sauces," to the middle independent clause, "I dislike the texture of raw tomatoes." It correctly implies contrast between the two clauses. The coordinating conjunction *so* correctly connects the final independent clause, "I avoid salads that contain them," to the rest of the sentence, demonstrating a cause-and-effect relationship between the first independent clause and the second. Because any of the other choices imply an incorrect relationship between the clauses, they would render the sentence nonsensical, unidiomatic, or both.

13. **C)**
Choice C is correct. The preposition *except* (meaning "not including") should be replaced with its homophone, the verb *accept* (which means "to agree to take [something that is offered to you]").

14. **C)**
Choice C is correct; the apostrophe is placed incorrectly in the contraction *Lets'*. An apostrophe only appears after a final *s* when indicating a plural possessive noun. *Let's* is a contraction of the words *let* and *us*.

15. **D)**
Choice D correctly matches the singular noun *cat* with the singular pronoun *its* and the singular verb *eats*; this choice also correctly matches the plural noun *dogs* with the plural pronoun *their* and the plural verb *sleep*. Choice A incorrectly matches the singular noun *cat* with the plural pronoun *their* and the plural verb *eat*; this choice also incorrectly matches the singular noun *dog* with the plural pronoun *their* and the plural verb *sleep*. Choice B incorrectly matches the plural noun *cats* with the singular possessive pronoun *its* and the singular verb *eats*; this choice also incorrectly matches the singular noun *dog* with the plural pronoun *their* and the plural verb *sleep*. In choice C, the singular

subject *cat* does not match the plural verb *eat* and the plural pronoun *their*.

16. **D)**
Choice D is correct. The correct answers are *There* and *there*. The word *there* is an indefinite pronoun that indicates a place, as called for in the sentence context. The contraction *they're* means "they are," and *their* is a plural possessive pronoun. Correctly completed, the sentences look like this: *There is nobody over there. Did you think you saw someone?* Each of the other choices would result in an ungrammatical sentence.

17. **D)**
Choice D is correct. The preposition *under* begins the prepositional phrase "under the bed," which tells where the cats hide. Choice A, *whenever*, is a conjunction; choice B, *our*, is a possessive pronoun; and choice C, *hide*, is a verb.

18. **A)**
Choice A is the clearest way to rewrite the sentence. The original version makes it sound as if the basketball is walking to school. Choice B makes it sound as if the gang members are walking to school (maybe they are and maybe they aren't). Choice C is too long and awkwardly phrased. Choice D leaves out important information about the people who stole the ball.

19. **B)**
The correct choice is B; the answers are *hole*, meaning "a hollow place in a solid body," and *whole*, meaning "complete or total." The noun *hole* makes sense in the phrase "a hole in your sock." The adjective *whole* correctly modifies the noun *day*, creating the idiomatic English phrase "to ruin your whole day." None of the other pairs of words make sense in the sentence. *Howl* is a "loud cry uttered by an animal" and *whale* is a "large marine mammal with a horizontal tailfin and blowhole."

20. **B)**
Choice B is correct. The adjective *four* correctly modifies *teammates*. The preposition *for* correctly completes the phrase "practicing for the big game."

21. **B)**
Choice B correctly pairs the plural subject "my teacher and the school principal" with the plural verb *have worked*. Choice A incorrectly pairs the plural

subject "my teacher and the school principal" with the singular verb *has worked*. Choice C contains a verb error ("have been worked together"), and choice D also contains a verb error ("had working together").

22. **A)**

    Choice A correctly capitalizes the proper nouns *Austin* and *Texas*. In choice B, the common nouns *weekend* and *graduation* are incorrectly capitalized. Choice C incorrectly lowercases *Austin* (in the proper noun *Austin, Texas*) and incorrectly capitalizes the common possessive noun *brother's*. Choice D incorrectly lowercases the proper noun *Texas* and incorrectly capitalizes the common noun *weekend*.

23. **D)**

    Choice D is correct. *Mourning* should be replaced with its homophone, *morning*: *How are you feeling on this sunny Saturday morning? Mourning* is a verb that means "grieving for a loved one who has died," and *morning* is a noun that means the opposite of *evening*.

24. **A)**

    Choice A correctly uses the possessive pronoun *yours* (meaning "the one that belongs to you"). Choice B misspells the possessive proper noun *Shelby's* by omitting the apostrophe. Choice C incorrectly uses *your* in place of *yours*, and choice D incorrectly uses *you* in place of *yours*.

25. **D)**

    The correct answers are *brakes* and *break* in choice D. The verb *brakes* means "uses a vehicle's brakes [to stop]." The verb *break* means "to damage or ruin." Choices A, B, and C are incorrect. The noun *brain* refers to "the organ that functions as the operating center for nervous, sensational, and operating function in a vertebrate animal." The word *bray* can function as a noun or a verb and means "the loud harsh cry of a donkey or mule" or the action of uttering that sound.

26. **C)**

    Choice C is correct. The common noun *summer*, the name of a season, should not be capitalized. Months' names (like *October*) are proper nouns, but seasons' names (*spring, summer, fall,* and *winter*) are common nouns.

27. **A)**

    Choice A is correct. The subordinating conjunction *because* joins a dependent clause to an independent one. Choice B, *love*, is a verb; choice C, *family*, is a noun; and choice D, *and*, is a coordinating conjunction.

28. **B)**

    Choice B has two independent clauses joined by the coordinating conjunction *and*, making it a compound sentence. Choice A is a simple sentence with one subject (*ride*) and one verb (*does [not] take*). Choice C is a complex sentence (one dependent clause and one independent one, joined by the subordinating conjunction *although*). Choice D is a compound-complex sentence: it has one dependent clause ("If you . . . Bay Bridge") and two independent clauses ("it will . . . longer" and "you will . . . traffic").

29. **B)**

    Choice B is correct. *Rite* (a noun meaning "a religious practice or custom") should be replaced with its homophone, *right*: *You're right: the best time to write . . . Right* can be an adjective that means "correct." When it appears later in the sentence, it acts as an intensifier and means "immediately or close to." The word *write* means to "mark on a surface" and is used correctly.

30. **C)**

    Choice C uses the following punctuation marks correctly: an apostrophe in *isn't*, a colon, an apostrophe in *there's*, a comma, another comma, and a period. In choice A, the comma after *home* should be changed to a semicolon or a colon. In choice B, an apostrophe is missing from the contraction *isn't* and from the contraction *there's*. In choice D, the apostrophe in the word *isn't* is misplaced (it is at the end of the word). Also, the question mark after *home* should be changed to a period; the clause "My cat . . . home" forms a statement, not a question.

31. **A)**

    Choice A is correct. The past-tense verbs *rained* and *reined* sound alike, but have different spellings and meanings. None of the other choices contain a homophone pair.

32. **C)**

    Choice C correctly uses the present-tense verb *bear*, which means "tolerate" or "endure." Choice A incorrectly uses *bare*, an adjective meaning "naked," in place of its homophone *bear*. Choice B incorrectly uses the past-tense verb *bore* in place of its present-tense form *bear*. Choice D incorrectly uses *burn*, meaning "cause to catch fire," in place of *bear*.

**33. D)**

Choice D correctly pairs the singular subject *no one* with the singular verb *wants*. Choice A incorrectly pairs the singular subject *one* with the plural verb *hope*. Choice B incorrectly pairs the plural subject *two* with the singular verb *hopes*. Choice C incorrectly pairs the plural subject *all* with the singular verb *hopes*.

**34. D)**

Choice D is correct. *Yours* is a possessive pronoun that means "the one that belongs to you." Choices A, B, and C contain the pronouns *I*, *they*, and *it*, but they are not possessive.

**35. B)**

Choice B is correct. The verb *affect* means "to have an impact on [someone or something]." The noun *effect* means "result" or "impact." Choice A is incorrect. These words are commonly confused. *Effect* can be used as a verb, meaning "to make something happen" (for instance, "to effect change"). Likewise, *affect* can be used as a noun, most commonly in psychological contexts describing someone's demeanor: "the patient had a flat affect." These uses are far less common. It makes more sense for a medication to have an impact on a person, and a medication cannot have a demeanor, so choice B is a better choice than A. Choice C incorrectly uses the verb *effected*, and choice D incorrectly uses the noun *affect*.

**36. B)**

Choice B correctly compares three or more items using the suffix *–est*. Choice A incorrectly uses *most* with a one-syllable adjective, *soft*. Choice C incorrectly compares six items (more than two) using the suffix *–er*. Choice D incorrectly pairs *most* with the comparative adjective *softest*.

**37. A)**

Choice A is correct. The word *summer* should be lowercased—it is a common noun. So are the words *spring*, *fall*, and *winter*. The names of months are always capitalized, but the names of seasons are not.

**38. B)**

Choice B, *went*, is the correct answer. It should be replaced with *gone*, the past participle of *to go*.

**39. A)**

The correct answers are *mortal* and *mourning* in choice A. The adjective *mortal* (meaning "deadly") correctly modifies *wound*. To be "in mourning" means "to mourn or grieve for a loved one who has died." The verb *mooring* means "securing [a boat or aircraft] with lines or anchors." The word *morning* is "the earliest part of the day, after the sun has risen but before noon." None of these other pairs of words make sense in the sentence.

**40. D)**

Choice D is correct. *Sweet* should be replaced with its homophone, *suite*: There are two bedrooms, a bathroom, and a sitting room in our hotel suite. *Sweet* is an adjective that means "sugary." *Suite* is a noun that means "a group of connected rooms."

**41. A)**

Choice A is correct: *I* and *she* are subject pronouns, and *her* is an object pronoun. In choice B, the three words are verbs. Choice C includes an infinitive (*to*), a preposition (*for*), a conjunction (*but*), and a verb of being (*was*). Choice D includes a noun (*test*), an adverb (*too*), and an adjective (*busy*).

**42. A)**

Choice A is correct. The plural verb *were* agrees with the plural subject pronoun *we*. Choices B, C, and D are all ungrammatical. Choice B is a singular verb. Choice C is past-perfect progressive, which indicates that the action was ongoing in the past, but before the other action—it is awkward and goes too far into the past. Choice D is past progressive, which also indicates an ongoing action in the past.

**43. B)**

Choice B is correct. The verb *bring* should be replaced with *take*: Please take that unsafe toy away from your little brother. *Bring* means "to carry [something] from one place to another," and *take* means "to remove [something] from someone or move it from one place to another."

**44. D)**

Choice D correctly uses the verb *affect*, which means "to cause a change." Choice A incorrectly uses *effect*, which is a noun that means "a result of a cause." Choice B incorrectly uses the verb *infect*, which means "to transmit a disease to [someone]." Choice C incorrectly uses the verb *inspect*, which means "to examine or study."

**45. A)**

Choice A is correct. *New* and *knew* sound alike but have different spellings and meanings, which makes them a homophone pair. Choices B (*royal/rayon*), C (*sweet/sweat*), and D (*manner/manure*) are not homophone pairs because they do not sound enough alike.

**46. D)**

The correct answers are *am* and *are* in choice D. The singular first-person subject pronoun *I* matches *am*, the singular first-person form of the verb *to be*. The plural third-person subject *my brothers* matches *are*, the plural third-person form of the verb *to be*.

**47. C)**

Choice C is correct. *Principle's* should be replaced with its homophone, *principal's*: My elementary school principal's name was Mrs. Woodnancy. *Principle* is a synonym for *belief*, *value*, and *rule*. *Principal* means "leader or head [of a school]."

**48. C)**

The interjection *hey* interrupts the sentence's flow as a new idea occurs to the speaker. Choice A, *considering*, is a verb; choice B, *English*, is a proper noun; and choice D, *biology*, is a common noun.

**49. A)**

Choice A correctly connects two independent clauses, "DeQuan loves eating pizza" and "meat toppings make him feel queasy," using a comma and the coordinating conjunction *but*. Choice B has a misplaced modifier: the dependent clause "[t]hough he avoids meat toppings." That clause incorrectly modifies *pizza* when it should modify *DeQuan*. In choice C, the verb *makes* is incorrectly conjugated: it should be plural to match the plural subject *toppings*. Choice D is a run-on sentence; it lacks a comma before *but*.

**50. D)**

Choice D is correct. The correct answers are *principal* and *principle*. A *principal* is the head of a school, and a *principle* is a value or maxim. In choice B, the masculine noun *prince* does not agree with the feminine pronoun *she*. In choice C, the adjective *invincible* (meaning "unbeatable") does not make sense in the sentence.

**51. D)**

Choice D uses the following punctuation marks correctly: an opening quotation mark, an apostrophe in the contraction *I'm*, an exclamation point, a closing quotation mark, and a period. Choice A incorrectly omits the apostrophe in the contraction *I'm*. Choice B incorrectly omits a closing quotation mark following *over!* Choice C incorrectly uses a question mark instead of an exclamation point to end the direct quotation, which is not a question.

**52. C)**

Choice C is correct. *You're* (a contraction meaning "you are") should be replaced with its homophone, *your*. Hundreds of years ago (in days of yore), if you were female, your destiny was not yours to decide . . . *Your* is a second-person possessive pronoun that means "belonging to you" or "owned by you." The noun *yore* is used correctly in the sentence; it means "long ago" or "former times."

**53. A)**

Choice A is correct. *Flour* is an ingredient in many recipes, and some bakers decorate cakes with fresh flowers or flowers made from icing. Choice B reverses the two homophones so that each is used incorrectly in the place of the other. Choice C uses *fleer*, which is not an English word, and *flowing* (meaning "moving freely") does not fit the sentence. Choice D misuses the word *flair*, which means "style," and incorrectly adds an –s to the word *flour*.

**54. D)**

Choice D is correct. A *metal* is an element like gold or silver. *Metal* also refers colloquially to many hard substances. The verb *meddle* means "to interfere with [something]." A *medal* is an award. Gold might be used to make a medal, but it is not a medal by itself. The noun *mettle* refers to a person's grit or determination. None of these answer choices make sense in the context of the sentence.

**55. D)**

Choice D has one dependent clause ("Because . . . awake") and two independent clauses ("I can't . . . evening" and "I need . . . morning"), so it is a compound-complex sentence. Choice A is a simple sentence with one subject (*mug*) and one main verb (*is*). Choice B is a compound sentence: two independent clauses joined by the coordinating conjunction *and*. Choice C has one dependent clause and one independent one, joined by the subordinating conjunction *although*, so it is a complex sentence.

## BIOLOGY

1. **D)**
   The electrons in a water molecule are more attracted to the oxygen atom, which gives the oxygen atom a negative charge and the hydrogen atoms a positive charge.

2. **B)**
   The fatty acid tails of phospholipids are nonpolar, and nonpolar molecules are repelled by water and other polar molecules.

3. **A)**
   Both plant and animal cells have carbohydrates, nucleic acids, proteins, and lipids. Plants and animals have similar organelles, including the Golgi apparatus. However, plant cells have a cell wall, whereas animal cells do not.

4. **C)**
   In a frameshift mutation, insertions of nucleotides in numbers other than three will shift all the following codons read by the tRNA, producing a dysfunctional protein.

5. **C)**
   Oxygen acts as the final electron acceptor during the electron transport chain. In the process of making energy (ATP), ATP synthase passes electrons on to oxygen.

6. **A)**
   DNA is organized into chromosomes using histone proteins. First, DNA is wound into nucleosomes by histones. Next, the nucleosomes are wound into chromatin, which is wound even tighter to form chromosomes.

7. **D)**
   During prophase, the nuclear envelope disappears and the chromosomes begin to condense into chromatin, which makes them visible using a light microscope.

8. **B)**
   Transcription is the process of converting DNA into mRNA so that the genetic code (DNA) can be translated into protein on ribosomes.

9. **C)**
   Egg cells have a haploid (1n) number of chromosomes. A skin cell would have a diploid (2n) number, so the skin cell would have 14 × 2 = 28 chromosomes.

10. **B)**
    The oxygen and hydrogen in a water molecule share electrons, creating a covalent bond.

11. **C)**
    There is a 50 percent chance that their child will have red-green color blindness. The children with the phenotypes $X_cX_c$ and $X_cY$ would be color blind. The children with the phenotypes $X_cX$ and $XY$ would not.

    |  |  | Mother | |
    |---|---|---|---|
    |  |  | $X_c$ | $X$ |
    | Father | $X_c$ | $X_cX_c$ | $X_cX$ |
    |  | $Y$ | $X_cY$ | $XY$ |

12. **A)**
    Organic compounds must contain carbon. They may contain other elements, including phosphorous, nitrogen, or oxygen.

13. **B)**
    The light reactions of photosynthesis occur in the chloroplast. Each chloroplast has stacks of membranes called thylakoids where enzymes convert light energy into chemical energy.

14. **B)**
    The Calvin cycle is the part of photosynthesis where ATP is used to convert $CO_2$ and water to sugar.

15. **A)**
    New nucleotides are added in the 5' to 3' direction. In order to add a new nucleotide, there has to be a free 3' end. The leading strand is synthesized continuously because the 3' end is always free. The lagging strand is synthesized, and it fragments as the DNA strands are unwound.

16. **D)**
    Meiosis produces gametes.

**17. B)**

Each tRNA molecule has an anticodon that is complementary to the codon on the mRNA strand. Once the mRNA strand is correctly aligned on the ribosome, the tRNA binds and the appropriate amino acid is added to the protein.

**18. A)**

Because cystic fibrosis is a recessive trait, the offspring would have to inherit two recessive alleles in order to have the disorder. Since the mother can only pass on dominant alleles, all of the children will have at least one dominant allele and thus will not have cystic fibrosis.

|        |   | Mother |    |
|--------|---|--------|----|
|        |   | C      | C  |
| Father | C | CC     | CC |
|        | c | Cc     | Cc |

**19. C)**

Carbohydrates, such as fructose, are sugars. DNA polymerase is a protein, vegetable oil is a lipid, and mRNA is a nucleic acid.

**20. A)**

Mitochondria produce energy for cells in the form of ATP. The electron transport chain, which is responsible for most of the ATP produced during respiration, occurs across the membranes of the mitochondria.

**21. B)**

ATP is unstable: when a phosphate group is removed from the molecule, energy is released.

**22. A)**

Telomeres are the ends of chromosomes. An easy way to distinguish *telomere* and *centromere* is that "telo" means terminal, and telomeres are at the terminus, or end, of chromosomes.

**23. D)**

At the beginning of telophase I, homologous chromosomes are located at opposite ends of the cell. As telophase I progresses, the 2n cell divides into two cells with a reduced number (1n) of chromosomes.

**24. C)**

Ribosomes are the small organelles that synthesize proteins.

**25. A)**

Each codon contains three nucleotides.

**26. A)**

NADH is one of the molecules used to carry electrons within cells.

**27. C)**

Each tRNA molecule has an anticodon that binds to the complementary codon on the mRNA strand. A bonds with U (not T, as in DNA), U bonds with A, and G bonds with C.

**28. B)**

If an organism has 8 pairs of chromosomes, it would have a diploid number (2n) of 16. The haploid number (1n) would be 8.

**29. B)**

DNA is replicated during the S, or synthesis, phase of the cell cycle.

**30. C)**

When incomplete dominance occurs, neither allele is dominant, and the offspring will have a phenotype that is a blend of the two alleles.

# CHEMISTRY

1.  **B)**
    $Br^-$ is element number 35, which means it has thirty-five protons. $Mg^{2+}$ has twelve, $Na^+$ has eleven, and $N^{3-}$ has seven.

2.  **D)**
    Both Se and O are found in group 16, so they have six electrons in their valence shell. They will add two electrons to fill the shell, resulting in a charge of −2.

3.  **A)**
    Ionic bonds contain an atom that has lost electrons to the other atom, which results in a positive charge on one atom and a negative charge on the other atom.

4.  **C)**
    An unsaturated solution is when a solution contains less than the amount of possible dissolvable solute.

5.  **D)**
    Electronegativity increases from left to right and bottom to top on the periodic table, with fluorine (F) being the most electronegative element.

6.  **C)**
    Toxicity is a chemical property: measuring the toxicity of a material will change its chemical identity.

7.  **A)**
    The balanced equation is $Pb(NO_3)_2 + K_2CrO_4 \rightarrow PbCrO_4 + 2KNO_3$, showing 1Pb, $2NO_3$, 2K, and $1CrO_4$ on each side of the arrow. The answer choice is 1, 1, 1, 2.

8.  **A)**
    $Ba(OH)_2$ is a base; bases usually include a hydroxide ion (OH).

9.  **D)**
    The answer is 20 moles of $KNO_3$. Set up railroad tracks using the conversion factor given by the chemical equation.

    $$\frac{10 \text{ mol } Pb(NO_3)_2 \quad | \quad 2 \text{ mol } KNO_3}{1 \text{ mole } Pb(NO_3)_2} = \mathbf{20 \text{ mol } KNO^3}$$

10. **D)**
    After twenty days, there will be 100 × ½ = 50 g left. After the next twenty days there will be 50 × ½ = 25 g left.

11. **B)**
    The half-life is the amount of time it takes for half of a radioactive sample to decay. After one half-life of four days, the sample would include 100 g ÷ 2 = 50 g.

12. **C)**
    The number of protons determines which element it is.

13. **D)**
    Both Mg and Ca are found in group 2, so they have two electrons in their valence shell. They will lose those two electrons in order to have a full valence shell, resulting in a charge of +2.

14. **B)**
    Covalent bonds occur when two atoms share electrons.

15. **D)**
    *atomic mass − atomic number = number of neutrons*

16. **A)**
    A solid has a definite shape and definite volume.

17. **A)**
    Solutions that have a sour taste and react strongly with metals are acidic.

18. **A)**
    The joining of two reactants ($2Li + Cl_2$) to form one product (2LiCl) is a synthesis reaction.

19. **D)**
    Electrons are negatively charged subatomic particles.

20. **A)**
    Group 17, called the halogens, have seven electrons in their valence shell and need one electron to complete the shell.

21. **A)**

The London dispersion force is a temporary force that occurs when electrons in two adjacent atoms form spontaneous, temporary dipoles.

22. **D)**

The answer is 30 moles of $O_2$. Set up railroad tracks using the conversion factor given by the chemical equation.

| 20 mol $KClO_3$ | 3 mol $O_2$ | = **30 mol $O_2$** |
|---|---|---|
|  | 2 moles $KClO_3$ |  |

23. **A)**

Condensation occurs when a substance goes from gas to liquid.

24. **D)**

Cereal in milk is a heterogeneous mixture because the elements are not evenly distributed.

25. **B)**

The breaking down of one reactant ($2H_2O_2$) into two products ($2H_2O + O_2$) is a decomposition reaction.

26. **C)**

The elements F, Cl, and Br are halogens in group 17, and thus have seven electrons in their valence shells.

27. **B)**

The reaction is a synthesis reaction that has the form A + B → C. Potassium (K) and chlorine gas ($Cl_2$) combine to form potassium chloride (KCl).

28. **A)**

The valence shell of the noble gases, group 18, is full, so they do not need any electrons to complete them.

29. **D)**

Deposition is the phase transition that occurs when a gas becomes a solid.

30. **C)**

The zinc and copper reactants switch places with each other on the product side, so this is a single displacement reaction.

ANSWER KEY

## ANATOMY AND PHYSIOLOGY

1. **C)**
   The pulmonary valve directs blood flow into the pulmonary arteries and prevents blood from going back to the right ventricle.

2. **A)**
   Nerve endings, blood vessels, and nervous tissue are found in the periosteum.

3. **B)**
   The appendix is attached to the cecum.

4. **D)**
   The urethral meatus is toward the front, or anterior, relative to the anus.

5. **D)**
   The left subclavian artery branches off directly from the aortic arch.

6. **D)**
   Afferent neurons receive information from the sensory organs, like the skin.

7. **B)**
   Inflammation increases the blood flow to the damaged area, increasing its temperature and bringing white blood cells to the site.

8. **B)**
   The dermis is the layer of the skin where blood vessels, hair follicles, and glands are found.

9. **C)**
   Calcium is released as bones are degraded, which helps balance the calcium level in the body.

10. **A)**
    The soma houses the cellular organelles.

11. **D)**
    Melatonin is produced by the pineal gland and causes drowsiness.

12. **A)**
    Apocrine glands are located in the armpit and also in the groin.

13. **B)**
    The A-band has thick myosin filaments that do not shorten with muscular contraction.

14. **B)**
    The corpus luteum, which remains in the ovary after the egg is released, produces progesterone and estradiol after the egg is fertilized in the fallopian tube.

15. **D)**
    The large intestine absorbs water and electrolytes before waste is moved to the rectum to be expelled.

16. **C)**
    The cerebrum is the largest and outermost part of the brain.

17. **A)**
    Costal cartilage connects the ribs to the sternum.

18. **B)**
    The lungs will never be absent of air, even during expiration.

19. **A)**
    The eight carpal bones are in the wrist and connect the bones of the forearm (ulna and radius) to the hand.

20. **C)**
    Myoglobin stores oxygen to allow aerobic respiration to occur when there is no blood coming to the muscles.

21. **B)**
    Mitochondria are present in muscle fibers to provide the energy needed to contract the muscle.

22. **A)**
    The corpus callosum is a bundle of white matter that joins the two hemispheres of the cerebrum.

**23. C)**
Platelets, also known as thrombocytes, play an important role in blood clotting.

**24. D)**
Lumbar vertebrae are also called the lower back vertebrae.

**25. A)**
The triceps is the agonist; it contracts to extend the elbow.

**26. B)**
Dura mater is the outermost layer of the meninges, which protect the spinal cord and brain.

**27. B)**
The bladder's external sphincter is mostly made of smooth voluntary muscle. The internal sphincter is made of involuntary muscle.

**28. A)**
The liver produces bile, which is needed for the digestion of fats.

**29. A)**
Neutrophils are a type of leukocyte, or white blood cell, whose role is to digest bacteria.

**30. C)**
The thyroid gland controls the use of energy by the body.

## PHYSICS

**1. A)**
Convert 60 miles per hour to meters per second.
$$\frac{60 \text{ mi}}{\text{hr}} \times \frac{1609 \text{ m}}{1 \text{ mi}} \times \frac{1 \text{ hr}}{3600 \text{ sec}} = 26.8 \text{ m/s}$$
Plug the variables into the appropriate formula and solve for acceleration.
$v_f = v_i + at$
$26.8 \text{ m/s} = 0 + a(4 \text{ s})$
$a = \frac{26.8 \text{ m/s}}{4 \text{ s}}$
**$a = 6.7 \text{ m/s}^2$**

**2. C)**
Plug the variables into the appropriate formula and solve.
$W = Fd$
$W = (400 \text{ N})(10 \text{ m}) = \textbf{4000 J}$

**3. C)**
Plug the variables into the appropriate formula and solve.
$F_g = mg$
$F_g = 80 \text{ kg}(3.8 \text{ m/s}^2) = \textbf{304 N}$

**4. B)**
Radio waves are **electromagnetic waves**.

**5. B)**
Convert 17,500 miles per hour to meters per second.
$$\frac{17,500 \text{ mi}}{\text{hr}} \times \frac{1609 \text{ m}}{\text{mi}} \times \frac{1 \text{ hr}}{3600 \text{ s}} = \textbf{7822 m/s}$$

**6. A)**
Plug the variables into the appropriate formula and solve.
$PE_g = mgh$
$PE_g = (0.0025 \text{ kg})(9.8 \text{ m/s}^2)(400 \text{ m}) = \textbf{9.8 J}$

**7. B)**
Moving charged particles produce a **magnetic field**. A changing current produces an electric field.

**8. C)**
Plug the variables into the appropriate formula and solve.
$F_g = mg$
$F_g = 1 \text{ kg}(9.8 \text{ m/s}^2) = \textbf{9.8 N}$

**9. B)**
Plug the variables into the appropriate formula and solve.
$P = \frac{W}{t}$
$t = \frac{W}{P} = \frac{100 \text{ J}}{100 \text{ W}} = \textbf{1 s}$

**10. A)**
Plug the variables into the appropriate formula and solve.
$I = \frac{P}{A}$
$I = \frac{P}{s^2}$
$I = \frac{0.5 \text{ W}}{(2 \text{ m})^2} = \textbf{0.125} \frac{\textbf{W}}{\textbf{m}^2}$

**11. C)**
Plug the variables into the appropriate formula and solve.
$v_y = v \sin\theta$
$v_y = 47 \sin 39 = \textbf{29.6 m/s}$

**12. B)**
Plug the variables into the appropriate formula and solve.
$a_{rad} = \frac{v^2}{r}$
$a_{rad} = \frac{(2.5 \text{ m/s})^2}{1 \text{ m}} = \textbf{6.25} \frac{\textbf{m}}{\textbf{s}^2}$

**13. A)**
Plug the variables into the appropriate formula and solve.
$F_c = m\left(\frac{v^2}{r}\right)$
$v = \sqrt{\frac{rF_c}{m}}$
$v = \sqrt{\frac{(0.80 \text{ m})(0.5 \text{ N})}{0.088 \text{ kg}}} = \textbf{2.1 m/s}$

**14. B)**
Plug the variables into the appropriate formula and solve.
$n_1 \sin\theta_1 = n_2 \sin\theta_2$
$n_2 = n_1 \left(\frac{\sin\theta_1}{\sin\theta_2}\right)$

$n_2 = 1.00(\frac{\sin 30°}{\sin 12°}) = $ **2.40**

15. **B)**

    Plug the variables into the appropriate formula and solve.

    $v = \lambda f$

    $v = (100 \text{ Hz})(400 \text{ m}) = $ **4 × 10⁴ m/s**

16. **B)**

    Plug the variables into the appropriate formula and solve.

    $N = \frac{Q_{TOT}}{q}$

    $F = 9 \times 10^9 (\frac{(17 \times 10^{-9})(22 \times 10^{-9})}{(0.08)^2})$

    $= $ **5.26 × 10⁻⁴ N**

17. **B)**

    Plug the variables into the appropriate formula and solve.

    $V = IR$

    $R = \frac{V}{I}$

    $R = \frac{3000 \text{ V}}{0.1 \text{ A}} = $ **30,000 Ω**

18. **C)**

    Plug the variables into the appropriate formula and solve.

    $V_t = V_1 + V_2 + ... = 18 \times 1.5 \text{ V} = 27 \text{ V}$

    $V = IR$

    $I = \frac{V}{R} = \frac{27 \text{ V}}{10 \text{ Ω}} = $ **2.7 A**

19. **D)**

    Plug the variables into the appropriate formula and solve.

    $KE = \frac{1}{2}mv^2$

    $KE = \frac{1}{2}m(3v)^2 = 9\frac{1}{2}m(v)^2 = $ **9KE**

20. **D)**

    Plug the variables into the appropriate formula and solve.

    $F_f = \mu_k N = \mu mg$

    $F_f = 0.40(47 \text{ kg})(9.8 \text{ m/s}^2) = $ **184 N**

21. **D)**

    Plug the variables into the appropriate formula and solve.

    $J = \Delta p = p_2 - p_1$

    $J = mv_2 - mv_1 = m(v_2 - v_1)$

    $J = 0.5 \text{ kg}(5 \text{ m/s} - (-3 \text{ m/s})) = $ **4 kg m/s**

22. **D)**

    Plug the variables into the appropriate formula and solve.

    $\Delta V = Ed$

    $E = \frac{\Delta V}{d}$

    $E = \frac{30 \text{ V}}{0.002 \text{ m}} = $ **15,000 V/m**

23. **C)**

    The normal angles of incident and reflected light rays are always identical.

24. **D)**

    Plug the variables into the appropriate formula and solve.

    $R_t = R_1 + R_2 + R_3 + ...$

    $R_t = 17(12 \text{ Ω}) = $ **204 Ω**

25. **A)**

    Plug the variables into the appropriate formula and solve.

    $F = qE$

    $E = \frac{F}{q}$

    $E = \frac{3 \times 10^{-9} \text{ N}}{1.602 \times 10^{-19} \text{ C}} = $ **1.8 × 10¹⁰ N/C**

26. **A)**

    The asteroid is moving at a constant velocity, so the acceleration is **zero**.

27. **C)**

    Plug the variables into the appropriate formula and solve.

    $F = qE$

    $q = \frac{mg}{E}$

    $q = \frac{(5 \text{ kg})(9.8 \text{ m/s}^2)}{(4 \times 10^4 \text{ N/C})} = 0.00123 \text{ C}$

    $= $ **1.23 × 10⁻³ C**

**28. C)**

Convert 1 revolution to radians.

1 rev = $2\pi$ rad

Plug the variables into the appropriate formula and solve.

$\omega_f = \omega_i + at$

$\omega_f = \omega_i + at$

$t = \dfrac{2\pi \text{ rad/s} - 0 \text{ rad/s}}{1 \text{ rad/s}^2} = 2\pi \text{ s} = \mathbf{6.28\ s}$

**29. C)**

Constructive interference of two identical waves in phase will double the amplitude but leave the frequency unchanged.

**30. C)**

Plug the variables into the appropriate formula and solve.

$n_1 \sin\theta_1 = n_2 \sin\theta_2$

$\theta_2 = \sin^{-1}(\dfrac{n_1}{n_2} \sin\theta_1)$

$\theta_2 = \sin^{-1}(\dfrac{1}{1.5}(\sin 45°)) = \mathbf{28.13°}$

Follow the link below to take your second HESI A² practice test and to access other online study resources:

https://www.ascenciatestprep.com/hesi-a2-online-resources